A novel by Tanaé B

Copyright © 2014 by Tanaé B.

All rights reserved. This book or any portion thereof
may not be reproduced or used in any manner whatsoever
without the express written permission of the publisher
except for the use of brief quotations in a book review.

*This is a work of fiction. Names, characters, places and incidents
either are products of the author's imagination or are used
fictitiously. Any resemblance to actual events or locales or persons,
living or dead, is entirely coincidental.*

I dedicate this book to the love of my life, in hopes that we'll find our way back to each other one day…

PROLOGUE
"WHEN YOU FIND"

............while the rain glistened against his thick eyelashes. I had never seen him look so pretty. That thought made me recall my mother's voice in my ear. It was a childhood memory that made me cut my eyes at her at the time, but now almost made me laugh out loud. It was a conversation about the beautiful Michael Jackson, may he rest in peace.

My mother had tried to explain to me that men are not supposed to be pretty. But it fit Michael just as it fits Dominique. In fact, Dominique really reminds me of the 1977 version of Michael with his tall, lean figure & his full, curly fro. Dominique licked the rain from his lips and snapped me out of my daydream.

"You gonna let me come in?" he asked with big eyes.

I couldn't just leave him out in the rain, although I'm sure his hair would catch all of it. I stepped aside and he walked in as if he was right at home. Technically this had been his home for a significant period of time. I guess I expected him to act unfamiliar with it like one does with an old friend they haven't seen in a long time. Why did he come here? What does he want from me?

"Why did you come here …?" I spoke loudly. "What do you want from me?" He chuckled like he was sharing a private joke with himself.

"I guess you not too happy to see me then," he responded, still smiling. "I bet Butter will be happy to see me. Where is he anyway?" Butter, short for Butter Pecan, was my pit-bull. I didn't realize it had been that long that Dominique didn't know…

"Butter……….died. A little over a month ago, actually." I watched Dominique's face fall and his eyebrows furrowed. His bottom lip got tight. I could tell he was about to be angry with me. "It really did happen so unexpectedly ---"

"He died and you don't even tell me? I mean, you hate me THAT much. You could not even come to me and speak to me even to tell me ---"

"How dare you!" I said, louder than I expected. "How dare you try to tell me how I'm feeling? I swear you are so condescending. You think you know everything, sometimes it really makes me sick to my stomach." I didn't want to be around him when I was feeling so vulnerable. I was bound to let tears fall at any minute. I couldn't give him the satisfaction.

"Now who's telling people how they feel?" I could see his anger fading as he said this. He looked down at the floor and kind of half smiled. "You almost sound like your mother just then, you know." I rolled my eyes.

This is the part where Dominique changes the subject so that he doesn't have to deal with confrontation. I remember that when we first met, he'd told me he doesn't get into arguments. I couldn't understand how any human being could prevent that from happening. How could he let someone make him so angry and not say anything about it? But I've come to know his technique very well. I can even see it coming sometimes.

"Please, don't start," I said.

"I run into her the other day," he ignored me, "and she seem like she doing good. She was really surprised to see me. Of course, she would not let something like this stop her from hugging me so tight."

He laughed again, it seemed, to himself. Dominique was always joking about how my mother would've had him if I hadn't roped him in myself. As if he was some gift to women. Sometimes I think I'm crazy to think such harsh things about the man I love, but then I think about what he's done to me. Unforgivable things …

"Are you going to tell me why you came or not?" I asked rudely.

"I love you." I looked up. It's nothing I've never heard before. "I……..I love you, Téa. I don't hear myself say this to you in a long time. Too long. Don't you think?" I didn't answer. "I want you to know that I been thinking about you every day I been away from you. This wasn't a way for me to put distance for us, but that's what it did. But I'm back now. I'm back and ---"

"And you expect me to be waiting here for you so that we can pick up where we left off at like nothing happened?" I could feel the tears forming in my eyes. I sighed loudly. "I think you should just go, Dominique." He shook his head at me like I was a child.

"That's the thing you keep doing," he said, still shaking his head. "You keep pushing me away. You keep acting like you don't want any things to do with me and you want me to leave you alone forever, when really all you want is for me to stay!"

I knew it was true as he said it. I felt it in my heart, but I couldn't let him do that to me again. I wouldn't. I refused to let him pull me in and make me believe that everything was all good and it wasn't.

He came to where I sat on the couch and grabbed my hand in his. I fought the urge to pull it away.

"Stop it. Stop letting you foolish pride get in the way of what we both want. I want you. Swear of God, you're all I ever wanted."

"You left me!" I cried. I snatched my hand away from him and used it to hide my tears. I couldn't help but sob right in front of him.

It hurt so bad just thinking of when he abandoned me. Everything was so perfect. That alone should have been a sign that things wouldn't turn out good for me. Dominique had me feeling like I was the only woman in the world. I never even THOUGHT of love until Dominique. Ultimately, I found love in him. It created a new me. I thanked him for the love he gave me and all I wanted to do was give him the same in return. And I did. Mind, body, and soul. I gave him all of me. By the time I realized it was over, there was nothing left.

"I know I left you, but evvvvery body deserve a second chance. Don't they?"

"I was done giving out second chances by the time I met you, Dee," I said with a blank expression. "How much hurt can one's heart take?"

"I never meant to hurt your heart. When I hurt you, I hurt myself. I try to stop both of us from hurting ever again. You see?" He came closer to me. "Let me make this right. Let me make you feel happy again…"

The tip of his nose grazed mine. He stared directly into my eyes before he let his lips fall on mine. It was the softest kiss I've never felt. I knew I was being a fool, but all of a sudden my feelings for him came surging and I allowed myself to be kissed. Our hands entwined as he kissed me once more. I could feel his heavy breathing on my neck. It whispered a song to me with every exhalation.

Dee's hands slid slowly up and down my thighs, and I allowed his tongue passage into my mouth. He still tasted the same. Like raspberries and vanilla. I felt my body warm up immediately from his touch. My juices began to flow and I know what I wanted and Dominique knew too. I was ready to feel and remember him again.

Dominique's large hands slid down and cupped my ass, as he picked me up. His lips never left mine. We were both breathing heavily now, knowing what was about to come. He led us into the kitchen and sat me down on the counter where we had made love many times before. Every time felt like the first time. A new, wonderful experience.

I threw my head back and rested it against the wall while Dominique slid my sleeveless top down to my belly button. His mouth grabbed at my nipples with hunger. He massaged my right breast while he devoured the left one. His slim waist was pressing in between my legs. I wanted nothing but this, and all of a sudden I came to my senses. At this very moment, I realized that what I was doing was wrong. I yelled at Dominique to stop but he couldn't resist.

"Shhhh...." he whispered into my neck, trailing kisses down to my chest.

I felt my eyes brim with warm tears. I tried to cover my face with my hands... I didn't want him to see that something was very wrong. But in my attempt to hide my emotions, he discovered the diamond ring on my finger. Grabbing my hand with so much force I almost fell to the floor, he lifted it to my face and spat, "What is this!" I could see the flare in his nostrils... I knew this wouldn't end well.

"I tried to tell you, Dee, you wouldn't give me a chance!" The tears were beginning to roll. Dominique began backing away, his head in his hands.

"Please... don't say this is happening," he said, more to himself than me. "Is this what I think it is?" I tried to swallow the lump in my throat but it was completely dry.

"Yes, Dee. I'm engaged now…" I managed to say.

"To who, Téa."

His head was down and I couldn't imagine how he must be feeling right now. But he left me! He left without saying anything and took my entire world with him. I was lonely, cold. I couldn't eat. I couldn't sleep. I couldn't even see color anymore. Everything was black and white.

And just when I'd thought everyone had left me, Percy came into my life. And he made me feel beautiful again. He made me feel like I meant something, after feeling like dirt for so long. I never expected that Dominique would come back into my life and I would have to explain how I'd carried on a relationship with the person he hated the most.

"WHO THE FUCK ARE YOU ENGAGED TO, TÉA!" he yelled suddenly, and punched the wall. I could see that he was holding back tears. I didn't want to do this to him, but I knew I had no other choice.

"Percy!" I screamed and couldn't stop myself from crying now. "He… He was there for me! He knew how I felt and he said I deserved better! And I did, Dee… I did. Why couldn't you be there for me?" I sobbed into my hands.

"Percy?" Dominique stood and snatched his coat up.

"Wait! Where are you going? You're just gonna run away again?" I ran after him and stood in front of the door so he couldn't get past, but he simply pushed me out of the way. "Please don't leave me, Dee," I tried one more time. He continued to walk to his car without a word. It wasn't until he slammed the door and started the ignition that I could see the tears flowing down his cheeks. His eyes were red-rimmed.

"This. Is TOO MUCH. FOR ME. Téa... I should not have come back..." he almost whispered.

"You're upset. Stay here for the night... please. You shouldn't drive," I tried to reason with him. I would do anything to get him to stay at this point. "Damnit, Dominique, do you want to get into a car accident!"

"It would not matter if I did. The pain would feel nothing compare to what I feel right now." He stared ahead as his words registered and burned my heart to its core. He abruptly pulled off and left me standing there with nothing but my tears.

ONE
"BEGINNING"

.........dealing with another one of my episodes. I don't really like to put a label on things anymore, but the truth is that I am depressed. Sometimes, there is an obvious reason for it. Other times, I just don't know why I feel the way I do. Today I don't know. I just know the pain has gotten to that point again where I can't escape it. Escapism has become a huge part of my life. I escape through movies, books, art, music. I've even escaped through my own dreams. But this time there was nothing. This is when the pain boils over into tears.

I've never been the type to share. I don't call up my mother every time I'm sad and say "Mami, I'm having that empty feeling again." But there comes a time when one simply NEEDS to ask for help. I wasn't doing myself any good by staying isolated from the rest of the world. But I needed a good cry. So I let the tears flow freely for a while before cleaning myself up and dialing Casandra's number. I watched television with the volume muted while the phone rang and asked myself why I insisted on carrying the weight of the world on my shoulders.

Casandra is my best friend of six years. Lord knows her family has done everything for me. They treat me like their second daughter. Even took me in for a little while when my mother kicked me out of the house. I listened to Casandra ramble on about the traffic for a few minutes before I spoke up and said "Please come get me. I can't stay in the house today. You don't know what it's like here." It was like having every reason in the world to feel beautiful but feeling so much less than that.

"As long as you know I'm gonna be dancing and I can't sit down and talk to you like I need to…"

"I don't care, just please get me out of here. I just need a change of scenery. Badly."

I had bitten all my fingernails off and started biting the skin on my fingertips. My mother thought I did this because I was nervous, but it was really stress. Casandra and I hung up and I began googling "natural ways to uplift your spirit". They told me to listen to music I enjoyed, but I tried that and it was as if the music has lost its energy right along with me. They told me to eat chocolate and get some fresh air, so I grabbed an ice cream bar from the freezer and waited outside on the porch for Casandra.

The warm sun on my chest and arms definitely brightened my mood. I think people take the sun for granted. I'm going to miss these beautiful summer days once September hits. The sun makes me feel beautiful. The sun makes me want to get up and do something. Amazing things happen under the sun. I rested my head on the railing and let it shine directly into my face. I can't wait to see all the golden brown skin Mr. Sun has created. *That brown skin means everything in the world.* If only my beautiful Black people knew.

Casandra honked as she pulled up to the curb. I stood up and knew immediately that she was taking in my outfit. A tight, white belly shirt, cotton gray harem pants, grey and black high top Adidas. There was no doubt that she was judging my large, silver hoop earrings. She frowned at what the wind had done to my fro. Or maybe she was just frowning at my fro in general. But she said nothing. Normally she would, but she probably didn't want to upset me anymore.

"I want you to smile today, pretty girl. Okay?" She leaned over and kissed my cheek as I buckled myself in.

"I will smile. I can't guarantee I will be happy though." I looked down as I said this, fumbling with my seat belt. Casandra pulled off, blasting the Off the Wall album. This was definitely for my benefit. I love her, but even she can't fill this void.

■■■

I grew up on the south side of Chicago. When life was good, all I had to worry about was making sure my stuffed animals weren't all over the floor. There were so many. I would create television shows with them and my Barbie dolls. And when they didn't want the roles in my shows, I'd cast my mother's bottles of lotion and nail polish. Her huge dresser and nightstand served as their apartment building. I guess you could say my imagination went far beyond the normalcy of imaginary friends.

When my mother announced to us that she had a baby on the way, I was in kindergarten. I went to morning kindergarten for a while, but that stopped because she wanted more sleep in the mornings for her and the baby. So I'd sit in front of the TV all day watching CatDog, Real Monsters, and Hey Arnold. Peanuts was my favorite. Maybe I wanted to be one of Charlie Brown's friends, because I'd go make my bologna and mayonnaise sandwich as soon as they'd grab their lunch and head to recess.

I'm not sure why these thoughts came to my head suddenly. Maybe because it was a much simpler time. But life did get hard not too long after. Random memories will probably pop up in my head as I go along. Just try to keep up when they do appear. They may be of some significance to you.

My thoughts are being interrupted by my phone vibrating on my thigh. I hop out of the car as we've reached our destination, and I'm immediately grateful Percy called when he did. We were facing a crowd of people and I feel so awkward walking past so many strangers.

"I'm still seeing you later, right?" I can hear him smiling devilishly through the phone.

Percy is a gorgeous man and he knows it. He knows he has IT. He can sing and dance. He's tall and fair-skinned with big brown eyes and little ringlets of hair surrounding his face. He's handsome and nice enough, but sometimes I feel like we live in two different universes when we talk. Or maybe it's just that he lives in his own universe that revolves around Percy. I'm not supposed to be judging people so I push that thought out of my head.

"If you still want me to, sure. I don't know how much fun I'll be. I'm not in the greatest mood." Casandra and I squeeze in between double-doors with about 30 other people. I think to myself, *I hope I'm not the only person who will be off to the side. I don't wanna draw attention to myself.*

"You know I got you. It's my job to keep a smile on your face so just let me take care of that. You just worry about taking care of me after I take care of you." I scowl, even though Percy can't see me.

I hate how he talks to me like he makes decisions for me. He has been trying for a long time to get me in bed and he still doesn't take my celibacy seriously. I wasn't asking for a ring before I'd give it up, just love at least. Was that so much to ask for? I could feel myself getting upset again. Everybody around me had stopped chattering so I told Percy I'd call him later.

"Where are we?" I ask Casandra. She's looking in the same direction as everyone else, paying attention to who's speaking.

"Les Gémeaux workshop," she whispers, and puts her finger to her lips to shush me.

"Are you kidding?" I laugh.

I didn't exactly follow them, but I thought the twins were adorable and very talented. I knew they were on tour with Beyoncé, which is really saying something. So it's nice to see they still do things like this that are considered to be on a smaller scale. I stood up on my toes to get a glimpse but that wasn't necessary. They were towering over everyone.

"Oki, so we gonna take some picture and say hi to everybody and then we gonna start," says Damien with a huge smile. "*D'accord? D'accord.*"

Everybody crowded around the twins and I went in the opposite direction to go sit on the floor with my back to the wall. I pulled out my phone and pretended to browse twitter.

"Shit!" Casandra was running up to me frantically. "I left my camera in the car, could you please go get it?"

"Couldn't you just use your phone...?" She saw me already comfortable in my position on the floor. I wasn't trying to move.

"No, I need my GOOD camera for a picture with the twins." She had the biggest *duhh* look on her face.

"Well you already have your car keys in your hand, why don't you just go for it?" I say with a laugh, so she doesn't get angry.

"Hurry, they're gonna get away!" She throws her keys at me. I'm almost positive they aren't going anywhere soon, but I reluctantly stand up and take the keys. I guess it's the least I could do since she took me away from my misery and all.

When I walked out the door, I checked my surroundings to make sure nobody was watching, and I made a beeline for her car. The sooner I got back in the comfort of my little bubble, the better. I grabbed the camera, made sure not to slam her door like she hates, and ran back across the parking lot.

"Be careful," I hear a voice behind me say. I turn around and see nothing but plaid. The giant in front of me giggles at the confused look on my face, and I peek upwards to find myself staring into one of the twin's eyes. I try to laugh too so I don't look embarrassed.

"I will be..." I say, and turn to re-enter the double-doors, leaving him outside.

I must pause here to let you know something. I do this a lot. And by "this", I mean that when guys talk to me, I rush out of there afterwards without even noticing until after the fact. I don't know why I do it, but I must seem very rude. I'm only telling you this because I hate to come off rude to people who did nothing to me. I don't want them to think I'm trying to get away from them. But this is probably the main reason I have such bad luck with guys. I'm always rushing to leave the conversation. Anyway...

"Here." I hand Casandra the camera and she jumps up and down before grabbing Damien's elbow and asking for a picture with him and his brother. I'm watching Damien give her a hug when the giant I bumped into a few minutes ago comes back inside and stands right beside me.

"Your hair is like mine," he says with a grin.

I smile back and say "Yeah, it is." He narrows his eyes and shakes his head

"She's mean," he tells Damien, still smiling at me. It was almost as if he was tattle-telling on me. Damien smiles at me while he signs Casandra's t-shirt. I'm standing there looking lost as usual because I don't know what to say to that. I watch him for a second but he has moved on to another girl.

"Take a picture of us, please?" asks Casandra, handing me the camera.

"That's what I'm here for." I walk backwards and wait for Damien to get his brother's attention to take the picture. Casandra stands in between them and cheeses. I snap two, tell her they were cute, because she needs reassurance, and sit back down by my wall.

"I want to take a picture with HER," the giant says and points to me. He has a mischievous look on his face.

"That girl ain't trying to get up and take no picture, good luck with that," says Casandra.

The giant motions with his head for me to come over. I just put my face in my hands, embarrassed from all the attention he was showing me. He was showing me attention, right?

"C'mon. This is once in a lifetime." I raise my left eyebrow. Who does he think he is? "It's once in a lifetime for me to get this opportunity to take some picture with you." He winks.

I feel my cheeks burning red. I see Casandra out the corner of my eye with a Kool-Aid smile on her face. I know in her head she was saying, *Check you out, pulling niggas.*

"I make you take a picture." The next thing I know, I'm being lifted in the air and slung over this man's shoulder. Now I need to pause again, because I have a confession. The way he wrapped his large hands around my waist and lifted me up so easily made me tingle between my thighs. But that's for you and me to know.

I screamed for him to put me down but I was faking it. He puts me down, laughing, and lays his arm over my shoulder. Casandra flashes our picture. He's smiling. I'm smirking.

"Bro, c'mon. It's time."

And just like that, I'm completely forgotten. He runs off to where his brother is and now it's strictly business. I sit down again and fade back into my own world.

■■

I watched Casandra pop, lock, grind, roll, twirl, whatever. You name it, she did it. I can't understand why her parents never took her dancing seriously. I mean, she was so talented. They shot her dreams down with a quickness when she told them she wanted to major in dance. They refused to pay for her education if she did. She was lucky to find a way to still enjoy it. I could see how worn out she was when quitting time came around.

She cuddled up next to me on the floor and begged me to carry her home.

"Get your sweaty arms off of me, you stink," I say with a laugh.

I can't help but notice that afro sticking out above everyone else's heads. I see the giant talking to a model type. He looks as if he's explaining something very important to her. They're smiling at each other. This is the part where I begin to pity myself. I know it sounds strange, but I've always been self-conscious about myself because I look young. I'm 21, but everyone assumes I'm 16. And why would a grown ass man ever talk to a woman who looks 16…

"Come on, girly." Casandra stands and pulls me up. "I'm tired, I have a paper to do when I get home."

I could hear her talking to me but I was focused on something else. He is showing someone a dance move now. It's amazing how some people, including him, can work a room the way they do and manage to speak intimately to everyone there. You know what I mean? The kind of way where you automatically figure he's only spoken to you that comfortably, but truth is, it's normal for him. Everyone sees that side of him. I can tell he's one of those people, just watching him.

Now he's making his way over to us. I pretend to dig in my bag for something because I don't want him to know I was watching him. Casandra is mumbling something about grabbing food on the way home. I turn my back on them.

"Thank you so much, I had so much fun!" Casandra gushes. "I really love you guys, you have to come back soon."

"Oh, thank you, baby. We come back when it a little hotter outside. This weather is crazy! What about you, did you have fun?" he asks, and I know he's talking to me even though my back is turned.

"I'm sure watching isn't as fun as dancing," I respond.

"Well maybe next time you dance with us. I can make you dance, it's not a big deal you know. It's easy." I giggle at this without thinking. I didn't want him to think I was laughing at the way he talks, but he laughs too. "What's your name?"

"Téa..."

"Téa? My name is Dominique." He held out his hand and I blushed as I shook it. "Why you so shy, Téa?" *Because you're saying my name in your sexy French accent.*

"I'll be in the car when you're ready okay?" Casandra gives me this look that makes me glare at her.

I already know what she's thinking. But this is the thing. Dominique has talked to every other girl in here, not just me. Even if he was somehow interested in me, I'm not stupid. He's all over the country. Shit, he's all over the world right now. I'm sure he'll find something better.

"Actually I better go anyway. I know Casandra is really tired. It was nice meeting you and your brother," I say with a smile.

"Wait." He grabs my hand to stop me.

Oh shit.

"Téa." He smiles. "Sorry, did that hurt you?" I shake my head slowly. "You should let me see you again."

I look around to see if anyone is still here. Believe it or not, I had forgotten I was in a room full of people. I didn't want anybody to see this because I didn't know how I was going to react. I don't want to reject him publicly.

"I don't mean to be rude but aren't those people over there waiting for you?" I slowly but surely remove my hand from his tight grasp. People were starting to look at us!

"Yes, but I don't go nowhere until you give me the answer." I was trying to resist his smile and failing miserably.

"I have a boyfriend," I say flatly. But Dominique doesn't miss a beat.

"I don't want to know your boyfriend, I want to know you," he said, leaning back onto the wall.

I could tell he was serious and not joking at all. Just then, I felt my phone vibrating in my pocket. It was Casandra. I picked up to hear the sound of her groaning, "I'm soooooo hungryyyyyyyy." I hung up.

"Sorry, I gotta go."

Dominique quickly snatched my phone from me and held it above his head while holding his other hand in front of my chest. As if I was really about to attempt to grab it.

"This is very childish," I said, but I did find it kind of cute.

I knew that the entire ride home, I would be trying to convince myself that Dominique must really be into me and that he probably doesn't do this with other girls he meets at workshops. But once I get home, I will completely erase these thoughts from my head and tell myself OF COURSE he does this with other women and I'm nothing special. Why would he choose me over anyone else? He doesn't even know me. If he's planning on starting a sexual relationship with me, he'll end up disappointed. Once that happens, it'll be like we never met. He'll be out of my life.

Dominique, still holding my phone in the air, dialed his number and waited for his phone to ring. He then immediately saved my number, *very clever,* and put it back into my jeans pocket.

"I'm gonna call you, *Téa,*" he said, and ran off. All I could do was shake my head and laugh. I watched his coily locks bounce until he joined Damien on the other side of the room and I left.

****

Percy was already sitting on my porch when I got home. I unlocked the door and let him in while he had what seemed to be an important business call. I knew my Grandma was asleep so I put my finger to my lips to tell him to keep it quiet. Percy and I haven't been "dating" very long and in my opinion, we weren't that serious.

I only get to see him once or twice a month now that he and his brothers are busy in the studio again. We never discussed what kind of relationship we had and lately I've been feeling like it's not really going to go anywhere. But I know I needed companionship. I had been lonely for too long…

Percy hung up the phone and wrapped his arms around me from behind. He inhaled the scent of my hair. It was peppermint.

"I'm sorry about that, baby," he apologized. I was used to it. I knew he had things to take care of. I was grateful that he took the time to see me when he could.

"It's fine, are you hungry?" I asked.

"Indeed..." he trailed off. I feel him slowly kissing me down the back of my neck. As strange as it sounds, things like this don't get me excited anymore. I don't feel the usual heat one feels welling up inside them when their significant other touches them so tenderly.

The first time, I figured I just wasn't into the guy I was with enough. Maybe he just didn't know how to turn me on. But it kept happening. With every new guy I was with, I would be aroused until things started getting sexual...

I lost my virginity a few months before my 19th birthday. I was one of those girls who wanted to wait for the perfect person to come along and fall in love with me before I gave "it" up. But after hearing boys tell me "You might as well get it over with because that's a dream that will never happen" for so long, I finally listened to one. Big mistake. The experience was horrific. He'd assured me that he'd taken a girl's virginity before and he knew what he was doing. But the whole thing was so rushed. And ROUGH. His kisses were more like attacks.

He sucked my nipples so hard and bit them even though I asked him not to. When I went home in pain later that night, I noticed that the skin had actually opened on one of them! There were bruises all over my chest and one huge purple one on my neck. You would've thought I'd gotten my ass kicked. The killer part is that he'd only gotten halfway inside of me. It hurt so bad, I wouldn't let him go any further. After a while, I went completely numb. I sat there and bit my fingernails while he stroked away. "This feels so good right now."

He came in less than 15 minutes. I couldn't wait to put my clothes back on and get out of there. I guess the disappointment was showing on my face because he said, "If it makes you feel any better, you got some good ass pussy." I knew I wouldn't be seeing him again. A couple of months after I turned 19, I started dating what I thought to be my first love, a local rapper named Trey. Trey was two years younger than me, and a virgin.

That relationship consisted of a lot of fumbled kissing and dry-humping. Of course he tried to make more happen, but what could he do? He had no experience. He didn't know where to start. I tried to help but he quickly took matters into his own hands by trying oral sex on me for the first time. I'll just say that my first experience with that was a rather… dry one. We broke up two days later. It had nothing to do with sex, I promise.

So here I was single again. This time, I had the mind frame of talking to whoever I wanted and not belonging to anybody. Calvin, who I called Red because of his light complexion, would be the next guy I came in contact with sexually. He lived in Country Club Hills, a Chicago suburb about 35 minutes away. Last summer, he would drive all the way to my house in the city, come and get me, and take me back to his place. We had a little routine going.

First, we'd watch a movie while cuddling on the couch. After a while, I would feel his hands trailing up my waist and slowly moving towards the center of my thighs. Then we'd have sex. After sex, we would cuddle again while watching a basketball game. When it started getting late, we'd go pick up some Wendy's. Red would turn on oldies and we'd eat and listen to them all the way back to my house. Sometimes, Red would text me to let me know he made it back home and to also remind me how tight I was and how it made him feel.

The first time we had sex, the pain was excruciating. I had only had sex twice and both times were a year prior to this. It was the same every time. I had to get used to pain. It was like losing my virginity over and over again. I never got to feel pleasure. I didn't *expect to feel it immediately, but I was getting scared that it would never happen for me. Any other attempts I made to have sex were ruined before a penis could even enter me. I just couldn't get into it.*

I ultimately came to the conclusion that I couldn't enjoy sex with someone I didn't have deep, true feelings for. And I was okay with that. I'd rather wait for love than keep trying different guys and adding more bodies on me, knowing that it wouldn't change anything. So I became celibate. I don't care for the Western ways of life, therefore I don't believe in a marriage license. But I would refrain from sex until someone loved me. Until then, Pornhub helped me sleep at night. Whoops, I let my thoughts take me away from reality again.

"Percy, stop. My grandma is right upstairs." I remove his hands from my waist and open the refrigerator. "Let's see what we have here." I heard Percy sigh and sit down at the kitchen table.

"You're 21 years old, when are you gonna move out of your grandma's house?" he asked almost with disgust.

He seemed to forget that not everyone his age is fortunate enough to have a record deal and receive royalty checks and go on tour. Some of us are just college students working part-time, trying to keep our cell phone bills paid. Well, I am.

"You know I've been saving up for a studio apartment," I say with a frown. "I'm almost there. Some motivation would be nice."

"You're not trying hard enough, babe. Those 20 hours a week you're working aren't gonna get you anywhere. That's for sure." And they tell me that *I'm* a pessimist.

"Well...I'm selling my portraits too..."

"Here we go again with this art shit." He stood up and I already knew what was coming. "You act like you *wanna* be stuck here forever. This is exactly where you'll be in five years drawing pictures."

I didn't just draw pictures. I drew nice quality portraits and sold them for decent prices. I was slowly building my fan base on the internet, which could help me get noticed by important people. And art is my life. It means a lot to me and I hate when he talks about it like it's worthless.

"Percy, I don't wanna fight." I'm looking at my feet because honestly, I can't stand to face him when he's angry with me. He makes me so conscious of all my flaws, twice as conscious of them as I already am. "Look, I have pizza left over from last night. Let's just relax on the couch and watch a movie, please. Can we just chill out for once? That's all I wanna do."

"I know, babe. I'm sorry. It just frustrates me so much when there are so many things you could do. I mean, you have a great voice. You could always come to the studio and lay down a few tracks. I can see you being so much bigger than what you are with these drawings." He grabbed both of my hands. "I just wish you could see what I see."

What's so bad about this is that he actually thinks he is helping me. What's even worse is that I actually thought he was helping me too. He kissed my forehead.

"C'mon." He led the way downstairs to the family room. I purposely popped a funny movie in the DVD player. I figured we could both stand to lighten the mood a little.

I snuggled into his chest. We weren't even halfway through White Chicks when Percy started licking my ear.

"Percy, c'mon. Watch the movie."

"I'm watching," he mumbled.

"No, you're not." His fingers worked their way under my tight shirt. "Pay attention."

"I wanna feel you…" he kissed my neck, then my chin, then my lips.

"You need to stop." I got off his lap and sat on the other end of the couch. Percy stood up so quickly, I thought he was going to bump his head on the ceiling.

"I don't have time for this shit." He snatched up his jacket and headed towards the door.

"Where are you going?" I asked.

"To go find a bitch that's ready for me. You supposed to be a grown ass woman, what the hell are you afraid of?"

I was so shocked by his words and how angry he was that I just stood there, not knowing what to say. I couldn't even believe he was saying all this.

"You stuck in that little girl phase, so maybe you need a little boy to come over and cuddle with you every night. Call me when you ready for a grown man." And he left.

This is one of those moments where I stood in the same position for a long time, trying to register what had just happened. After a while, I turned the television off and headed upstairs to my bedroom. I wasn't going to cry, because I didn't feel for Percy enough to do that. I was just going to go to sleep. I needed it to be tomorrow so that tonight could be forgotten.

TWO
"CLOSER"

...............rolled over and squinted as the sun beamed in my eyes. These are the best mornings. Waking up in a warm bed with the blinds wide open, lighting up my whole room, always brought a smile to my face. It was serene. I knew this was God's way of telling me that today was going to be a big day for me and I didn't want to miss another second of it. I was in pure bliss. I sat up in bed and clasped my hands together.

Good morning, Jah. Thank you for waking me up this morning. Thank you for all my talents, blessings, and most importantly my health, and my family's health. Please continue to watch over and bless me and all my family, friends, and loved ones. Also, please continue to watch over and bless Adrian and all his family, friends, and loved ones. Thank you, Jah. Selah.

I secretly hoped that God didn't find me rude for not kneeling sometimes. I wiped the sleep from my eyes and dragged my arm across the bed, searching for my phone and the remote control. My daily summer routine was to check all my push notifications, watch Steve Wilkos, Jerry Springer, Cheaters, Maury, and Bill Cunningham respectively, and make breakfast. Breakfast was the same for me every day: maple brown sugar oatmeal with chopped pecans, whole wheat toast, pineapple juice, and a piece of fruit. I'm a bit of a health nut. What can I say, my body is my temple.

My phone was showing two texts and one missed call. As you can see, I'm very popular. The first text was from Casandra. It read *So you just not gone tell me what happened last night hoe?* I almost spit my juice out at that. I thanked her in my head for helping me start my morning off with a good laugh.

The second text was from my father. His read *Hello my beautiful daughter. Please call me when you get the chance.* To anyone on the outside, this would seem like a sweet message sent from a very loving father. Not that my father isn't loving, he is at times. But this man has more ulterior motives than a loan shark.

My relationship with my father was a lot different when I was younger and didn't know anything. When I say it was different, I mean it was better. I was the perfect little daddy's girl. He took me everywhere with him and I was clearly his favorite. According to everyone else, I am his spitting image. Unfortunately, that comes back to bite me in the ass every day now. You see, my father's father was a womanizer. He had many children by many women.

My father had brothers and sisters he didn't even know about. My grandfather beat on my gran. She tells us all the time that she hates him, even though he's no longer living, and that she had tried to kill him once by poisoning him. He had three sons by her. My father, my uncle Troy, and my uncle Don.

Uncle Don committed suicide when he was 16. He decided to shoot himself one day because, at his tender age, he "couldn't handle everything anymore". That's why my mom gets so angry when I'm upset about things. She's afraid my depression will lead to suicidal thoughts as well.

Why am I ruining this perfectly good morning thinking about these things? I'll save them for a later date. I don't bother replying to my father. I just check my missed call. I don't recognize the number, which can only mean one thing. Wow, someone must be an early bird. He called me just before 8am. I turn the volume on the TV down and call the number back. There's loud noise in the background when Dominique answers the phone.

"Hello?"

"Did someone call from this number earlier?" I ask, knowing damn well that it's him.

"Yes, this is Dominique. Good morning, Téa." I was sure he'd probably forgotten my name by now, like everyone else does. He…is…good.

"Good morning. What made you call so early?" Was that rude to ask?

"Well me and Damien wanna invite you to come chill today, you know?"

"Oh, you do?"

"Yeah. So do you know the United Center?"

"Yes…"

"You gonna meet us here, oki? We gonna be here 12 o'clock to 5 o'clock. So just come whenever you want. Come laugh. Have fun. Chill. You know? Bring a friend if you scared." I hear Damien laughing in the background.

"Why would I be scared?

"I know you scared of me, but don't worry. You gonna like me. Text me when you almost here, oki?" There is a lot of screaming suddenly, and then he hangs up. I sit on my bed staring at my phone because I'm not really sure about what just happened. I decided to just laugh it off.

I can't believe I will be spending my afternoon with the twins. Not that I'm star-struck or anything, but I would've never guessed I'd even be acquainted with them before yesterday. It's weird how these kinds of things happen. I mean, Casandra had been fascinated by them for a while now. And while I was in awe of their talent, they weren't frequently a part of my thoughts. Yet, they were inviting *me* to spend time with them. It's only right that I invite Casandra along.

I texted her and waited for her excited response. Ten minutes later she was calling me. I should've known. She talked about what she was going to wear and told me she thinks she should try to come on to Damien so that it could be a double-date and he wouldn't feel like an extra wheel. I'm sure it was mainly for her benefit though. Besides, there was no date. And no extra wheels. We were simply going to laugh and have fun and chill, right?

"So what do you think is going through Dee's mind, huh? I mean, never in a million years would I think..." Casandra trailed off. I threw myself backwards onto my bed and allowed my body to bounce several times before I exhaled loudly.

"Oh, I don't know. I'm not really worried about it, Casandra. After Beyoncé's show this weekend, they're leaving to go who-knows-where and we will never see each other again. What's the point of getting excited?"

It's much easier to be this way about things. I call it letting myself down easy. If I were in a contest or a talent show, I would tell myself and everyone else "So and so is going to win. I'm ready to accept my second place trophy. I wouldn't be upset about a bronze though." This way, I don't have to get hurt when they do hand me that bronze trophy.

"You are so modest, Téa. I swear. You're crazy beautiful, you're smart. And not the kind of smart where you get good grades, but like actually educated. You know, there are probably so many people who look up to you and you don't even know it."

I knew Casandra was shaking her head on the other end of the phone. I sigh. It's true that I have a beautiful soul. I know this. I even look beautiful sometimes. I mean some days, I can really look in the mirror or walk down the street and just know that I'm bad. But a lot of other days, I feel like I would probably get picked last to be on someone's team. If that makes sense.

"Thank you, I appreciate that. Look, I want us to try to be there around 1pm so I gotta get ready, okay?"

"Whoa, whoa, whoa. I'm not gonna be ready by one. Not hardly."

I knew this was her way of telling me I was going to have to take the bus. It's times like this when I wish I would have just taken range again in high school. If I wasn't lazy, I would have gotten off my ass one of those days when I didn't have anything to do and gone to the DMV for my license. But I never did that, so I guess I'm shit out of luck.

I immediately get up and hop in the shower, now that I have a long bus ride to take. I put on some Corinne Bailey Rae and let her voice float throughout the house. The smell of my mango mandarin-scented body wash made my senses awaken. I breathed in deeply. Never had I felt more relaxed.

I rubbed my conditioner through my hair and let it soak in. Silently, I wondered if Dominique would get the chance to enjoy the smell of my hair as much as Percy did. I still couldn't believe he had stormed out the night before the way he did. I just hope this is a blessing in disguise.

I towel-dry my body and use an old black t-shirt to dry my hair. I like to wear it up and in a big puff when it's this hot outside so it can stay out of my face. I wasn't like Casandra. I'm not about to go out of my way to look extra beautiful just because we were hanging out with the twins. I have nobody to impress. Besides, people were supposed to like you for who you *really* are, right? So I'd wear my tight shirts and baggy pants. I'll rub cocoa butter lotion on my face instead of wearing makeup. And Casandra better not have anything to say about it.

The bus ride wasn't as long as I thought. It seemed to go much faster with my music playing in my ear. That, and I was also thinking about my studio apartment. I'd led Percy on to think that I was getting close to it but I had actually already signed a lease. I was just waiting to move in.

I texted Dominique like he said to when I was about 5 minutes away. I also texted Casandra to find out where she is. The girl was losing her mind over having "nothing" to wear. There are some guys on the sidewalk when I'm stepping off the bus and I can feel their eyes on me. I pretend that I don't know they're there.

"Whassup, Lightskin," one says to me. I smile and say hi only because I don't want him to think I'm a stuck up bitch like people assume every light-skinned female is. I know that it really doesn't matter because he doesn't know me, but I hate for people to have those thoughts about me.

To my surprise, Dominique was standing right outside the doors. I immediately felt an adrenaline rush. I can't believe I just got so nervous out of nowhere! I didn't know if I should say "Hey" or just wave or greet him with a hug or shake his hand. I was just lost.

Dominique was smiling very hard at me. He came down to my level and reached his arms out to pull me in for a hug. Thank God he took control because Lord knows I'm submissive and I will continuously wait for someone else to make the first move.

He smells so damn good. Like a combination of powder, sweat, and cologne. He was wearing a black beater and black jeans. I also noticed that his underwear was black too, from the way his pants were hanging a little off his waist. It was sexy.

"How are you?" he asks.

"I'm great, thank you." Before I can get another word in, he continues.

"We gonna perform here tomorrow. With Beyoncé." I could tell he was very proud.

"Yeah, I know! I know a lot of people with tickets. I'm not one of them, unfortunately." Dominique grabs his heart and pretends to be shocked at this. At this point, I know I've been giggling too much at everything he says and does and I try to stop myself, in fear of seeming over-zealous.

"Oh no, why you don't have a ticket?" I open my mouth to answer, but he stops me and grabs my hand. "C'mon, let's go inside."

So now Dominique LeBeau is leading me through the United Center with his hand in mine. He's being awfully close with someone he only just met. While we're walking he says, "I can get you a ticket, you know."

"Oh, no you don't have to go to any trouble to do that. I probably won't even be able to. I have a lot of things to do this weekend."

Dominique opens a giant glass door on our side and peaks his head through. I can hear him whisper, "Damien! Come." There are several people setting up equipment inside the stadium and I wonder if I came at a bad time. But of course I remember that Dominique invited me.

Damien is saying something to Dominique but he is speaking too low for me to distinguish his words, but they are smiling. I automatically assume they're joking about me. I know this is foolish but I can't help that I'm more insecure than I should be at times.

"*Bonjour, mon chérie!*" Damien greets me with a smile bigger than

Dominique's and kisses me on both cheeks. I couldn't help but giggle. "They have the sound check right now so me and my brotha just gonna chill. It's cold in here, no?" asks Damien, rubbing his arms. Dominique pulls a red Cola crewneck sweater over his hair and shakes his head.

"Damien is always unprepared." I laugh because I know this is a joke. And even though it isn't that funny, he was cute when he said it. "So why are you so busy this weekend?" asks Dominique.

"Umm...where do I start? Well I'm an artist." Both of their eyes get wide at this, which makes me beam with pride. "I draw portraits for people and I have a lot of them to do this weekend. Not to mention I have to go to my real job. And I'm in the process of packing up all my stuff at home so I can move out."

"Ooh, where are you going to go?" asks Damien.

The fact that they seem genuinely interested in the boring things I'm talking about makes me appreciate them. Part of the reason I was intimidated by hanging out with them is the fact that their life is so much more exciting than mine. My average week consists of going to work, eating, drawing, eating again, browsing Tumblr, watching Desperate Housewives and One Tree Hill on Netflix *while* eating, etc. An exciting week would include all of that plus ice cream. I'm aware that I have been a bore to guys in the past and it's one of the things I'm very self-conscious of.

"Not far," I respond. "I really just want a nice studio apartment with my bed, a kitchen, bathroom, and just a whole lot of empty space for me to work in." I'm getting worked up now, demonstrating everything I'm saying with my hands. "I want a really high ceiling where I can hang all my drawings up on one side of the wall and use the other side to do a huge kind of mural. You know?" They nod their heads slowly, their eyes still widened. Damien is smiling.

"I will pay you to draw Damien," says Dominique.

"I will pay you to draw me too," Damien laughs. I look at Dominique.

"Really? Why not yourself?"

"Well, I don't like my face. I prefer my twin face." He doesn't look hurt or upset when he says this. He states it as if it's a simple fact and there's nothing wrong with him feeling this way. It makes me feel a little bad but I try not to look sympathetic because he might not like that.

"You do know that you are identical, right?" I say, narrowing my eyes and smiling.

"Even still, Damien's face is better." He shrugs. I decide to drop it.

"Well I would love to draw the both of you together. How about that?"

The two of them haven't stopped moving since I got here. They were very energetic. I'm sure if I weren't there, they would be off somewhere dancing. I could tell from Dominique's sweat that they were probably doing so prior to my arrival.

"Are you hungry?" asks Dominique suddenly.

"Yes, finally. Let's go get something to eat," says Damien, and he grabs my hand. My phone rings and look who it is. Casandra.

"Hello?"

"Hey, are you with Damien and Dee yet?"

"Yes, I am. Actually we're about to go get something to eat." Damien is dramatically pulling on my arm, dragging me out while Dominique is holding the door open waving his hand for me to hurry. I'm trying to speak clearly to Casandra but they are making me laugh so hard. Their facial expressions were killing me.

"How are you gonna go out to eat without me? Tell them to wait for me!" She sounded highly annoyed.

"Um, why don't you meet us there? You're driving right." She sighs deeply.

"Meet you where, Téa."

"Damien, wait!" He has me halfway out the door already. "Where are we going?"

"What? What is Damien doing?" she asks. Dominique runs from the door and grabs my phone.

"*Bonjour, comment allez-vous*......we are going to go to seafood restaurant on Hubbard. Do you know Hubbard......Okay so we gonna take um, the train so meet us there in one half hour, okay? D'accord? Oki. See you, bye-bye." He hands me back my phone. "C'mon girl, you gonna eat." He puts his arm through my left arm and Damien puts his through the other.

■■■

It wasn't cold, but it was getting slightly cooler outside and I knew that my day with the twins would be ending soon. They had talked my ear off the entire train ride over. I enjoyed it though. It was nice when you could meet someone and not have to deal with awkward silences or try to keep the conversation up by yourself.

I was surprised at some of the things Dominique told me. They seemed a little too personal to be disclosing to someone so soon but he didn't have a problem sharing. In that 30 minutes it took to get to the restaurant, I learned where he grew up, what all his tattoos were of, the names of all his ex-girlfriends, and that his relationship with his father was shaky. Something we had in common.

Damien and Dominique were amazingly easy to be around. They made me feel more comfortable than my own family did. I admit I was a little closed off when we first met up, but I quickly began feeling more at ease. Damien sat across from me and Dominique at a booth that was made to seat at least 8 people.

I ordered cream of broccoli soup, which I later regretted when I thought about what it might do to my breath, and grilled salmon with a baked potato and some naturally-flavored soda. The boys were such twins, telling the waiter they wanted King crab legs simultaneously.

Casandra made it there before our food had gotten to us. Damien stood and kissed both her cheeks as he did with me and Dominique gave her a wave. I silently snickered at this. Not because he didn't feel Casandra was worthy of a hug, but because he felt that I was. Casandra sat snugly next to Damien even though the bench was a good 12 feet long. She told him she had tickets to Beyoncé's show tomorrow and she would make sure to wave to him from the second row.

A couple of times while Dominique was in the middle of talking, he rested his hand on my thigh. It wasn't sexual at all. It was more like a *Pay attention, I want you to hear this* touch. He never made eye contact with me when it happened and I never questioned it.

I noticed that whenever he or Damien spoke, they got so excited that they would come out of their seats a little bit. They were like little kids in grown man bodies. I sipped my drink and laughed while watching them. Casandra, on the other hand, was eating her food slowly with an irritated look on her face. I was hoping it wasn't because Damien hadn't said a word to her the entire time.

I whispered in Dominique's ear and told him that when I had went to the bathroom, I told one of the waiters that it was Damien's birthday and asked if they could bring him a cake and sing to him. He couldn't control his laughter and almost ruined the joke. But soon enough, after we finished our meal, 5 waiters came to our table yielding a giant fudge brownie sitting in New York vanilla ice cream and sprinkled with nuts.

Damien had no idea they were coming to our table, because it wasn't his birthday of course. I almost pissed my pants when he started clapping and singing along with the waiters, watching to see where they were going to end up. When they stopped at our table and gave him the brownie, a resounding "WHAT, IT'S FOR ME?" was heard throughout the entire restaurant.

I could no longer hold back my tears. Casandra started to catch on and almost spit out her food laughing. Dominique's whole body was stretched out along the bench with the table cloth covering him so nobody could see him turning red with laughter.

The waiters continued to sing, Damien yelling Dominique's name in confusion the whole time. When they finished, we all clapped and I yelled "Happy birthday, Damien!"

"Do you know I'm gonna kill you," he says to me with a grin. "I can't believe you did that. That wasn't nice."

"I'm sorry, I really wanted a free brownie." I've laughed so hard, my cheeks were starting to hurt. Dominique has finally recovered and is wiping his eyes with a napkin.

"You don't have to pay for your meal, you know," says Dominique. I immediately get quiet because no guy has ever said this to me before, therefore I don't know how to respond.

"Of course I do. Why wouldn't I?"

"Me and Damien have it." I look at Casandra to see what she thinks I should do. She puts her hands up as if to say go for it.

"That wouldn't be fair," I say. I pull my wallet out and search for my card. Dominique closes it.

"Me and Damien ask you to come out with us, so it is fair."

"And you give me this delicious dessert so I have to do you a favor," says Damien.

"If you guys are sure…" I dip my spoon into the brownie and taste it. Oh my goodness, it was so mouth-watering. "You have to try this." Damien unexpectedly takes my spoon and scoops up some brownie to taste himself.

"I'm sorry. But you're gonna be my sister anyway. I can tell," he says with his mouth full.

"Let's go outside," says Dominique before I can even begin to wonder what Damien means by that.

So here we are. Me and Dominique step outside the front doors of the restaurant and are welcomed by the cool breeze. He leans against a black railing near the curb and I sit on the wooden bench beside him.

"So," he says.

"So. You got me out of there quick," I respond. I look up at him and smile, wondering. What was Dominique LeBeau thinking about?

"It's not like that. He just have a big mouth. He is good at messing things up for me."

"What was he talking about? You can tell me. You don't have to worry about me thinking too much of it," I lied. I would analyze whatever he said in my head all the way home then re-analyze it and read into it as far as possible.

"It is not normal for me to go to a restaurant with a girl I don't know."

"I didn't think it was. But there's nothing wrong with it. Is there?"

"No, no. You make me and my twin laugh so much. We had fun before we have to go back to work tomorrow." Dominique sits down next to me on the bench and it suddenly feels like it's on fire.

"Oh, good! I'm glad you enjoyed my company. I had fun too. It was nice hanging out with both of you."

"Hanging out is cool, you know, but I want you to know me more."

The front door to the restaurant opens and Damien and Casandra step out. Damien informs Dominique that they have to get back to the center. He nods his head and looks at me again.

"You know we gonna be friends and grow from that. You want that?" He grins and waits for my response.

"I…would LIKE that," I say with a laugh.

"Good. I want that. I have to go now." Dominique leans in gives me a peck on the lips so quick and coolly, that I literally miss it. He and Damien are already 20 feet down the sidewalk, running towards the subway before I can open my mouth to speak.

"What was that!" I try to yell and still be discreet because there are so many people around. He turns to face me while walking backwards at a steady pace.

"WE GONNA GROW, GIRL!..........WAIT AND SEE!.........IT'S POSSIBLE!" I can do nothing but cover my face and laugh because everyone is staring at us. I touch my finger to my bottom lip, trying to remember his lips being there. "IT GONNA BE BETTER NEXT TIME!" I see Casandra shaking her head and smiling out the corner of my eye as I watch Dominique and Damien disappear down the subway steps.

"I can't believe this is happening to you," she said.

I couldn't believe it either. I don't even know what I did. It's hard enough to get normal guys who go to school with me to look at me. The ones who do look don't interest me. But who knew that my pickiness would eventually land me with a man who met all of my standards? I thought I was supposed to die lonely and bitter.

"Well, c'mon. I know you want a ride home." I was still holding my hand to my lips and they were hot. I snap out of it and we begin walking to where she parked.

"Were you okay in there? You looked really miserable," I say. "I wasn't leaving you out of the conversation, was I?" She shook her head.

"No, girl. It's not you. I just thought since we were sitting so close at a table together that Damien would have to acknowledge my presence."

"But he did. He was the first to greet you as soon as you walked over."

"He greeted me the way he greets a fan," she scoffed. She unlocked the car and I hopped in, becoming aware of how tired I was. Believe it or not, today was an eventful one for me. I couldn't wait to get in my bed.

"Are you aware that just yesterday, that is all you were? A fan?" I laugh. She just rolled her eyes at me and pulled off from the curb.

Dominique actually likes me, for reasons unknown, but even I wasn't expecting much from him. I've known the guy for 2 days! She'd only been in Damien's presence for a few hours and she was ready for a proposal. I leaned back in my seat, let my window down, and felt the breeze rush through my hair. I promised I wouldn't read too much into everything Dominique was doing, but he had given me a lot to think about. I had a text from Dominique by the time I made it home that evening. It read

I hope I did not make you mad

Why would I be mad?

I really want to kiss you so I don't think first.

Dominique is on his way to his hotel room and wanted to make sure I had made it home safely. We end up talking on the phone because it's easier for Dominique to get his point across when speaking English instead of writing it. He tells me that since they've been in Chicago for 3 days, they'll be getting right on the road once the show is over.

Of course. I try not to sound disappointed but he must have sensed it, because he immediately says that the next stop is in Michigan. It's not too far from me, and he plans on visiting. Despite all of my confusion and wondering what the next couple of days would bring, I went to sleep with a smile on my face.

■■■

My earliest memory of my father is of being at his apartment that he lived in alone, playing a racing game with my brother on his Sega Genesis. We were visiting for a couple of days like we did every week. He and my mother were going through their first divorce. I was almost 4 years old and my brother was 6. I vaguely remember eating apple cinnamon oatmeal for breakfast and having fried chicken and rice for dinner a lot.

I remember watching The Mask, The 9th Brother, and The

Preacher's Wife regularly because those were the only movies we owned. I remembered coming home from school one day with one of my really bad ear infections and vomiting all over my father's bed. And I remember him combing and twisting my hair for me because nobody else was there to do it.

These are fond memories. Even the story of me vomiting was a fond memory, because of how my daddy took care of me. Today, in my earliest memory of my father, wasn't how our usual day would go though. We were going to visit Daddy's friend, a woman who lived down the hall. We had never met her before.

She didn't talk to us other than saying hi and leading us to her daughter's bedroom to play. Her daughter had a tent and she locked me in her closet so that she could lure my brother into the tent and seduce him. We were only little kids, and my brother got out of there quick before she could try to kiss him. We went home.

I never thought about the fact that my father was with another woman until now. Sure, he was divorced and he had every right to be with her. But we were his kids and he took us to her house and we didn't know her. We were barely introduced. I went home that night to my mother's apartment; her new boyfriend was over.

I didn't like him because he felt he had the right to discipline me. He yelled at me when I did something wrong. I don't know what ever happened to him. All I know is it hurts that I felt guilty for letting another man teach me how to tie my shoe, and my father can't even feel guilty about not taking care of us.

As you can guess, my parents got back together somewhere around 2 ½ years later. We moved out my mother's apartment that had the little pond with the ducks swimming beside it. A house on Central Park in Chicago became our new home. I didn't know it yet, but I would have several memories there too. Memories I'd wish I could forget.

Like I said before, life was great until my sister came. At the age of 7, I was forced to be a lot more mature than other 7 year olds. My mother had work at midnight that required her to sleep throughout the day, and I practically raised my sister. I bathed her, clothed her, fed her, changed her diaper, put her down for naps, played with her, cleaned up after her, and accepted all her punishments.

My childhood was stolen. Not only by my sister, but by my parents. Once I was in my room, playing with everything on my dresser again, when I heard my mother cry out and some bangs against the wall. When I went in the living room to see what was going on, they were acting like everything was normal. But in my head, I could see him pulling her by her arm and swinging her into the wall, and I cried.

I wouldn't find out until I was much older that my father hit my mother a lot. It didn't surprise me when I found out. On too many occasions, my mother had called his best friend or his brother or even the police to come pick him and all his belongings up. My sister and I were in bed one time when they came and arrested him around 11 at night. I'll never forget the cutest officer with an Elvis hair cut popping his head in and saying "You'd better be doing homework!"

There would be more incidents like this until my mother finally decided we were going to move. More incidents where my mother would change the locks but my father would persuade me to let him borrow my key for a while. Then of course, he'd make copies of it and BAM. He's back in our lives again. We'd been in that cramped little house, living unhappily for seven years.

I was now 13 and it was coming to the end of my 7th grade year. All our boxes were packed. A nice, big house in South Holland awaited us. We would be moving within the next couple of days. Tonight, however, my cousin was over and my father was out. Who knows where. And we were having a good time, for a change.

My father came home drunk, which is another thing I would later find out he did a lot. Along with driving drunk while we were in the car. He saw me next to the computer, showing my cousin how to use our internet. I wasn't allowed to be on computers when my parents weren't around, because I was caught in a chat room talking to strangers once when I was 12. I wasn't actually on the computer, I was just pointing things out to my cousin. But my father didn't care. He was drunk and had nothing better to do, so he told me to get into "the position" on the floor. My eyes instantly welled up with tears.

I got on the floor, positioning myself as if I were about to do a push-up, and stayed there with my back perfectly straight. If it wasn't perfectly straight, I would get hit with the belt until it was. If my stomach even dared to touch the ground, I would get hit with the belt until I was in the air again.

This wasn't the first time he made me do this, but it was the worst. I was down there for two whole hours. I screamed and cried out the entire time. My father laughed and said "I'm a terrible ass father, ain't I?" My cousin and my brother and my sister could do nothing but pretend this wasn't happening right in front of them.

I would have been down on that floor much longer if it weren't for a sudden crash and glass falling from our front window. My father went outside to see what happened. Some preteen boys who lived in the neighborhood had thrown a rock from all the way across the street and put a large hole in our glass. My father went after them, but eventually gave up and called the police.

"The police about to come over, so go ahead and get up and go clean yourself up." I thanked God for that. Thank God for rocks.

I didn't see my father again for months, but I hated him the whole time. We were finally in our new home and only came back to Chicago to visit my Grandma on weekends. One day, he found out I was over her house and asked me to come outside. I didn't speak to him or hug him back.

"Aw, you don't love me no more?" he asked with a goofy smile on his face. My face never changed. I gave him a hard look and let him know that I was serious. I hated him for what he did to me. I hated my mother for not thinking it was wrong. Here I am, a 75 pound little girl, and it was okay for him to punish me that way because "they punished people in the military that way all the time." Needless to say, this wouldn't be the last time my father did something to fuck up our relationship.

I'm up talking with my Grandma, reminiscing on happier memories than these ones before it's time for me to leave. Today was my big moving day. Téa was finally going to be on her own, free to waste all the time she wanted, eat all the food she wanted, clean up whenever she wanted, decorate as she wanted, and go out late without having to hear someone's mouth. I could tell my Grandma still wanted me there with her, even though we never got along. She would be a little lonely, but I needed this change. I needed to start living for me.

When my phone started ringing, I was shocked to see Dominique's name on my screen. We exchanged a couple of texts, but I hadn't heard his voice or seen him in a little over a week. I was convinced that we simply had a little thing while he was here and it was all over now.

"Long time, no speak," I answer the phone.

"Where are you? I'm in Chicago, I'm gonna come and see you."

"Well, thank you for letting me know beforehand," I say sarcastically. I don't want to be angry with him or anything, but it's one of my biggest pet peeves when someone thinks they can just come and disrupt my day. "Today is not a good day, Dominique. I'm super busy."

"What you busy with? I can come and help you get it done so you can spend time with me."

"It's not that simple. I'm moving into my new apartment today."

"I will help you."

"No you won't."

"No, really. I want to help. Where do you live?" He was serious. As much as I wanted to see him again, I didn't want him to think it was okay to just barge in on me like this. Because then, he would keep doing it.

"My friend from down the street is already helping me and he's looking forward to getting paid today, so that's okay. Thank you though."

"Girl, if you don't tell me what's your address, I'm gonna get it from your friend." I giggle.

"Dee. I'll call you when I get moved in okay? Bye…" I wait for him to say something and when he doesn't, I hang up.

45 minutes later, my doorbell rings. That means my friend is here and it's time to hit the road. Imagine my surprise when Dominique's jaw line is all I can see when I look through the peephole. I open the door quickly.

"You are not serious," I say, with my face in my hands. I peek through my fingers and see him leaning against my railing, smirking.

"Hi, baby. You ready?" I can't stop laughing at how amazingly serious he was, standing in my doorway.

"You really did this. How did you even get my address?"

"I told you I will get it from your friend," he says, entering the house and sitting down at my kitchen table.

"You don't even have her number!"

"She give it to Damien. Damien give it to me." He shrugs.

"And what am I supposed to tell my friend? He's gonna be pissed."

"Oh I meet him a few minutes ago. I pay him and told him he could go." My eyeballs are popping out of my head now.

"DEE. YOU DIDN'T."

"I did. I just did that."

"Oh my God, wait. Who on Earth is gonna drive this UHAUL?! I can't do it!" I smack my forehead and start pacing. I'm about to lose my mind. I'm trying my hardest to laugh it off and not get angry with him but he was really trying it today.

"Why are you so worried? I can drive it for you." He grabs my shoulders tightly to stop me. "You are crazy, girl you know?" I stop and stare at him. "What you thinking about?"

"How to murder Casandra and still be discreet. Okay, c'mon. I don't have no other choice now, so let's go."

"*Allons!*" he says, pushing me forward a little.

"You are so annoying."

■■■

My apartment was still so big and spacious after all my things were inside, I was in love with it. Of course I didn't have much, just two beds, my desk, my dresser, my clothes, laptop, printer, flat-screen TV, and some miscellaneous things.

All my new place needed was a new color on the wall and some decorative curtains maybe, and she would be perfect. I watched Dominique bring in my mattress all by himself. He was dripping with sweat from the heat and he had removed his shirt. I made him an ice cold glass of water.

"I can't believe I just gave you some water from my very own sink," I say with exaggerated excitement. He downs the water while I lean against the table he's sitting at and stare at his shiny chest. "You know, maybe you shouldn't be doing this. I don't want you to hurt your back or anything. I mean, you do have to dance for a living."

He looks at me with one of his silly, wide-eyed faces and says, "I'm good." He stands at the door, about to go and get the last of my art supplies. "She still watching us."

An older lady from two houses down had seen me and Dominique pull up and start moving in. She must have gotten the wrong idea when she saw Dominique throw me over his shoulder, the same way he'd done back at the workshop, and carry me inside screaming and laughing. She waved and told us we were a nice-looking couple. I told her in a polite, clear way that we weren't together. I expected Dominique to say the same, but he just pulled me closer.

"She's probably thinking we're getting our own place together for the first time and we're gonna keep her up at 3 in the morning with all the sex we're having," I say laughing.

"Maybe we are," Dominique says, without a smirk or a smile. He bites into one of my green apples and looks at me with a straight face. "Sound good." I hit him in the arm and the corners of his mouth turn up.

"I'm not having sex with anyone any time soon." He doesn't say anything. "You look tired. Let's take a break."

■■■

"We should play with these when we're finished." Dominique pulls a deck of UNO cards out of one of my boxes labeled "Miscellaneous". I suddenly feel bad about my sex comment earlier, which I sensed had made things a little awkward. Here he was, in my apartment alone with me, and he wanted to play UNO. Not only that, but he was giddy with excitement about the possibility of playing with them.

"Maybe, if you can get the rest of that box unpacked without stopping to ask me a question," I say with a smirk. Of course he couldn't do this.

"Who is this?" he asks. I turn to see him holding up an obituary. I already know whose it is. I've only had one friend pass away and I have refused to attend a funeral ever since.

"That's Adrian," I say flatly. "He was my friend. He died of cancer."

I met Adrian almost seven years ago, when I was just a freshman in high school. The person I called my older brother was like a younger brother to him. He had previously attended the school I went to, but was now 20 years old. I was 16. He thought I was a cute girl, but never overstepped any real boundaries because of my age. This didn't stop him from talking to me on the phone all night though.

The first time it happened, I thought it was weird that he wanted to call me. But I soon realized he was very charming and hilarious. He made me laugh more than anyone else. Our conversations were FILLED with endless laughter. He began to flirt with me more and more, but still referred to me as his little sister in front of his friends.

Our relationship so far had only been through a phone. I never knew it would always be this way. There were several occasions when we wanted to plan a day to hang out, but those plans never materialized. After knowing him for two years, I started to feel a little pressured to want to be with him.

He was constantly looking for my reassurance that he was attractive and that I "wanted" him. Unfortunately, we had a falling out when I finally got tired of him acting immaturely when he didn't get the responses he wanted. We lost contact for a couple of years. There was absolutely no communication, not even through friends. I didn't care.

Adrian randomly hit me up over Facebook one day and I, not one to hold a grudge, was glad to befriend him again after such a long time. It wasn't long before we talked on the phone and I heard the difference in his voice. He told me that there was a tumor pressing against his vocal cords. I sat in disbelief as he explained how his cancer had been in remission but now it was back.

I couldn't believe he seemed so okay with it. He was the same old silly Adrian, cracking jokes as usual. His voice had simply gone from a deep baritone to an airy falsetto. I started staying up talking to him past 3am again when his cancer treatment caused insomnia.

He kept asking me to come visit, but I always had an excuse that I was busy or didn't have transportation. I wasn't lying. But now I wish I would have just gone. He told me that he still had the Michael Jackson magazine he bought me for my birthday and never gave to me and that I should come pick it up. It never happened.

I hadn't spoken to him in two months when I got the news of his passing. It was two days after his birthday, which I had selfishly forgotten while on a trip to Jamaica. The last time he spoke to me, he was checking on me. He was the one with cancer, and he was checking on me. The first time I ever saw my precious Adrian in person was at his funeral. He looked nothing like himself. I'm only just now beginning to stop feeling guilty for never going to see him.

"I'm sorry," said Dominique. He placed the obituary on the dresser. I smiled to let him know that I was okay.

"So where is Damien? He didn't come with you?"

"No, Damien has his own life you know. We are not always together."

"What! You left Damien by himself? I don't even believe *this*," I joke.

"He is a big boy, oki. But he come to Chicago with me." I laugh.

"I knew it! You can't travel anywhere without your twin. You guys are too close. It's very cute though. So where is Damien at in Chicago? You could've invited him over, you know."

"He with his boo. He do his own thing."

"I had no idea Damien had a boo…"

"Damien have a lot of boos," Dominique smirks.

"Casandra is gonna be so upset…" I sound concerned at first but we both burst into laughter.

Everyone around her knows that Damien wasn't really interested in her that way but knowing her, she'll try to flip it and say that he hasn't shown her much attention because he is distracted by this other girl. Casandra is a very attractive, fun girl so it's hard for her to accept that not every guy is going to like her. Dominique finally pulls the last item out of the last box and sets it on my kitchen counter. I gasp.

"*Fini*," says Dominique, and he bows while I applaud him.

"Yay, I can't believe we're finally done! I couldn't have done it without my super talented sidekick..." I raise both my hands in the air.

Dominique high-fives me, then gracefully pulls my arms behind my back, brings my body closer, and kisses me tenderly. It surprised me but I was somehow prepared for it. It was as if I had been waiting for his lips to make contact with me again since the first time. It was short, but sweet. He playfully growled and nibbled at my neck afterwards until I pushed him away laughing.

"I wanted to kiss you the right way," he said, referring to his surprise kiss by the subway. He definitely did. My mind begins to go into overdrive.

"I know it's kind of soon to be asking you this…but…what are we doing, Dominique?" He looks up, directly into my eyes. "I mean, this is so unlike me. I don't let anybody, let alone a guy, get this close to me so soon. We've only known each other for two weeks. And you're not just a regular guy that saw me walking down the street and wanted to talk to me. You're fucking travelling the world right now. But you found the time to come back to my little city and help me move. Correct me if I'm wrong, but I feel like someone who does that must really have feelings. I feel like I'm on the outside watching all of this happen to me. It's surreal."

"Oki, calm down Téa. Just breathe," he says, trying to cover up his laughter. "You right, I don't really know you. You don't really know me. But I can tell you one thing. You different from most girls. I can see that. Already." He is looking down at me with this sexy smile and I can't believe I'm the person on the receiving end of it. "Yes, it is different. I don't know what this is but I know that I like this. That's the important thing, right?"

"Yeah. You're completely right."

"So stop worrying and let's chill. Here. Come draw me a picture like one of these." Dominique picks up a portrait I drew of Aaliyah. He looks through all of them before he comes to one of Beyoncé. "You should let me show this to Monster. It's so good."

"Noooooooo," I say, waving my hands side to side. "Don't do that," I laugh nervously.

"Why not? I know you not afraid." I look down. "Don't hide the talent you have. It's scary in the beginning to let people see who you really are, but you won't get nowhere if you scared. Trust me. Let people see you, girl."

"So you don't think that drawing is pointless? You think it will actually get me somewhere?" I ask, thinking of what Percy said.

"Of course. You will be a big artist one day. And if you don't, I will buy all your art. Don't ever think you gonna fail or some shit like this."

I couldn't tell if he was just being sweet because he liked me, or if he really thought I was talented. But I knew he didn't put me down the way Percy had done. He gave me motivation. Just those few words made me feel like I had a purpose.

"Listen, I don't have cable yet but do you maybe wanna watch a movie on BluRay?"

"Yes, actually I have been waiting to ask you if I can borrow your Iron Man 3 that I saw in your box." I crack up at the guilty look on his face when he pulls it out of the pocket of his sweatpants.

"Are you "borrowing" my stuff already?" I shake my head. "We can watch it now. When do you have to go back?"

"We leave to go to Canada tomorrow afternoon. I can stay for the rest of the day, it's not a big deal."

Dominique and I take advantage of the fact that my living room is 5 feet away from my bedroom. We sit on the floor and lean on the front of my bed. Dominique's long legs are sprawled all over my rug. I pop in the movie and start feeling like I'm experiencing déjà vu. I silently prayed that this scenario doesn't play out the way it did with Percy. It doesn't.

I didn't have to keep asking Dominique to stop touching me, I had to keep asking him to stop talking! He wouldn't shut up through the first 20 minutes of the movie. He was ranting about how he didn't get to do battles as much as he used to and he missed that. He went from battles to talking about his *maman* because he missed her too. I could see that the tour was beginning to take a toll on him.

"I nevvvvvvver get to relax like this and watch a movie. I *am* a movie. I am always moving." I laugh at his joke, but I can also hear the sadness in it.

When Dominique finally runs out of things to say, he rests his head in my lap. I feel my eyelids getting heavy and I slowly doze off. When I wake up an hour and a half later, we are still in the same position on the floor. I look at the clock and see that it's only 5pm. He's breathing lightly and he looks so peaceful sleeping, I decide not to wake him. I take the cap off his head and just sit there, stroking his hair, and asking myself what the fuck is happening.

THREE
"THE TRUTH"

"..........for when he wakes up. He does eat pizza, right?" I ask Damien. He has been on the phone with me for the past 30 minutes. It is now almost 7pm and Dominique has been asleep on my rug the whole time. I knew I liked to wake up to good food so I decided to order a pizza. It felt wonderful telling the delivery guy my very own address. Damien had called me to make sure Dominique was behaving, but ended up staying on the phone with me so he had someone to talk to on his way over.

"Yeah, he eat pizza but don't get him any soda because he will be up all night talking to *me*," he responded. I grinned, because I imagined that would be 10 times worse than when he wouldn't stop talking earlier.

"I won't, I promise. So what were you up to all day?" Damien didn't have a problem talking himself. 75% of our conversation had come from him. I found it impossible to believe that he did this with any girl Dominique had a thing for. In fact, they both had latched onto me emotionally pretty quickly and I couldn't help wondering if maybe they were both kind of lonely. They had many friends on tour and met a lot of people every day, but they had nobody to sit down and talk to. I suddenly became that person.

"So much. I'm very tired. My bro is gonna have to drive us back. I was with a crazy girl today. She don't know how to stop."

"Say no more," Damien and I had become very comfortable with each other quickly, but I don't think I was ready to hear about his sexcapades.

"I think I'm outside, Téa."

"Okay, I'll come get you. Bye." I hung up and opened the front door, waking Dominique from his peaceful slumber. I smiled as I watched him stretch his long, muscular arms to the ceiling and yawn. He was very adorable waking up.

"Hi," he said.

"Hi."

"How long was I asleep?"

"A good two and half hours. You look very rested."

"I can't move my legs," he said, and I knew his limbs were asleep from lying in the same position on the floor for so long. "What are you doing?"

"Standing outside the door so Damien knows where my apartment is. Here he comes."

Dominique stands up slowly and steadily and runs his fingers through his hair. Damien finally makes it in with a huge smile on his face. These twins are always smiling, it's incredibly contagious. He rubs my cheek with his index finger as he walks past me and sits down at the kitchen table to make himself a plate.

"Damien eat like a pig. I never see nobody eat more than my twin." Dominique rolls his eyes and pffttsss his lips.

"It's fine. Don't be afraid to dig in. Just think of this as me repaying you for dinner."

I grab myself 4 slices and pour a glass of pineapple juice. Damien & Dominique have started arguing about who has to drive back, so I tune them out and scroll through Instagram on my phone. I see that Dominique posted a picture while we were watching the movie. It was of my rug and the TV screen, and part of my legs and feet. The caption said

This rug so soft. I gonna stay here forever. Goodnight lmao.

I felt my cheeks getting warm at "forever" but told myself to calm down because he was only talking about a rug.

"We never played UNO and I really wanted to do that, Téa," says Dominique. He's pointing his finger at me, accusingly.

"This guy," says Damien, using his thumb to point at Dominique. "He so rude. How you put up with him?"

"I'm gonna choke you if you put that finger on my plate one more time, Damien."

"Téa, I am sorry, but cover your eyes. It's gonna be bad, oki?" says Damien. His voice is serious but his face is comical. I didn't mind seeing them argue because they did it in their cute, broken English.

"You gonna be the one to tell everybody if something happen to me, that DAMIEN DID---." Dominique can't finish his sentence because Damien is trying to stuff a slice of pizza in his mouth.

"Oh, shut up."

"Does this mean your argument is settled?" I ask, laughing.

"Yes, Dominique is going to drive." I tell Damien that he can take the entire box of pizza with him. I even give them one of my jugs of pineapple juice, which I happen to be very stingy with.

"Please be safe okay, no arguing while behind the wheel," I warn. Damien kisses the side of my lip and thanks me for the food before walking out the door. Dominique immediately uses his finger to rub Damien's kiss off and kisses me full on the mouth.

"You bring out me and my twin silly side some way, girl," he says, and winks. "Don't forget about me when I'm not here, oki? *D'accord?*"

"How can I?"

"*D'accord?*"

"Okay."

"Say it." I roll my eyes.

"*D'accord!*" He nods his head.

"We gonna have you speaking French soon," he says, caressing my chin. "Bye, baby."

I smile and wave then close the door behind him. Here I am again, stuck in the same position at the door like I was when Percy left my house. But this time, I had a grin on my face. And I was certain I had begun to fall.

■■■

That night, I had two dreams. In the first dream, Dominique was my boyfriend (naturally). It was his mom's birthday and I was at her house with other family members. I had this really nice gift for her, but I had to leave for good right after the party. I had told Dominique this in advance so he would know that was his last chance to see me. He forgot about me. Just as I'm about to leave, I see through the window, him and Damien running at full speed towards the door. Dominique runs in and hugs me and gives me a kiss.

So then it got weird. Instead of there being grass next to the sidewalk outside, there was swamp water. Yeah. So Dominique went in the water and there was this other guy out there smoking weed. Next thing I know, I look out the window and see the police arresting the other guy. I go outside and see them bring Dominique over in handcuffs too. He and the other guy are both crying. I just hugged him really tight around his waist, because I'm only 5'1, and kept telling him he just has to post bail, which will be nothing for him, and he can get out. That was the end of that dream.

In the second dream, I was graduating from high school. Me and all my classmates were at school getting ready for it. It was at nighttime. But instead of rehearsing for it like any other class would do, we were preparing by running a mile around a track. I was running with a dress and one heel on.

I didn't actually see the graduation happen in my dream either. I just remember my friend coming over and kissing me on my forehead, then I was home at the dinner table with my Daddy and my brother. I told them that I was upset because nobody came to my graduation. My daddy got mad at me because he couldn't believe I didn't tell anyone that I would be graduating that day and that I let him miss out on something important like that.

My phone vibrating on my face is what woke me. Today wasn't like the other day where I woke up with the sun shining and with a smile on my face. I was very groggy this morning and there were grey clouds outside my window. I check the time on my phone before I see who's calling. It's after 12pm. I can't believe I've slept this late.

What's even worse is that my daddy's name is popping up on my screen. Coincidence? I figured I've been avoiding him enough and pick up.

"Hello?"

"Good afternoon, daughter," he says, putting emphasis on the "daughter".

"Hi, Daddy."

"Was you sleep?"

"Yes, but I need to get up anyway. I have a lot to do today. What's up?" I ask, trying to get this conversation over with.

"What you gotta do?" He completely ignores my question.

"Well... I have to go get another Bristol pad to draw in and some graphite pencils. Then I gotta ship some orders out. I hope I can get to the post office before 3."

"Orders?"

"Yeah, well." Now I have to break things down for him. "People can order prints of my drawings online and I have to ship them out."

"Oh, I see. So you got a lil business going on and you couldn't tell your daddy?" he says jokingly, but he's serious. And now he wants to get in on it. I already know.

"I mean…" I trail off.

"Listen." He gets loud all of a sudden. "I got an idea on making money. It's about making family calendars." He pauses, waiting for my thoughts on it but I have no idea what he's talking about.

All I know is that it sounds like one of his wack get-rich-quick schemes that he always comes to *me* for because he doesn't know how to do anything. Last time he came to me about "making money", it was to start some kind of local lottery pyramid shit. I'm not sure exactly. I just know it was illegal and that he had me printing up all kinds of charts for him that he never used because the lottery never happened anyway.

"Umm, Daddy, I'm really busy right now. You know, I work part-time but I'm also doing my art, trying to get my clothing line started, and I'm even writing a book. I know that may not sound important to you, but it means a lot to me and it's very time consuming and takes a lot of hard work. So I just don't really have time for that…I'm sorry."

"Well, if you busy, you busy. You know?" I took this to be rhetorical. He inhaled sharply. "Well I'ma let you go ahead and…take care of your business. I'll talk to you later okay?"

"Okay."

"I love you."

"Love you too."

"Byeeee."

"Bye-bye." I hang up and roll my eyes. I flop back onto my pillow for five minutes, then force myself to get up and get ready.

As I shower, I reflect back on my dreams and wonder why? I was big on writing down my dreams as soon as I woke up. I used to write down who I saw in them and a very detailed summary of what happened in them, so that I could read and remember later. I even looked up the meanings of some of the key things from the dream that stuck in my brain. Maybe I would do that later.

Right now, I wasn't feeling up to it. I was mad at myself for waking up late because now I wouldn't be able to eat breakfast and would probably be irritable for the rest of the afternoon.

I made it all the way to the post office before I realized it was Sunday. I could have kicked myself. I wanted to scream, but I had somehow developed a sore throat on the bus ride over. It was obvious I was just having a bad day. Anything that could go wrong would go wrong.

I thought about the tips I told myself to follow when I started feeling depressed. Number one was to continue to smile and not let little things ruin my entire day. So I exhaled slowly and pasted a smile on my face. It started to feel forced, so I decided to smile at people as they walked past and say good afternoon. That felt better.

I felt like it was working because my bus came three minutes after I got to the bus stop and I didn't have to wait in the windy weather. I told myself that things were starting to look up already. Maybe I would go home and fix myself something nice to eat and cuddle up in bed and write for the rest of the day, since it was so ugly outside.

I thought of other positives about the day to keep myself in a good mood. When I stepped off my bus, I walked the two blocks to my apartment and my heart stopped. I didn't know how I would react the next time I saw Percy, but I also didn't know it would be so soon.

Percy was leaving an apartment across and a little down the street from mine. I kept walking, hoping that he wouldn't see me but he spotted me immediately. *Maybe this will be a pleasant encounter*, I whispered to myself. One could only hope. He crossed the street and walked over to me. He was smiling so I guess he had put things behind him also.

I was taken aback when he grabbed my waist and pulled me in close without even speaking. My nose was in his neck and I couldn't breathe. He was holding me so tight, I couldn't find a way out of his grasp and I could feel his tongue on my neck. He had my arms pinned to my side. I got scared because I realized it was getting dark outside and we were all alone.

"What the fuck are you doing, get off of me!" I grunted. By now, he was backing me up into the front gate of my building and kissing down my chest. "Stop it!" He finally let me go and laughed. As soon as he unwrapped his hands from around my wrist, I jetted inside of the gate and locked it. "Are you crazy?"

"I see you still scared of a lil dick," he spoke. He was still laughing hysterically. I thought he might be drunk because I've never see him like this before, but I hadn't smelled any alcohol on his breath. "You must be a lesbian."

He started walking off, and I watched him until I was sure he had turned the corner. Then I ran inside and dialed Casandra's number and begged her to come over. I was crying because he'd made me feel stupid and dirty and worthless when he grabbed me and touched me the way he did. I was frightened out of my mind because at one point, I actually thought he might rape me.

Casandra didn't ask any questions. She just got there within the next 20 minutes and put some tea on, even though I didn't drink hot tea. She said it would calm me down and I was hiccupping by the time she got there, so I let her make it. She gave me a cold, wet washcloth to wipe my face with and sat next to me on my bed.

"I'm calling Dominique," she said, point blank. I shook my head profusely.

"He's busy, Casandra. He doesn't need to be worried about me. He's gonna think it's way worse than it is. It's not that big of a deal for you to do all that."

"Oh, it's not?" She raised her eyebrows. "Percy assaulted you, Téa."

I said nothing. I knew she was right, but I didn't want to bother Dominique with this. He wasn't my protector. He wasn't even my man. Was he?

"I just don't want him to think I'm gonna be calling him every time something goes wrong like he's my Superman or something. It's asking a lot for him to just drop what he's doing and fly out here to be with me."

"Whatever you say, Téa. But I don't think you should be alone. What if he tries to come back? You know I can't be here with you all the time." Just the thought of him coming back for me made me tear up again. Casandra stood up. "That's it, I'm calling him."

I didn't object this time. She walked into the kitchen and dialed his number. I couldn't hear his voice, although I really needed to at that moment.

"Don't tell him I'm crying," I plead.

"Yeah, this is Téa's friend. Casandra……Right…I'm great, and you?……. Well a LOT is up….Actually, that's why I'm calling. She had a little run-in with this guy and she doesn't need to be alone right now. He knows where she lives." I sigh because she is making it sound really bad and I don't want him to think I'm in grave danger. "I felt like that would be a good thing to do….She doesn't want you to worry but I just thought I should inform you…..Cool……Nice talking to you too, Dominique….bye." She hangs up and reclaims her spot next to me on the bed.

"How annoyed was he by the fact that you called him?" I asked sarcastically. She starts separating the tight curls in my hair.

"He was quite pleasant, actually," she says. "When I told him you don't want him to worry, he said he's not and that I did the right thing by calling him. He's gonna try to fly out as soon as he can."

"So he wasn't mad at all?"

"No, girl, why would he be mad? I'm pretty sure he has more than a thing for you and men always have to protect what they feel belongs to them. So he obviously feels that way."

Casandra stays to cook me dinner, even though I tell her over and over again that she doesn't have to. She stays with me as long as she can, but eventually she has to leave of course. I tell her I'll be okay. She kisses my cheek and begs me to get some sleep. "I'll even let you keep the tea," she says with a smile, and I walk her out.

The next couple days drag by. I don't have work until Friday but I force myself to get up at the crack of dawn anyway. I look up a couple watercolor paint tutorials. I watch some natural hair videos and deep condition my own. I bake a chocolate cake. Anything to keep myself happy.

Four days after my encounter with Percy, I get a call from Dominique and he tells me he is outside my door. I open it and he grabs my face and kisses my forehead before I can say anything. He just holds me and I can feel my heart pounding quickly because I'm finally smelling his scent again.

I'm so happy, I could cry. I was lying to myself this whole time. I've been lying to myself ever since I'd met Dominique. I had been pretending that I could care less what would become of us and that Dominique probably could too. But the truth was that I could see it in his eyes that he had never cared for any woman the way he cared for me. And truth was I had fallen head over heels for the man on some Jack and Rose, in-love-within-two-days type shit. I was just in denial because I know how guys can lead you on to believe it's more than what it is, and it's not. But this…this is.

"You shaking," Dominique finally speaks. He pulls away from me and looks down, directly into my eyes. He's staring into my soul. "Don't shake, I'm here now," he laughs.

His face moves in towards mine and something is different about this kiss. It's warmer. No…it's more tender. Or maybe it was the emotions that had built up all the way to the brim and were finally being released, shared between the connection of both our lips. Mine parted and the slip of his tongue brought a sensation that travelled from my mouth down to the center of my thighs.

It was so overwhelming, I stopped it. I walked over to the kitchen table and sat down while Dominique watched me with a confused stare.

"So how did you get here?" I asked. I knew I was breathing hard and that he could probably see my chest going up and down quickly. If he noticed, he didn't mention it. He just walked over to me and kneeled down in between my legs so we were face to face.

"I rent a car," he says, kissing my chin.

"Well, did Damien come with you again?" My hands instinctively move towards the back of his neck as he's kissing me, but I quickly realize what I'm doing and sit on them.

"Nope." His left hand is now resting on my right thigh and his other hand is on my lower back. He's kissing my collarbone ever so gently. My blood is beginning to boil.

"Umm, Dee…" I ease myself backwards in the chair, but he only leans forward. My phone vibrates against the table and I thank God for Casandra calling because it was getting hard to ignore the way he was making me feel.

Dominique picks up my phone and smirks at me as if to say *This isn't over*. And I believe him. So I get up and pretend to pull food out of the refrigerator to eat while he talks to her. This is a total fail because my refrigerator is almost completely empty.

"What's wrong, baby?" Dominique is suddenly behind me with his hand on my shoulder. I whip around and back up towards the counter. I didn't mean to make it so obvious that I wanted him to stop touching me, but I did and he finally got it. "Why you running away from me?"

"I'm not, it's…..not that. There's just no food here to eat?" I say it as more of a question than a statement. "What did Casandra say?"

"Do you need me to go get something?" he asks, generously.

"Oh, would you?"

"Yes. Just tell me what you want and I'll give it to you." What is that sound? Oh, that's just my bottom lip trembling. I try to think of what to tell him to get but my brain isn't functioning properly. "Just text it, oki? I'll be back soon." He leans in for a kiss but I open my mouth to speak.

"Do you know where to go?"

"GPS." He leans in again.

"Okay, be safe!" I pat him quickly on the chest. He narrows his eyes in a way only he could and slips out the door. I breathe a sigh of relief and grab my phone to call Casandra back.

"He's trying me, Casandra," I blurt out as soon as she answers. "He's trying to rope me in and I can't do it."

"What are you even talking about?" she asks.

"Dee… he is seriously trying to seduce me. I mean he came in here and was just all over me. I don't know if I can hold back for much longer." Casandra laughed so hard, I could almost feel her spray through the phone. She laughed for a good minute and even slapped her knee a couple of times before she responded.

"Téa. You sound like a crazy person. You made it seem like he was trying to tie you up and hold you hostage. He wants you. What's so bad about letting him have you?"

"I don't know… I mean, you know my feelings about sex. It just feels wrong to do that with him when I haven't known him for that long. I've known plenty of guys so much longer and never did anything with them."

"And you know why? Because none of those guys were *the one*. I'm just saying, I hear you go on and on about this guy and I can see in his actions that he feels for you. Dee just does it for you and you have to admit that." She was right. Whatever IT is, he is definitely doing it. "I don't see anything wrong with you having sex with him if you love him."

"Who said anything about love?" I was just being self-conscious because I thought she would tease me for even thinking I could be in love so soon. "Look, I'm just very fond of him."

"Oh really. Where is he right now?"

"He went out for a second to pick up some groceries for me."

"Are you fucking kidding me? The man is out grocery shopping for you and you act like you can't let him eat your pussy?"

"Casandra…"

"Casandra nothing. He isn't just fond of you. I'm sure he doesn't go out of his way to book flights and go see women he is *fond* of." Her voice gets softer. "I get it, Téa. It's been a long time since you've had real feelings for someone and it's been a long time since you let a guy get that close to you. But trust me when I say you don't wanna let a good thing get away from you. Stop being afraid and GET YOUR MAN."

Something about those words made something go off inside of me, and I knew she was right. What were the chances of another guy, who is perfect in my eyes, feeling this way about me and actually having the means to express it to me?

I would certainly never meet another Dominique. And I didn't want to. I wanted him. All of him. I didn't know how I was going to go about it, but I was going to have him. I repeated this to myself over and over again in my head until he returned with the groceries.

"I try to tell her how much semon…salmon, SALMON," he corrects himself, "you want but she no understand me." I grab the bags out of his hand and set them on the table.

"It's okay, baby. Come over here with me." I pull him by his hand until he follows me over to the bed. "Lay with me," I say.

"Okay but you don't wanna eat?"

"We will…." I pull his hand so that his body gives in and he sits next to me. Then I strategically slide to the other side of the bed and lay on my side to face him, hoping he'll get the gist and do the same. He does. Now we are in the center of my bed lying face to face and I see his arm go up and stroke mine. He smiles and shows off his beautiful teeth.

"You confuse me, girl, you know that?" he speaks. "You de first girl I don't know what she want. Evvvvvvery time I see you, you show me something. Something new. All de time."

"I'm not good at making up my mind…"

"Why you not good at it?" He sits up a little, so attentive. When he puts all his weight on one elbow, a curl falls in front of his left eye and it takes everything in me not to move it out the way.

"I don't know. I guess you were right about me being scared. You were definitely right actually." I look down but Dominique pushes my chin back up, forcing me to look him in his eye.

"I know you scared, you wanna know how? Cause you don't tell me anything. Look, I tell you all about my family and you don't tell me nothing about yours. So. Tell me now." My laugh echoes off the walls.

"What am I supposed to say?"

"Tell me evvvverything. Who your father? Who your mother? How many brudder and sister you have?" I inhale and exhale.

"My father is Jerry. My mother is Sonya. I have one older brother, one younger sister, one older half-brother, and one older step-brother." The shock on Dominique's face makes me giggle.

"Oh my God. I never know this if you didn't tell me! Where are they?"

"Well I don't live with any of them. My younger sister lives with my mom and stepdad in the suburbs. My brother lives in Texas. He just graduated from college out there. My half-brother…well, my father doesn't claim him. I've only been around him 4 times in my whole life." Dominique's smile drops a little when I say this, probably because of my noticeable dismay. "My older step-brother has his own place, but we hang out from time to time."

"You didn't tell me where your father is," says Dominique.

"My father…" I start, but I'm not sure if I want to finish. "I don't really like to talk about him."

"But why?"

"He's just a poor excuse for a man."

"I know what you mean. I can say the same thing for my fodder. And I tell you why. So tell me about yours." Dominique wraps his large hand around my small one. "Don't be scared to tell me things. I can't know de you now if I don't know where you come from." My eyes almost glaze over at his sincerity. If his looks didn't get me into bed one day, his honesty certainly would.

"I don't know... we just never see him. Even when we were kids and he lived at home with us, we never saw him. When my parents finally divorced and we moved, he didn't have a choice but to find his own place to live. He dropped by my Grandma's house one day to "visit" us and never left. It made me so mad how he just decided for her that he was gonna live there. I was mad at her for not making him leave. Well, months later, he told us that he was asked to be out of the house within a week. And he's lived from couch to couch ever since then.

"He do something bad to you? I see it in your face."

"He did a lot of bad things. My mom did too. Worst thing she did was stay in that abusive relationship and make us endure it with her." I shook my head. "But my mom has taken care of us all on her own since then. My dad was ordered to pay child support but he was injured a lot working such a physical job. It started to take a toll on his body and he eventually had to stop working. So my mom barely gets any child support now. He admitted to me that at one point in time, he didn't even have enough money to pay his cell phone bill after child support and the IRS took money. He actually tried to make *me* feel guilty for the fact that he had to give us money."

I was getting so angry just thinking about a phone conversation we'd had when I poured my heart out to him and he refused to apologize for the things he's done. Dominique hurried to wipe a tear before it could leave the corner of my eye.

"I'm sorry baby. If it make you sad, you don't have to talk about it." He puts his arm around my waist and pulls me closer, kissing me on the forehead.

"I can't believe you almost just made me cry." I playfully smack his chest, trying to lighten the mood.

"Don't hit me cause you not ready for that," he says, squeezing my arm tightly. "That Percy muthafucka really no ready for it."

"You don't have to fight anyone for me, Dee. He's nobody. Not even worth it."

"But still. He not gonna mess with you cause you mine now." His hand, still wrapped around mine, begins to play with my fingers. "We belong to each other. Now hand me some sugar." I give Dominique the craziest look before I realize what he's trying to say and burst into laughter. His eyes widen. "I say it wrong?" he asks.

"You mean to say 'give me some sugar'," I explain, still laughing.

"Well, GIVE. ME. SOME. SUGAR. Muthafucka," he laughs, and kisses me in the middle of my laughter. His lips move swiftly from my mouth to my chin to my neck. Three sweet kisses from this beautiful being were enough to make my night. He looks at me and smiles for what seems like minutes. "You make me tired."

"How I make you tired, you the one making me talk." I stick my tongue out.

"Don't do that again." Dominique puts my head in his chest and strokes my hair. "If you keep being bad, somebody gonna take care of that." I blush at his threat. "Go to sleep, girl. I love you." He said it so effortlessly as if he'd been saying it for the last five years. It replayed in my head a million times before I felt him smack my ass.

"Don't be mean."

"I love you too Dominique."

"Goodnight."

■■■

I slipped out of bed around 8am after the longest, most fulfilling slumber I'd had in years. We had gone to sleep pretty early, but I guess Dominique was still tired from work and jetlag. He didn't move a muscle when I slid out of his tight grasp.

Being fully energized for the first time in a long time, I decided to work on a new piece. I had plenty of pictures saved in a folder on my computer that I wanted to draw, but it takes a while to get around to them when so many people are requesting custom portraits. Finally I was able to work on something that inspired me.

I grabbed my laptop, my pencils, my 14x17" drawing pad, my sharpener, erasers, and my watercolor paints. I chose the "Oldies" playlist on my iTunes library and made sure to keep the volume low so it wouldn't wake Dominique.

I slowly sketched the outline of the face, glancing back at the real picture on the screen of my laptop every couple seconds. The eyes were easy. They were the most simple feature on the face. The nose was much harder. I wanted it to be perfect. I carefully drew in the lips, which stretched almost from cheek to cheek, smiling. Little chin hairs.

"Sunshine" by Enchantment played softly while I drew the tendrils of hair falling in front and to the side of the forehead. The portrait was forming so nicely, I screamed with excitement. On the inside of course.

I shaded in the high cheek bones and the flawless jaw-line. The stress lines above the brows gave me a little trouble but I finally got them right. The hair took up most of my time. But it had to be perfect. When I completed the shading, I pulled out the paint and started adding drops of color to the paper. Beiges and pinks and oranges, with a speck of blue to give it a little diversity.

It was so beautiful. Masterpiece was an understatement and I couldn't be more proud. I'd never done a drawing in such a short amount of time. Dominique woke up from his peaceful sleep just as I was signing and dating the bottom of the drawing. When he saw what I had done, he quickly came over to admire my work of art.

I laid down on the floor and looked up at the ceiling while Dominique touched the corners of the paper. I knew he was not only seeing it, but feeling it as well. He didn't speak, but his eyes said everything. I watched him run his hands over the charcoal hair, which smeared it a bit, but made it even more remarkable.

"You do this for me?" he finally asked.

"All for you," I say. He opens his mouth to say something else but no words come out.

"You are so beautiful to do something like this…… God make you so beautiful in a lot of ways." I am humbled seeing him in awe of his portrait. I smile.

"God gave me a beautiful person as inspiration. I didn't do it all on my own, did I?"

"I inspire *you*?" he asks.

"Yes. You do." I hold my hand out. He takes it and I pull him so that he's kneeling on the floor, hovering over me. "Thank you for opening your eyes and seeing me, Dominique."

"It's hard not to see you." He strokes my belly with both his thumbs before he lies down on top of me. Once again, I find myself with Dominique LeBeau between my legs. The sun reflecting off my purple and red curtains make for a lovely lighting effect that reminds me of mornings in Montego Bay.

"Do you know this song?" I ask. Dominique shakes his head. "It's called Carousel. It's by Michael Jackson." Dominique nods his head, recognizing the voice. "There's one part...when it comes to the bridge. Michael does a little run and his voice fades away, and the way the guitar comes in makes chills run down my spine. The bass line, it just makes me shiver. Have you ever felt that? I love music with real instruments because they have that kind of beautiful effect. I feel bad for the people who have never felt that before."

The song is coming to the part I described and I close my eyes. Michael sings. *And I can hear it calling me...* I sigh.

"You can feel it in your soul."

Dominique closes his eyes as well and slides down so that he is laying cheek to belly with me. He rubs his face against my skin and his bushy mane tickles me. He is like a child, weary of leaving his mother's side. We were so peaceful just lying there, that it felt like an out-of-body experience.

Suddenly I was in the air above us, watching myself stroke the back of Dominique's neck and watching him caress his cheek against my belly. I see part of his hair dip into my watercolor paints, lying on the floor next to my hip. I sit up slowly, so as not to disturb him too much.

"There's paint in your hair, baby." He looks directly into my eyes.

"Wash it for me."

I give Dominique a towel out of the linen closet and we both head to the bathroom. I tell him to soak his hair in warm water while I look through the small cabinet for my sulfate-free shampoo and my conditioner. Dominique does just that, and then stands. He's towering over me, hair dripping everywhere. He is stunning.

I glare up at him with my mouth agape. The next thing I know, he is pulling his wife beater over his head and grabbing my hand. I don't realize that I have closed my eyes until I feel his lips on my hand. I open them to see him kissing it, gentleman style. Then he wraps his hand around it and lures me into the shower. *Oh shit.*

You keep your eyes on me as you walk backwards towards the tub. I'm watching you as well. I notice the corner of your mouth curl up. There is a shy but certain smile on your face. Water pours into every wrinkle and crevice on your chest; you are a God. I'm not sure if I'm placing my hand or if you are guiding it, but it lands below your collar bone and slides down ever so slowly.

Your left hand is on my waist, pulling me forward. I can hear your voice in my head saying **Don't be scared**. *I'm not. I'm ready and willing. Bending down and wrapping your hands around my face, you kiss me once on my left cheek, once on my right cheek, and once on my head. I close my eyes and savor it before the feeling goes away.*

I can hear you pull the shower curtain back and goose bumps rise on my arms and thighs. We don't undress. You help me into the shower then step in behind me, towering over me. The lights are off but the sun is on, and we glow blue and green, just like the shower curtains.

You waste no time in lifting me up against the wall and wrapping my legs around your slim waist. You have me right where you want me. You have never kissed me so intensely. We are familiar with each other's mouths so there is no need to hold off on what we really want. Your warm, sleek...um um um. The taste of that sweet tongue is the best greeting I've ever experienced.

You tease me with it, slipping in and out, making my tongue chase after yours. You put my arms above my head and pin them to the shower wall. You don't want me to escape either. But when you suck hungrily on my bottom lip and grind your hips into my center, escaping is the last thing on my mind.

*I'm surprised at the pleasure I feel from the friction of your basketball shorts rubbing against my legging. Imagine what kind of magic we could make without them. You lick the water that has travelled down to my neck back up to my ear. There is a weak attempt to hold back your laughter when you whisper **Are you wet**?*

You nibble, suck, lick... your tongue on my ear sends me over the edge and I let out a weak moan. You are the first man to ever make me do that. I'm so overwhelmed, my hands fly up and grab at your soaking hair and I squeeze. You put them back up against the wall and make sure they stay there. I'm fighting.

I don't understand what kind of power your tongue possesses but it has got a hold on me. It glides slowly up the front of my neck, over my chin, and back into my mouth. Your lips, supple and soft, give me one last moist kiss and you let go of my arms. My eyes are still closed, my mouth still agape. I hear the shower water go off and I open them.

You throw me over your shoulder effortlessly, like you have done so many times before. You carry me through the kitchen to my bed and we are dripping water all over the house. But that is the least of my problems. All I'm worried about is how I'm going to handle what you're about to do to me. You slap my ass and squeeze to snap me out of my thoughts.

The sun is so warm, our bodies are already beginning to dry after you lay me down. You walk away and go back towards the bathroom. I lie on the bed, contemplating. I feel sexier and more confident than I have ever felt in the presence of a man. Maybe it's the way you look at me. I can tell you want me.

I hear your footsteps coming back toward my bed and sit up on my knees. Your hands are behind your back and your hair is falling over the front of your face. Just the sight of your beautiful skin makes me tingle between my thighs; I can't wait until you're back on this bed with me. When you're standing in front of my bed again, I put my hands on your waist and lay my forehead against your abs. I can just stay that way forever.

The bulge in your shorts is right before my eyes and before I can stop myself, my hand is rubbing it and stroking it. I look at you and you're looking at the ceiling, your hand in my hair. I kiss it. I can't believe what I'm doing. I have seemed to forgotten that I am submissive. But you make me want to do things and get close to you in ways I've never been before.

You soon take control again though, and I don't mind. You pull my hair back slowly until my head is inches away from your pelvis and force me down on the bed. My leggings are still wet and sticking to me, but you manage to slip them off. You remove my tank next and gawk at my breasts. They aren't big, but they're beautiful and I can see the appreciation in your eyes.

My nipples are still wet and hard, but you warm them with your luscious mouth. You are enjoying this as much as I am. Both your hands go up and down the sides of my waist as you lick around my nipple and back and forth. Your tongue is lightning fast, flickering back and forth in my cleavage. It makes my legs squeeze tightly around yours. Yes Lawd...you doing that.

You pull back and pick up what you were holding behind your back. You squeeze some of my cocoa butter lotion onto my belly and slowly rub it in. it makes my caramel brown skin glisten and glow. You repeat the same process on my thighs and calves.

I'm nervous when you get to my feet, because I've never let another get that close to them, but your hands work their magic on them as well. You go over to my dresser and pull a pair of socks from my drawer. I burst into laughter. **What are you doing?** You don't answer, only wink as you put them on my feet. You rise up and kiss the side of my thigh before you grab at my panties.

You pull them down. It is revealed that I am completely bare, with the exception of a small patch of hair above my clitoris, a symbol of my womanhood. You turn me over, then rub the cocoa butter on my ass. You find humor in the fact that my right cheek is spotted with brown freckles, but kiss them tenderly and reassure me that they are beautiful. You turn me back over and suddenly I'm nervous because I know what comes next. My legs are shaking and you haven't even entered me yet. **I haven't done this in a long time...please be gentle?**

I gonna always be gentle with you, baby. I gonna always be gentle with what is mine. *You hover over me, pressing your hard-on into my clit. Rubbing slowly... lie on top of me... put all your weight on me. Your nose and mouth are in my neck as you roll your body into mine. I slide your shorts down at an equal pace and grope your ass. I force you to grind harder onto my clit and it feels amazing. I don't want it to end, but you reach one hand down to feel my wetness.*

You circle around my pussy and I'm so slippery, I must be ready because it has never been so easy to slide a finger into me without a cry of pain. You must be able to that tell fingering is not my preference because you slide it back out. Face to face with me, you put your finger to your lips and close your mouth around it entirely. I watch you slide it out slowly, devouring all my goodness. Then you place your finger in my mouth and I taste nothing but you.

You kiss me greedily, like you might run out of me. But you never will. Slow down, there is enough of me to have for centuries to come. I don't realize the hard kissing is a distraction so that I don't notice the pain from the tip of your dick at my entrance. Of course I feel it, but it was a nice try.

I open my mouth to tell you to go slow, but you give one hard thrust before I can say anything. My eyes widen and I yelp. You bite my mouth to hush me. You thrust one more time until you are completely inside of me. It feels like my vagina is being pulled from the inside and I let out a faint **FUCK** from the excruciating pain. It's killing me but I realize that the pain would have lasted much longer if you had taken your time easing in.

You spread my legs wider to open me up some more but you never take your lips off me. Once I find a comfortable position and the pain is starting to disappear, you dive into this pussy and grind your pelvis against my clit until I start tremble. Something about the intimacy, the closeness of your body against mine matched with the overwhelming attraction and emotions I feel for you, made my body ache in an amazing way.

Never had I felt the slightest bit of pleasure from penetration alone. But it wasn't penetration alone, was it? It was you, Dominique LeBeau releasing all your hopes and dreams onto my body. Do you feel that baby? You don't have to say a word; I know you feel it when you slide out of me and struggle to catch your breath.

I smile to myself because I know I'm working with some good shit. I know it's time to change positions, and I roll over onto my knees so you can take me from behind. It's easier this way, you know. It takes a little work to get inside but once you're there, you stroke slowly to a steady beat. The beat of our hearts? No, that's much too fast.

You're taking your time but you're breathing real hard, Daddy. I can feel it on the back of my neck when you reach forwards and swirl your wet tongue across it. That move alone made me feel so good, I could've cried. ***C'est tout… c'est la vérité… juste ici,*** you moan. How long can we go on like this? You lean back again with your hand on my neck and pump faster, but you don't wanna come, do you?

Nah, fuck that. You pull out and lay on your back, waiting for me to assume the position. I crawl towards you and straddle your waist. You pull me down onto your tip and slide in with ease. You don't stop until you have completely filled me. A drop of sweat falls from my nose onto your chest. You try to guide my hips, but I shut that down. Let me find my rhythm... I can't believe how deep you are.

I'm beginning to get that feeling again. It feels so good, I need more of it. I need that feeling to come harder and faster. So I grind into you harder...and faster... You can't take it. Your hands leave my waist and grip the bed sheets. You're biting your lip. Let me do that for you. I stop before you can come, lean forward and kiss you full on the mouth.

You've taken this opportunity to take back control. We're back in missionary the way I like it and the look on your face tells me you're not stopping until I give you what you want. And the way you stroking that, I can tell you're gonna get it. When you put your lips on my breast and devour them like they won't still be here tomorrow, it gets me to that point.

I'm gonna scream... **Shit, baby...**, you say to the ceiling. It's getting better...and Better...and BETTER until... my God! Ohhh......yes. YES. You did that. I'm panting and I just lay there until you come seconds behind me. My whole body is shaking. I have never climaxed like this before. Masturbation has nothing on this shit.

You throw your face into my chest and just lie there, exhaling quickly. Your nostrils are flared and your forehead and hair are soaking wet from the heat of our love-making. Our love-making. You and I made hot, steamy, beautiful love butt naked in the middle of the morning with the sun gleaming on us.

You look at me and I'm smiling down at you. You give me a long, wet kiss and your lips feel like beauty, art, love, and pain all rolled into one. A thought suddenly comes to me. I tap you to get you to roll off of me and tell you **Don't move, I'll be right back.**

I grab two washcloths out of the linen closet and go into the bathroom to let the hot water run. Then I soak one towel with hot water and soap and the other towel with hot water only. I walk back to the bed with them, take the towel with soap, and proceed to clean off your wondrous manhood. I remember reading a book when I was younger, much too young to be reading that book.

The woman would always wash her man's dick for him when they finished making love and, to me, it showed that she owned it. That was hers. And this is mine. I wipe again with the other towel then wipe you dry. When I'm finished, you pull your basketball shorts back on and I climb on top of you to lie. **Thank you, baby.** *You're out like a light within minutes, and I doze off not too long afterwards.*

When I wake up, it is a little after 2pm and Dominique is no longer in bed with me. I rub my eyes and run my fingers through my hair, which is all over the place now. My twist-out had become very fluffy from my sweating. I was hot because I had forgotten to close the blinds before I fell asleep.

I grabbed my bath towel so that I could take a nice, warm shower. When I stand up, I see that Dominique has hooked up my old Gamecube and is sitting in the middle of the floor playing Mario Kart. I giggle and walk over to him to kiss the side of his cheek and mess in his hair.

"You are so beautiful right now, you know that?" I ask. He laughs.

"You think *I'm* beautiful?" he asks. "You are a Queen." He leans in to kiss me but I back up.

"Well bow down, PEASANT. Thou shalt not address the Queen in such a manner. The Queen is going to take a shower now." The slap on the ass I receive when I turn around is highly expected.

"You look good, baby!" Dominique yells after I have already disappeared into the bathroom.

What Dominique did to me earlier that day felt so good, but it left my vagina aching like never before. The hot water was easing the pain a little and I wanted to stay under it forever. I couldn't even wash my ass for five minutes without Dominique popping in to *tongue me down*. He wasn't about to get up in this again, if that's what he was thinking. My body needed a break. I wouldn't mind falling asleep tonight the way I did earlier at all though.

When I jump out and get dressed, I'm still in an excellent mood. Who knew dick could make you smile like that? Not me, that's for sure. Of course it wasn't just the dick. It was Dominique, period. This man rocked my world in more ways than one, and my heart pounded every time he put his hands on me.

It was a scary feeling, but one I wasn't ready to let go of any time soon. I needed that love that could breathe life into you. And that's what he had done for me today. He handled me in a way only a man who loved me could handle me. I would reminisce on this day for years to come.

"You know what?" I say suddenly, grabbing Dominique's attention. "I think I'm gonna cook. Yep. I'm gonna cook." I'm grinning from ear to ear, pulling pots and pans out and this is when Dominique knows he has cast a spell on me. "I'm gonna cook you the best spaghetti, fish, and garlic bread you have ever had in your life, sir. You not ready for this."

"Look at you, you cook for me---?" Dominique is cut off by the sound of the buzzer.

"That's probably Casandra, she was a little worried about me earlier," I say.

"Why?" Dominique asks, as he walks toward the front door. I blush a little, thinking about our phone conversation.

"Oh nothing. You open the door for her, I'm gonna go wash my hands real quick."

I went to the bathroom, closed the door behind me, and inhaled deeply. I put my back against the door and smiled. I had to take a moment to myself to ask God if this was real. Is this actually happening? Never had I felt so normal with a man. It felt like this is how things were supposed to be. *Please don't let it go away any time soon, God.*

I lathered my hands, rinsed, and dried them off on a towel. I couldn't wait to go back in the kitchen and spend the rest of the day with my man and my best friend. But my cheerfulness was short-lived. Before I could even crack the door open, I heard a voice that wasn't Dominique's. It wasn't Casandra's either.

"I thought I had the right apartment but I guess not," I heard Percy say. I kept the door cracked and looked out, shaking. I could see Percy looking past Dominique and glancing around the room. I prayed that he didn't notice anything that belonged to me but I knew he had once he said "What's your name?" Dominique looked confused, but answered.

"Uhh, Dominique. I'm not from Chicago."

"Yeah, yeah, I thought you looked familiar. You're one of those twins, from France right?" he asked. I cringed.

A million thoughts swam through my brain. I couldn't figure out what to do. I had to get in there. Dominique didn't even realize who he was talking to. And I didn't want Percy anywhere near my place or me, for that matter. Think, Téa. Think.

"Yes, that's me," Dominique says with a smile. Percy reached his hand up to give him dap and I knew this had gone on long enough. I slowly start making my way out of the bathroom. Percy sees me first and grins.

"Téa, man. Whassup?" he asks as if we are cool. I cling to Dominique's side and he puts his arm over my shoulder. Percy pulls out a cigarette and says, "I knew I had the right place."

"You know him, baby?" I look down at the floor, pissed off. I can't believe he would really try something like this.

"This is Percy..." I mumble.

So uhh...," Percy takes a drag from his cigarette, "Since you got this nigga answering the door with no shirt on, I'm guessing you fucking him, huh?"

Dominique's arm quickly falls from my shoulder and he pushes me behind him. His nostrils are flaring and I've never seen his face so angry. He is instantly in Percy's face and Percy backs up, laughing. I see his fists clenched together as he pulls his shorts up. I get scared when I see that because I don't know what he's going to do next and I don't want him getting in any trouble.

"Say that shit again?" he says calmly, but his lips barely move.

"All I said was she finally gave up the pussy. She finally sucked a nigga's dick or something," Percy replied, shrugging his shoulders. Dominique shoved Percy's shoulder with one hand but so much strength, Percy almost fell off the steps.

"You talk too fucking much boy, you gonna hurt yourself," says Dominique. Shit is going too far. I grab him by his waist and tell him to just let it go. "Stay over there."

"You better listen to your wifey before you do something you regret. You a lucky man. She never even let me lick it. Stay lucky."

Dominique stepped to him and sized him up. He stood 4 inches taller than him with a little more muscle. I knew it would take something small to send him over the edge, and Percy cued him when he inhaled his cigarette smoke and blew it directly into Dominique's eye. Dominique only had to swing once. I screamed. Percy stumbled and backed up away from the front of the building. Dee had caught him just below his nose and Percy spit blood.

"I'll let you get away with that one nigga. But best believe, if you try that shit again you going to jail. You don't wanna get arrested in America nigga." Dominique was smiling and nodding his head, the arms in his muscles still flexing. "Better watch yaself."

Percy pointed to me, then walked backwards down the sidewalk until he couldn't be seen anymore. I ran inside and Dominique followed behind me. My heart was in my stomach. It had dropped completely. I couldn't fucking believe this shit.

"FUCK THAT NIGGA, MAN," Dee said. "What's wrong, baby?" He looked at me, concerned. I was damn near hyperventilating.

"Every fucking thing was going so fucking well and he had to FUCK it up!" I scream. "I can't take this shit, Dee. He threatening you. He making me feel unsafe in my own home. I don't wanna deal with that." I feel my eyes watering. I wave my hands in front of my face in an attempt to stop it. Dee pulls me over to the bed and sits me in his lap on the floor.

"You don't have nothing to worry about, Téa. It's over. If he come back over here again, he stupid. Nothing gonna happen to me. He can't do anything." A tear slips from my eye. He wipes it. "If you start crying, I gonna sing to you." He rocks me side to side quickly and starts to sing off-key. I want to laugh so badly, but I'm still very upset. I do let a smile form on my face. "Why you still look mean?" Dominique tickles me under my chin, my armpits, and my stomach until I'm red all over from screaming and laughing.

"You made my stomach hurt, you fuckin…broccoli head." The Percy situation is still on my mind. But Dee says he's going to find a way to handle it, so I trust in that. I lay across his legs.
"Look. I got to show you something." He pulls his phone out and starts scrolling.

"I hope it's good."

"Ohhhhh yes, I gonna show you something good," he says, nodding his head and showing all his teeth. "It was a surprise. You don't know I do this."

"Oh Lawd, I'm scared now."

"Don't be scared, baby, don't be scared," he laughs and shakes his head. "Look." I sit up and look at the screen. The first thing I see is a picture of my portrait for Dominique up on a website. Then I see the name of the website and I can tell it's an online artist gallery. Underneath my picture is my name and all my contact information. My eyes get big.

"Dee, you didn't."

"That's great, right?" he says, excitedly. He doesn't realize that I'm not happy about this.

"What is this?" I ask with a frown on my face.

"It's a gal-er-ree. My friend help me with it cause it was hard to write but this is big. I wanted to help you, baby."

"By going behind my back and doing something without my permission?" My eyebrows are raised and now he can tell this was a problem. "Are you always so impulsive?"

"You don't like it?"

"No, Dee. You should've asked me first." I don't want to be mad at him, but damn. I hate when people do things like this. I never said I wanted that. I knew he was just trying to help but he went about it the wrong way.

"But Téa, it's big art gallery. HUGE. They ask for a picture of one piece, right? And a title of piece and name of the artist. And how people can contact you if they want a commissary."

"Commission?" I ask.

"Yeah, commission. And people all over the world look at this gallery and they buy stuff too. Celebrity too. Check your email. People probably already write you." I roll my eyes and check my email on my phone.

He was right. I had about 4 messages from people wanting to commission art from me and 13 purchases from my Etsy page. I looked back at the art gallery website and saw that my portrait had been viewed 1,478 times with 56 comments. All from today. I also noticed that Dominique had chosen to title my portrait *My Boo Though*. I punched him lightly in his shoulder and he put on his best "oops" face.

"Wow… I can't believe this." It's not easy selling my art and I had never gotten so many interested people in one day. Not even in one month. Dominique had actually done well.

"I just wanna help you grow, baby. You so good at what you do."

"Thank you, honey bun." I give him a small smooch. Dominique raises his index finger.

"One more surprise."

"Dominique, no. I can't take any more surprises today," I pretend to scream and put my hands on my head.

"Justttt wanna invite you to come to Monster next show with me in Vegas."

"Really?"

"Yeah, I get you VIP. You can be in the first row and get to be close to me." I roll my eyes.

"Actually I think I may need a break from you," I say, jokingly. "When is it?"

"In a week so get your summer clothes and pack them because it's not cold there like it is here in the Windy City."

"Boy, what do you even know about the Windy City?" I laugh.

"I know I'm tired of it. You should be tired too. All you do is work. Leave home and work, come home and work some more. You gonna have fun next week. I gonna make you."

"You don't have to persuade me to go anywhere with you, I'm there." I kissed the tip of his nose and stood up. "Damn, I still have to cook."

"I thought everybody from the States eat hamburgers."

"I used to, but I stopped eating red meat." Dominique looks confused. "You know. Pork and beef."

"Why you do that?"

"It's hella bad for you. My body couldn't take it anymore. Plus I started living a Rasta lifestyle this year and I'm trying to keep my body pure.."

"Rasta?" I smile at his interest.

"Yes, sir. *Rasta livity*. Our bodies are our temples. We have to keep them clean for Jah Rastafari to live inside us. Understand?"

"Jah... He is God?"

"Yeah, He's God," I smile. "I try to live the most natural life I can. That's part of the reason I wear my hair like this. I don't smoke or drink... I don't even take prescription drugs, unless my pain is unbearable. Well...." My cheeks burn red, "I do smoke a little herb from time to time."

"I knew you did, I can tell!" Dominique points his finger at me accusingly, but he is only joking. I was a little relieved that he wasn't turned off by it. "Wow man. You soo different. I don't know any girl like you. It's crazy. I love that about you."

He looks at me with a smile on his face for a while, and I just know he's looking at me in amazement. Maybe even wondering how he gets to have someone so amazing. It made me feel...supreme.

"Tell me something else about your religion," he asks.

"Hmm... well the most important thing you need to know is that it's not a religion. It's not Rastafarianism, it's a way of life. And we follow the teachings of King Haile Selassie: to not judge people for their wrongs, to always help our brethren and sistren, to love everyone regardless of their sexuality, gender, religion, race, ethnicity, financial status, uplift Africa, and to just live a righteous life. It's a lot about morals and values and what's in your heart. And your mind, of course. Gotta stay conscious. And we don't deal with the Western ways of life. Or Babylon, as you might hear another Rasta say. I grew up here, celebrating America's holidays because that's just how I was raised. But I don't do that anymore. I pretty much reject all of that stuff, along with marriage, religion, and corporate jobs. Sometimes I need a little extra help and I get part-time jobs like the one I have now, but hopefully not for long."

"So, question? You don't deal with marriage right? What happens if I want to marry you one day?" He grabs my hand and intertwines his fingers in mine. That mischievous smile is forever on his face.

"Then..." I pause and look down from embarrassment, "*Maybe* I'll let you be my King."

I look up at him with my eyes crossed and stick my tongue out. Dominique doesn't hesitate to taste it or my lips. His large hands grip my small ass and travel up and down my hips. I break away from him to say, "My thighs are so tiny. I've been doing exercises to build up muscle in them, but I don't think it's working."

"Your thighs are fine to me. *But*...if you do want them bigger, I can help you with that. For sure."

"How is that?" I ask, giving him a side-eye. I wait for him to suggest something sexual.

"I mean, we can plan a day where we exercise together or you can come to workshop with me and dance. Whatever you wanna do." He shrugs. "I'm down."

I hug him tightly around his waist and don't let go because Lawd... I love this man.

FOUR "FOR REAL"

………..shook out his afro like a wet dog. I was now drenched in water and shampoo suds slid down the bathroom mirror. Dominique gives me his innocent puppy dog eyes and goofy smile.

"Now why would you go and do that?"

Washing his hair had been almost an hour-long task because of his silliness. The man didn't know how to sit still. He went from sleeping half the day to doing death drops in the tub and skipping around the kitchen like he didn't have any sense.

Although his sudden burst of energy was entertaining, he was going to make us late. We had to be at the airport in 3 hours and we were already running 30 minutes behind. I turned around to grab a towel and he rested his very wet head against my lower back.

"I'm very sorry, but you have to understand," he starts, "this is how I dry my hair when I'm on tour."

"Yes, well you have towels now, honey bun," I say as I pat his head. He jumps suddenly when he feels my phone in my back pocket vibrate against his neck. I giggle at how he rubs his throat, pretending to be in pain, and see who's calling. It's my mother so I know I have to take it. I give Dominique the towel and leave the bathroom, closing the door behind me.

"Hey baby, I'm just calling to make sure you packed enough panties and personal items---."

"Here we go." I sigh.

"No, no, no. I just wanna help you out, Téa. Okay, you're going on a trip with a.......grown man. You wanna make sure you're prepared."

"Oh my goodness...." I saw this coming soon as I told her about Dominique. She always does this, treating me like I'm still in elementary school. "I'm almost 22 years old, Mami. I've slept in the same bed as a man before okay. I've been alone with a man before. Hey, I've even had sex with one," I say sarcastically. I wasn't really angry, just annoyed. I found myself pacing around the living room.

"Do you have enough pads?" she asked, completely ignoring what I said. "You don't want that man to think you don't take care of yourself. You don't want him to think you nasty and then tell other people and then you're known as The Nasty Girl." She gave me this same speech every time when I was younger and was invited to spend the night at someone's house or went on a trip.

"I'm not even going to be on my period." I throw myself on the couch and slide down slowly until I melt into the floor.

"Are you sure?"

"I've been going through this for 7 years, Mami. I'm pretty sure I know when my period is supposed to come. I'm practically a pro at this, okay." All this period talk was reminding me that my vagina still ached from days ago. She finally eases up and her tone changes.

"Hm. Well, okay. That's good. When am I gonna get to meet Dominique? You two seem to be getting serious." I instantly perk up.

"We are... you would've met him already but everything kinda happened faster than I would've expected. But I'm happy though…"

"That's good. Just be careful, okay? Have you talked to your father?" I can hear the irritation in her voice and I could tell he had been giving her problems again.

"Yeah… I did…"

"Um. That don't sound good."

"No, it was okay. He was just being his normal, weird self."

"Well I know you got your trip or whatever so I don't wanna put you in a bad mood. I was gonna tell you he been telling your sister all this crazy shit again, but I don't want you to worry about that. We'll talk about it when you get back. I'll let you get back to your packing. Have a safe trip, baby. Have fun."

"Thank you," I say. "I will."

"Love you."

"Love you too. Bye-bye." We hang up and I breathe a sigh of relief.

Lord knows I wasn't about to get into that with her right now. I'm glad that she feels she can confide in me now and tell me certain things she couldn't when I was younger, but hearing about stuff my father did is always so awkward. Some things you don't need to share with your children and she's been doing that a lot lately.

Dominique walks out the bathroom with the towel wrapped tightly around his head.

"Whyyy, Dee? Whyyy?" I cover my face with both hands. "The towel was just to stop your hair from dripping all over the place. I haven't rinsed you yet, boo boo."

"Back to the bathroom," Dominique says, and spins on his heel.

We managed to make it to Midway an hour before our 3:30pm flight. I had only been on a plane one other time for my trip to Jamaica, and I definitely didn't fly first class. I told Dominique that didn't matter to me, but he insisted. I was just glad to be there with him.

I knew him and the other dancers had been on somewhat of a break for the past week and he would be back on tour for a while before I saw him again. I was going to savor my time left with him and take full advantage of it. Unfortunately, Dominique had charged down significantly and only wanted to rest before his long day of rehearsal.

"Baby…" I speak in an almost whisper. Dominique turns over in his seat and faces me. His eyes are slits.

"What, baby?"

"I had a weird dream about you the other day. We were in a big house and there were lots of people and gifts and…..weed." I pause to make sure he's still listening. He opens his eyes and soon as he notices I stopped talking. "You got arrested."

"That's crazy," he mumbles.

"Yeah, your mom was there."

"What, what-was-she-doing-there." I could hear the drowsiness in his voice. I fully intended on keeping him awake though.

"It was her birthday. I wish I could figure out what the dream meant though. Maybe I was just subconsciously thinking about you. I don't know. But then that makes me wonder, why don't I dream about music? Or drawing? Or eating? Or doing other things that I love… why don't I dream about being a well-known artist or starting a family or my own business? It really makes you think. What do you dream about, baby?" I ask.

"I-dream-about-you-baby," he answers, eyes closed. His breathing gets louder and I know he's out. I lean over and kiss the tip of his nose and he wakes up long enough to peck me on my lips and go back to sleep. He only sleeps for a little while before we stop in Detroit for a layover.

We eat when we get off the plane and he shares his ear buds with me. I smiled at this internally because it made me think of how he shares with Damien and I hoped that maybe, just maybe, he felt even halfway as close to me as he does to his twin.

I sleep completely through the next flight and I'm woken up by Dominique shaking me gently. He's eating a chocolate bar in my face and I side-eye him as hard as possible. I'm so tired even after sleeping for so long. We land after 9pm but the weather is absolutely beautiful.

It's dark outside but I can feel a light breeze in the warm temperature. To my surprise, Damien is right there to meet us. He puts his arm over my shoulder and I wrap mine around his waist. His presence seems to give Dominique that extra boost he needs, because he lights up.

"Man, you need to fix your hair bro," says Damien, shaking his head. He looks down at me smiling. "You let him go out with you like that?" Dominique rolls his eyes.

"I fall asleep on the plane, bro."

"We going out tonight?" Damien asks me.

"Ohh, I'm not going anywhere tonight. I just wanna stuff my face with food and knock out." Damien and Dominique grab all of our bags and we walk to his Rent-A-Car. When we get to the hotel and check in, Dominique immediately orders room service.

The suite is huge and I start to feel guilty about staying in it because I know he only paid for it for me. I doubt him and Damien stay in suites on the regular just because. Then again, he did invite me so obviously he wanted to do something special for me. I needed to stop being so insecure and let a man take care of me for a change.

The twins naturally ate most of the food. I caught myself telling Dominique to make sure he used the bathroom before he left, then realized I sounded like his mom. I only meant that he'd eaten so much and he didn't want to have to use the bathroom on the way to the club. But he simply laughed it off and kissed me goodbye.

I settled back against the headboard with my plate of grilled tilapia, cabbage, and baked potato. I took a sip of my apple-flavored Izze and surfed through the channels on the flat-screen HD TV hanging on the wall. I watched Law & Order SVU until I finished my meal and fell asleep almost instantly.

When I open my eyes again, it's after 4am and Dominique is laying stomach down on my ass. "Wake up babyyyy." He hops up and down. I giggle tiredly.

"Why would you wake me up, take your crazy ass to sleep." I push him until he rolls off me. "Don't you have to be up in like four hours to go to rehearsal?"

"Nooooo, I no wanna go there. Don't make me," he moans. I hop out of bed and go to the bathroom to brush my teeth. If we were going to be up all night talking, I didn't want to have morning breath. I come back in and lay on the bed and he snuggles up to me, still fully clothed with his shoes and jacket on. When I realize he is snoring, I smack my lips. This motherfucker woke me up just to fall asleep on me. I couldn't even be mad. Feeling his breathing against my chest comforted me too much.

■■

Dominique didn't wake me when he got out of bed for practice. I wasn't up until 10am. The first thing I did was call Casandra. Even though I didn't want to go back to that day, I explained to her everything that happened with Percy. She couldn't believe it. But she was almost turned on by the fact that Dominique stood up for me the way he did and got in Percy's face. She said she'd always wanted a man who would do that for her, and I admitted Dominique definitely scored points for that with me. I lounged around the suite and talked on the phone for hours before I officially started my day.

I didn't eat "breakfast" until 3pm and hopped in the shower about an hour later. I had about two hours before the car would be around to take me to the venue so I soaked my hair in water, deep conditioned, sealed with olive oil, and put my hair into bantu knots. Dominique called me while he was on a lunch break and told me I looked beautiful right now, even though he couldn't see me.

I just laughed it off and told him he was silly. But in reality, he made my heart melt. I got dressed quickly and ate some chocolate ice cream. I was apprehensive when it was time to leave. It was the first time I'd ever wondered, *Do I look good enough?* The ride over didn't help. It left me wishing that Casandra was there with me so I didn't have to do everything alone.

I was in a solemn mood when I arrived but it quickly changed when I ran into Dominique. He was rushing to take pictures with a few fans when he noticed me walking in. Afterwards he sprinted over to me and reminded me not to go anywhere once the show was over and he would meet me.

"Where am I gonna go, Dee?" He kisses my cheek and runs off. I see the girls he took pictures with watching and whispering. One smiled at me. I felt weird but I smiled back and walked in.

More and more people started coming in and it was almost time for the show to start. I had my camera ready in the first row as soon as Run the World started. I was surprised at how excited I was to see Beyoncé make her entrance from underneath the stage. I wasn't the hugest fan of her but all the excitement of a live show always pumps me up.

When Dominique and Damien came out, I screamed as loud as any fan. It was so surreal to see him up there doing his thing, knowing that he'd been with me all week. After I recorded the beginning of the show, I put my phone away to fully enjoy it. I found myself yelling out things like "Yesss, baby!" and "Get it, boo!" while he danced. I danced right along with them and everyone else. I was truly having a great time.

I didn't know all of her music, but I knew all the radio songs and sang along until I started to lose my voice. They performed my favorite, Grown Woman, at the end and I belted that one out too. I completely forgot that I was alone. At one point during "1+1", a girl that I had conversed with a little and shared knowing glances with throughout the night grabbed my hand and sang along with me. It reminded me of just how powerful music could be. Live shows were definitely something to experience and brought out much emotion. Real, actual instruments were so much better than hearing the song normally.

When the show was finally over and the audience started to scatter, I waited where I was just as Dominique had told me to do. I browsed through some of the pictures I'd taken until I saw him coming towards me out the corner of my eye. When he was three feet away, a girl called his name and came over. I immediately observed that she was much taller than me and three times as curvy. She was a Latina with long, dark, wavy hair flowing down to her waist. She wore a lot of makeup and a revealing outfit that displayed a flat, toned belly.

I couldn't even hide my intimidation as her and Dominique kissed each other's cheeks. Mine were surely burning red when I saw her stroke his arm ever so gently and tell him he put on a wonderful show. Before he could even acknowledge my presence, a dancer yelled, "Twin!" and grabbed his attention. He walked hurriedly in that direction and I was left with the girl and her friend.

I was planning on ignoring them completely but the tall girl spoke up and said, "So how do you know Dominique?" Her smile was devilish and her friend was smirking. I didn't know how to answer her. I didn't know if I should say he was my man, because she had me feeling a little indifferent about that.

"Umm... I flew out here wi---."

"Oh yeah?" asked the friend before I could finish. "He flew Leslie out here too." She leaned on Leslie's shoulder.

"Yeah, me and Dee Dee are good friends," she said. Her friend tried unsuccessfully to hide her laughter. My throat was starting to feel tight. "I like your hair. That kind of hair works for you." I knew this was a backhanded compliment. When I didn't say anything, she waved and said bye.

Damien was making his way over as they were walking off. He must have seen the desperate look on my face and came to my rescue. My embarrassment heightened when I heard Leslie's friend from a few feet away say, "Bitch think that just cause he spent a night on her floor, she important." On the inside, I was so angry and confused, I could cry.

"Don't worry for that bitch, nobody likes her," Damien stated loud and clear for everyone to hear.

But my eyes were already welling with tears. I stopped them before they could slide down my face. I felt pathetic and so, so stupid. Damien rubbed my back and waited with me for Dominique to come back. When he didn't show, he grabbed my hand and took me to my car where my driver was waiting patiently.

"Don't let that make you feel bad. She nobody, oki? Don't let her take your smile," Damien comforts me.

I nod my head and thank him. I just want to go back to my hotel room and sulk. I didn't even want to see Dominique's face at this point but I was still upset that he just left me there and his brother had to take care of me. I'm not being ungrateful, am I?

Dominique doesn't get back to the hotel until two hours after I do. I look up when he walks in but immediately turn back to the television. I made sure he knew I was pissed. He tries to sit on my lap but I push him away and tell him to fuck off.

"I'm sorry, don't do that to me," he says softly, grabbing my hand. "What do you want me to do, baby?"

"Who is Leslie?" I ask, point blank.

"She is a family friend."

"Well Damien didn't seem too friendly with her. Do you pay for flights for all of the friends of the family who look like Sophia Vergara?"

"It was just a favor she ask me to do… it didn't mean anything."

"Well she thinks it does and she made it clear that she doesn't think *anything* of me. Had me convinced that you didn't either. Why would you leave me like that? Do you think I deserved to be humiliated?" I was almost yelling now.

"You have to understand I didn't mean for that to happen. I just go and take care of something. I thought I will be right back but it take a long time and I'm sorry. I love you, just believe me." He kisses my hand. "Forgive me, please. I don't want you mad at me."

I look away and shake my head. I want to forgive him but I didn't want him to think it was that easy to get back in my good graces. He pulled me out of my seat by my hand, lifted me up by my underarms and tossed me up. I screamed and laughed even though I didn't want to. I couldn't help it. He wrapped my legs around his waist and kissed my neck softly.

"Say you forgive me…"

"I'm not saying anything." He bites my neck. "DEE!"

"Say you forgive me…" He licks where he bit me at and I can feel myself succumbing to his advances. "Say it…"

"I forgive you…" I close my eyes. He lays me down on the bed and unzips my pants. He pulls my panties down with them and without warning, throws my legs in the air and puts his face in between them. "Dee…" I can barely say.

You kiss both of my inner thighs with those soft, supple lips then glide your tongue over them back and forth. Your tongue trails all the way to my clit and you play with it. You pass over it a few times before taking it between your wet lips tightly and letting go. Over and over. Again and again. I'm crying. My hands are flailing, trying to find something to hold on to.

Your tongue is relentless in searching for my pleasure. It goes up and down, inside and out, reaching for my core. Do you reach it, I don't know… it's so powerful, it has temporarily put me in a state of numbness. You slide your hands up my outer thighs to bring my feeling back. You're eating. When I release, I pull your hair with one hand and the sheets with another and cry out. It's so powerful…it has put me to sleep. Not powerful enough to make me forget.

••

"Knock, knock." I look up to see Casandra closing my bedroom door behind her. "Hey lady," she says.

"Hiii! Oh, I'm so happy to see you!" I stand up and hug her tightly until she's squealing.

"I'm happy to see you too, Munchkin," she laughs. "Your mama told me you would be here."

"Yeah, yeah. I definitely had to come back here and pick up some of my older pieces for this art show."

With my hands on my hips, I look around the room to see my artwork scattered everywhere, covering the bed and the floor. My mami had a few of them framed and hanging on the wall as well. My portrait of Damian Marley, entitled "Lion", was my first real piece. It was joined by three portraits of Michael Jackson, not drawn by me, but a nice touch because they were both Kings. A few photos of me & my siblings as children, two guitars, a book shelf, and a baton from being on the Majorettes team in high school completed the room.

"You didn't have to come all the way out here! I could've met you somewhere when I got back to the city."

"Actually, I did. I wanted to make sure I saw you because I'm packing later on today…and leaving tomorrow." I see her bottom lip quiver a little when she says this and I place my hand over my heart in shock.

"You're leaving already?" Casandra had given me the good news that her parents had finally agreed to support her dance dreams only a week ago. She had applied to UC Berkley months ago and gotten an acceptance letter. I guess her parents had started to see how seriously she was taking it and agreed to pay her tuition. I was extremely proud of her. I knew this is what she always wanted but it still hurt to know my best friend would be so far away from me.

"Yep…I'll be out of here. Living in a new place with a new climate. Hanging out with new people. Starting a whole new life. I don't know how I'm gonna do this without you, Téa," she says as a tear rolls down her cheek.

She's making me want to cry but there's no way I'm going to let her be sad about her success. I hop into her lap and wrap my arm around her neck and hug her.

"What are *you* gonna do? What the hell am I gonna do without you, you know I can't even reach the peanut butter without you," I say, making her laugh a little. "Look at us, Cas. So much has happened in the past month. I'm doing art shows! I'm working on starting my own crewneck line! You're going to dance school in California! This is just one step closer to fulfilling all of our dreams. This is good, okay? Let's be happy about it." She's nodding her head and wiping her tears.

"I know, I know. It is good…but it would be a lot better if I could go out drinking with my best friend to celebrate." I roll my eyes and muff her in the forehead and she falls on the floor, almost taking me with her. We laugh until our stomachs and our heads hurt and I'm crying.

"That's what you get for trying to peer pressure me," I say. I don't drink, but for once I wish I did so she wouldn't have to do it alone for her last night in Chicago. "We could always go out to eat or see a movie or something. As long as it's before 10pm."

"What's happening at 10pm?" she asks in a weak voice full of laughter, while adjusting her hair.

"Dee usually skypes me around that time." I watch Casandra pretend to stick her finger down her throat and gag. "Girl, whatever. I miss my man so much."

It has almost been exactly a month since we were last face-to-face.

Beyoncé had taken her tour overseas to Europe so I knew I wouldn't see him for a while, but golly. This experience alone lets me know I could never do a permanent long-distance relationship. Just going without Dominique's touch for this long made me sick. He was currently taking a break at home with his family in France, but he would be back over my way in a few days. I couldn't stand waiting, but skype dates would have to do until then.

"I just wanna make it clear to ya'll that I am the one and only reason you two are together," says Casandra. I cackle at this. "No, seriously. If I had never taken you with me that day, you would've never met and you wouldn't be the pretty little couple that you are now."

"Yeah, yeah. I'll remember that the next time me and Dee get into an argument so we can blame everything on you." I start piling everything I'm taking with me together and putting them into bags. Casandra absentmindedly starts to help with a curious look on her face.

"Speaking of arguments, what ever became of the one you had the last time you saw him? You guys ever work that out?" she asks.

"We talked about it again before I left but ultimately, I just decided to let it go. It's still fishy to me, but I don't wanna go into this relationship not trusting him."

"Aren't you already in a little too deep to be worried about that?"

"Perhaps," I say, side-eyeing her and smiling.

"You are such a creep."

"I just like your choice of words," I say, still smiling. She smacks me with an old drawing of Miley Cyrus.

"What are you doing for your birthday, silly girl?"

"Oh, nooo, you won't be here for my birthday!" I exclaim. Not that my birthdays are ever spectacular but I'm definitely down for staying at home, just chilling with a close friend and now I can't even do that. The seasonal job I was holding had ended two weeks ago, so I can't even work on my birthday to keep myself busy.

"Won't Dee be here by then?"

"Yeah, but I wouldn't hold it against him if he forgot it's my birthday. He knows it's September 14th but I told him that at the beginning, before we even established being in a real relationship, so I'm sure he doesn't remember."

"He seems to be pretty sharp about those things. I'm sure he'll remember. Well, I gotta get up outta here and go pack. I'll text you with some show times, okay?"

"Okay, honey bun." I give her a hug. "Thanks for coming." I watch her leave then I go back to work.

■■■

Later that night, Casandra and I go to see Insidious 2 even though we are both extremely paranoid when watching scary movies. The only time I can see them is when they are newly released and the theater is packed with people. That way I don't feel so alone and it always makes for hilarious reactions and good laughs. I enjoy the company of my best friend for one more night and almost hold her captive when she drops me off at home.

"Make sure you call me when your plane is about to take off, okay?" I say.

"I promise, Munchkin." She pats my cheek.

"I love you boo boo."

"I love you too! Bye bye…"

I close the car door and check the time before sprinting into my apartment. It was only a little bit after 9pm. Dominique hadn't texted me all day, but I assumed our skype date still stood. I washed the dishes, vacuumed the whole apartment, started my laundry, and changed my sheets while I waited. When I got done, I realized it was already 10:23. I fixed myself a bowl of chocolate ice cream so that I could gloat in Dominique's face and waited.

After 15 minutes, I started to figure that maybe he forgot. But I didn't see how that could be possible since we did it every night. I went to call him first, but he was still offline. I turned the TV on, angry. He wasn't exactly on my good side already because even though I'd let it go, my feelings were still hurt by the fact that he'd forgotten me. And here he was forgetting me again.

I watched Family Guy until after 2am. I got out of bed every hour to eat, drink, and use the bathroom. Before I knew it, it was 4am and I was still awake with red-rimmed eyes. I was in a zombie-like state. It reminded me of the time I stayed awake for more than 30 hours, involuntarily, and went to work wide-eyed and full of energy. I had to stand up and talk to people and entertain their kids all day while they waited in line, and after a while my tiredness caught up with me. I started falling asleep mid-sentence. It wasn't unusual for me to have problems sleeping at night. I've had insomnia on and off since I was 15. But lately, it had seemed like it was off. I guess after last night, it was on again.

I went to the kitchen to get myself an apple for energy and I hear a key in the door. My first instinct is that someone is trying to break in and to hide under my bed, but I'm so tired I can't even move. Dominique's nose peeks in through the cracked door before the rest of his face does. He's wearing a big smile that drops as soon as he sees the look on my face. I know I must look tragic and I cover my face with both hands.

"What are you doing here?" He ignores me and kneels down in front of me.

"What's wrong, why you crying baby?" I wasn't crying, but I start to tear up when I see the concerned look on his face.

"I'm so tired and I can't sleep," I cry. "It's hard for me to sleep without talking to you first…"

"Ohhh, babyyyy." Dominique pulls my head into his chest and rubs my back. "I'm so sorry baby, I didn't know. I want to surprise you and come early. I'm sorry. I missed you."

"I missed you too," I mumble softly.

"You gotta go to sleep baby, that's not good for you. Come on," Dominique says, grabbing me by my hand and pushing my chin up. "You not a vampire, you gotta sleep. It's not good for you." He pulls me in bed and lies down with me, wrapping his arms around mine from behind. A shiver runs down my spine and he kisses my ear.

"Dominique… are you gonna be here forever?" There is a long pause before he says, "*I wanna be.*"

"I hope so. Because you are *my happiness*. I don't wanna ever go back to how my life was before you. I can't ever go back to that. Don't make me…---," he cuts me off.

"I won't. Don't think about that now. Get your beauty sleep."

When I wake up the following afternoon, I am shocked to see Dominique asleep in my bed. I guess I was so tired and it was so late that everything that happened last night didn't seem real at all and I thought the whole thing had been a dream. The worst part is that I remember what I said to him before I went to sleep, and it scared me.

It scared me to feel so strongly about a human being who could instantly be taken out of my life at any time, God forbid. I sat up in bed and watched his chest go up and down. *My Dominique.* My Dominique was Superman. He was always coming to my rescue.

Six days later...

Damien and his newest arm candy were sitting on my rug eating McDonalds that they had picked up on the way over. My little sister was bouncing up and down on my bed texting and gossiping with her friend, who was annoying me by repeatedly smacking my birthday balloons that were floating nearby.

The only reason I'd allowed her to come is because I knew my mami kept my sister in the house all the time and she needed some fresh air and some fun. If Dominique wasn't taking so long out in the car, we could sing Happy Birthday to me, eat cake, and hit the road for this long drive to Six Flags.

"Damien. What the hell are you doing, bro?" I ask playfully. "I thought we agreed that you wouldn't eat like a pig anymore. You're eating burgers and fries, then you're gonna eat some birthday cake, and I KNOW you're gonna stuff your face when we get to the park."

"One second," Damien says to his friend. He walks past me, dips his finger in my cake, and rubs the icing all over my cheek. "Happy birthday, sister." I'm in such a great mood today that all I can do is stand there and laugh.

"Did you just stick your finger in my cake?" I peep at him from under an eyelid full of icing just as Dominique is walking through the door with his arms full. "What the fu....NO, NO, NO, NO, NO!" I yell. He comes in carrying boxes and expects me not to notice anything. "I told you not to get me anything!" I smack his arm as hard as I can and he pretends to cower against the door. "I meant it!"

He looks dumbfounded for a few seconds before saying, "But it's your birthday."

"You are so disobedient, someone needs to punish you." I can't help but smile. I'd thought of the idea to go to Six Flags at the very last minute so it was the only thing I expected to happen. But Dominique LeBeau *always* has a trick up his sleeve. He's hiding something underneath his shirt and it's so obvious, but I don't even question it. I start opening my gifts.

"That is from me," says Damien.

"No!" says Dominique. "It's my idea."

"But I pay for it," Damien says proudly. "It's from both." I open it to find endless amounts of shea butter, olive oil, and gel. I am literally turning red laughing at this gift because it is so perfect.

"Thank you very much, Damien," I say, kissing him on the cheek. I look through the gift bag and find little mint chocolates, dark chocolate Hershey bars, chocolate covered almonds, raw pecans, and chocolate roses. I knew for sure this was from my baby. "So you got me chocolate roses instead of real roses, huh? You think you know me well, huh?"

"I told you!" Dominique says excitedly, hitting Damien's chest. "Damien go shopping with me and he say 'You gotta get her flowers bro' but I know you think they don't make sense and I tell him. THOSE ARE THE ONES, bro." He points to his gift. I laugh at his explanation as I unwrap my final gift.

"This is so weird, opening gifts in front of everybody like this. I haven't done that on my birthday since I was 6," I say.

I've appreciated every moment of this day. My friends and family knew well enough that it was the simple things that brought me happiness. It kept getting better and better. And when I ripped the wrapping off the last gift, I couldn't see how it could get any better than this right here.

I slowly pulled out all the books and ran my fingers over the title. He had went out and bought 9-10 of my favorite books that I read as a child, including Little Bear and Dr. Seuss' Bartholomew & the Oobleck & Other Stories. Books that took me back to a happier, care-free time. I couldn't believe my eyes.

"Deeeee," I barely whispered. "How did you know?"

"I see your tweet. You tweet about missing so many things and I don't know why but you say they important to you. And Trini. She help me," he laughs and points at my sister.

"Trini," I signal her to come towards me, "Come here." I pretend to cry and squeeze her super tight. "Thank you Pookie." I stand up to give Dominique a hug and his shirt punches me in the neck. I hear a squealing sound come from beneath it. "Dee, your shirt just picked a fight with me," I say, confused.

"Is that a baby?" Damien jumps up. Dominique puts his hand up to stop him.

"No, it's not a baby. Why would I keep a baby in my shirt?" He lifts his shirt up to reveal the smallest, cutest puppy I've ever seen up close.

"Oh my God!" Me and everyone else close in on Dominique and try to pet the puppy, but he hides in Dominique's arms. "You got me a puppy too!"

"No, it's not for you. It's for me." He rubs the puppy's head gently and tells everyone to back up.

"Dee. Don't play." I reach for the puppy again and Dominique smacks my hand.

"Don't touch my baby. Don't ever touch my baby."

"Oop!" I laugh and say, "Deeeee. Stop playing. Are you serious right now?"

"I GUESS….we can share. Butter is mine but he have to stay here when I'm with Beyoncé."

"You so rude," says Damien.

"Okay? Do you see him with his nose stuck up in the air like that? Don't fuck around and get it caught in my ceiling vent." I can't take how silly, yet serious, he is right now. He lays Butter on top of my head and pets me. I glare at him. "I see you acting up today." Trini's friend takes him off my head and rocks him in her arms. "So exactly where is Butter gonna go while we're at Six Flags?"

"Dogs can stay at home alone," says Trini.

"Okay, but he's a brand new puppy. He'll be scared. And we don't even have anything for him to eat."

"I did not think about that," Dominique says with an *oops* face.

"Yes, I *know* you didn't sweetie. You and these impulsive decisions are going to be the death of me. We'll try to see if my mami and stepdad will take him, since we'll be out by their house in Gurnee anyway. Let's get this show on the road."

I grab Dominique's hand while he holds the door open for everybody and lean up to kiss him. I whisper a *thank* you in his ear and he whispers back, *no problem Queen*. He was working hard to keep my trust after losing it temporarily and I was taking notice. Is it bad that I'm starting to feel like he can have me either way?

When we got back home that night, Dominique undressed me and made love to me on the floor right in front of my bed. It was the closest I'd ever felt to him; closer than the first time. He warmed every part of my body and soul. And as we lay there with our legs intertwined and him still inside me, it felt like home.

For once, if only for a little while, I felt peace resonate within me. I knew that this was exactly where I was supposed to be. I hoped Dominique felt that too. After the pleasure came pain, more than usual. He carried me to the bed when I was too weak to get up on my own and covered me with my zebra throw. My body was aching like crazy and when I woke up to my period, I knew I was going to be sick.

I showered before Dominique woke up but when I got out, he was in the kitchen fixing himself a bowl of cereal. I don't eat cereal so I narrowed my eyes at him as if to say, "Where you get that from?" and he winked at me. He watched me as I walked to my bed and sneakily came up behind me and undid my towel. Before I could even give him a reaction, his lips were on me.

He held me in the air by my waist and his lips had a strong hold on my nipple. I held on to his head for dear life and screamed his name, but that only made him think I wanted more. He laid me down on the bed and I made sure my panties were still intact. I put my hand to his chest before he could lay another hand on me. He smiled mischievously.

"I don't want you to get too worked up…cause I'm on my period," I say and behold the disappointed expression on his face. His head drops onto my shoulder.

"Nooooo," he cries.

"Yesssss, honey. C'mon. Get up." I pat his head softly to get him to move so I can get dressed. But suddenly that familiar feeling comes over me…that feeling where I can sense that my body is about to give out on me and I speed past Dominique to the bathroom because I don't want him to see me this way.

I've been to the doctor every time this happens, but I still haven't been able to figure out why it started happening. I stopped eating beef last year because I thought that was the cause, but I guess not. First, all the energy is drained from my body in a matter of seconds. I can't even hold myself up. I have to sit on the floor. Then the pain starts. My cramps are magnified times 20 and the pain is so excruciating, I can do nothing but writhe on the floor and scream.

Dominique is banging on the door demanding for me to open it but I couldn't if I wanted to. I couldn't move at all. I struggled to reach for the Motrin in the bottom cabinet under the sink. It was the only time I'd ever take medicine. When this happened, I felt like it was the only choice I had.

I swallowed a tablet but I was throwing it up 10 minutes later because I hadn't eaten anything. Dominique was standing by the door the entire time. I heard him talking to someone on the phone and I prayed he didn't call an ambulance. I wanted to tell him what was happening but I couldn't even speak. He heard me retching into the toilet and banged on the door once more.

"Baby, what's wrong? Are you sick?" I moan yes. "What do you want me to do? Open the door, baby. Please. You scaring me." I try to reply but another spasm rips through my abdomen and cuts me off. "Did I do something? Did I hurt you last night?"

When my body is free of pain for a few seconds, I stand up weakly and unlock the door. Dominique almost knocks me over opening it. He grabs me by my shoulders and begs me to tell him what I need to make it better.

"Food," I say. I start to lean but he tightens his grip around me before I can tip over. Dominique carries me to the bed, lays me down, and sits next to me. He puts his hand to my forehead but I don't have a fever, of course.

"I can't cook," he says with a desperate look in his eyes.

"An apple. And some toast." I knew from my three other experiences with this that I needed a lot of fruits, vegetables, and grains. They seemed to ease the pain and were enough for me to take a Motrin.

Dominique worked quickly and kept coming back to feed me more when I couldn't lift my hand to do it myself. He even grabbed my laptop to look up how to steam vegetables so he could make me some broccoli. I could tell he was scared because he didn't know what was happening. Hell, neither did I. I just knew it was something that happened to me. I didn't want him to be too worried so I kept a faint smile on my face, but the pain was truly killing me.

After the beautiful meal he cooked for me, I was able to fall asleep. When I awoke two and a half hours later, Damien was in my kitchen cooking. I sat up in bed and stretched. When I stood up, I felt three times better than I did before I got sick. My mouth was very dry though, and I was starving.

"Hi, Damien!" I always wake up cheerful after I've recovered. "Wait, don't hug me. I have to brush my teeth first." I almost forgot I had vomited before I went to sleep. I finished brushing and came out and kissed Damien on his jaw. Dominique was walking in the door with three grocery bags. "Are you cooking for *me*, Damien?"

"Yeah, I heard you were sick. You feeling better?" he asked.

"I feel a lot better."

Dominique takes a bunch of vegetables and seasonings out of the bags and lays them on the counter for Damien. He sits down at one of the stools and looks at me and I just get so warm and fuzzy inside. I can't help but wrap my arms around his neck and kiss him a million times until he's giggling. He made me question if I deserved to be treated so well. I found a comfortable spot between his legs and leaned against him. "I have to make a doctor's appointment though to try to find out what's going on."

"Well don't worry, I cook for you for a long time til you want me to stop." Damien places a plate full of chopped kiwi, strawberries, mangos, raspberries, and oranges in front of me. "Appetizer," he says, giggling. I jump right in and have to smack Dominique's hand away when he reaches for a raspberry.

"I'm your man, you supposed to share evvvverything with me," he says. I point my finger at his face and snarl.

"You know DAMN well that doesn't include food."

They laugh at my seriousness and Dominique starts to rub my tummy while I eat. Damien begins to tell me how Dominique can't do anything without him and he's always calling him for help. He makes sure to add that he has no problem helping when it comes to me though. I go and grab Butter from his tiny bed and snuggle up to him.

"Hi, baby," I say, rubbing him softly. "Your daddy didn't even say hi to you today, did he? Your daddy doesn't love you like I love you. He's a bad daddy." I take Butter's paw and make him slap Dominique's face with it. Dominique just puckered his lips and allowed Butter to lick all over them. "You are gross," I say. I have to push him away when he tries to kiss me. "Those lips aren't coming anywhere near me until you brush those teeth."

"Bro, you don't get paprika. This is cinnamon." Damien scowls at his brother. "How you get cinnamon and paprika confused?"

"I just look at the color," Dominique says, shrugging his shoulders. I almost spit my fruit out laughing at him. He tries to hide his laughter by sneaking a strawberry and plopping it in his mouth.

"You know what, stay here. I go get it cause you can't do nothing right." Damien grabs his car keys and leaves out the door in a huff.

"Why are you always getting on Damien's bad side?" I ask, shaking my head.

Dominique stands up and goes to the bathroom to brush his teeth. I watch him walk away and Lawd. His walk and his figure are so sexy. I don't know what's different about it today, but seeing those broad shoulders and that slim waist was getting me hot. I was so upset that he couldn't put it on me at the moment. God, he was right here and I was right here and I couldn't ride him like I wanted to. I wait for Dominique to come out the bathroom and I grab his hand and lead him to my bed and tell him to sit.

"What did I do?" He thinks he's in trouble. Well, he is. I get behind him and start massaging his neck.

"You didn't do nothing, baby. I just wanna show you some love." I lean down and plant a kiss on the side of his neck. Still rubbing his shoulders, I say, "I really appreciate you taking care of me today. You went the extra mile." I felt his shoulders start to relax.

"I had to. I don't like seeing you hurt like that."

"I know. Nobody else has ever taken care of me that way."

I lick from the lobe of his ear to the top and bite gently. I could feel him shudder slightly and I smiled because he had no idea what he was in for. I kissed every area of his neck I could reach from behind him and licked his chiseled jaw line before kissing him full on the mouth.

I moved from behind him and positioned myself so I was facing him. I could feel him growing between my pelvis and I rubbed him while we kissed. His hands slid through my hair, down my back, and rested on my ass. He palmed and pushed, making me grind harder onto him. Then he stopped.

"But I thought you can't have sex?" *I put my finger to his lips and kiss him again.* **"I can't."** *I kiss his chin. I kiss his Adam's apple. I pull his shirt over his head so I can kiss his chest. I crawl off of him onto the floor. I kiss his belly button. I unbutton his jeans and look up to see him watching me. His breathing has sped up and he looks anxious. I know he finds it sexy to see me act this way with him. I pull his jeans down until they're around his ankles and I grope at his hard-on.*

He knows I've never given head before and that I consider this a gift that should be given out scarcely. No other man I have been with deserves this from me. I didn't think twice about ever putting my lips near their manhood, but when it came to Dominique, I wanted to please him more than anything. I wanted to do it better than any other woman before me had done. I actually craved his dick.

I pulled his boxers down enough to release his beautiful piece. It wasn't like any other dick. It glowed. It looked like a well-carved, golden brown piece of wood. It was shaped to fit my pussy perfectly and I knew it would fit my mouth perfectly as well. I stared at it for a long time, taking in all of its appeal. Then I kissed the head. Dominique released a short moan and closed his eyes.

I smiled up at him as I wrapped my hand around him and reached my tongue out. I licked circles around the head before wetting my lips and taking the whole head in my mouth. I clenched tightly with my lips then slid them off slowly, making a suction sound. He tasted sweet and salty at the same time.

I wet my tongue and licked the length of his dick on all sides. I held it up and took his balls into my mouth. Dominique threw his head back and let out profanities I couldn't understand. I sucked and released...sucked and released over and over until I was sure he couldn't take it anymore. Then I wrapped my lips around his dick again and slid it in and out while contracting my cheeks.

When I used to think about what it would be like to suck a dick, I didn't want my man to see my face or see my head bobbing up and down. It seemed to drive Dominique crazy though. He massaged the back of my neck as I bobbed. I popped his dick out of my mouth and tongued it down. His veins were so thick and popping out at me, I was afraid they would burst.

I remembered how good it felt when Dominique stroked my thighs while he was eating my pussy, and I did the same to him. I could see the effect it had on him when the look on his face became twisted and he clenched the hair by the nape of my neck. I took as much of his dick into my mouth as I could and swirled my tongue around. I knew he was about to come.

He slid out of my mouth on his own and came all over my left breast. The way it landed was so surprising and funny, I made an "O" shape with my lips and start cackling. Dominique is laying back on the bed with his hands over his forehead. The expression on his face is that of one who is lost in thought...

I go to the bathroom to grab some warm, wet towels and perform my regular after-sex ritual. Knowing that I could please him that way made me feel so in control. I felt like I had some kind of super power. Dominique looked too weak to move, but I knew we had to hurry before Damien got back. It had already been 20 minutes. I pulled Dominique up by his hands to get him to stand. He closed his eyes and shook his head quickly. The man was practically seeing stars.

"You okay, baby?" I ask, laughing.

"I don't know you have that inside you. How long you been hiding that?" he asks, with a serious look on his face.

I laugh again and pull his chin down for a kiss. He quickly takes my bottom lip in his mouth and sucks on it while firmly gripping my ass. I pull away slowly and say, "I'm gonna take a shower." He groans and slides his hands in his pants.

"I WANT TO SLEEP!" I hear him yell after I close the bathroom door behind me.

After I take a warm shower, I run myself a bubble bath so I can relax my muscles. My body was sore too. Not being able to get any had my vagina pulsating uncontrollably. When I got out, I remembered to call my gyne to make an appointment. I insisted that I go alone because honestly, I was scared about what she would say. Surprisingly, she was able to take me three days from now.

Dominique dropped me off at UIC, kissed me warmly, and rubbed my belly. When I got inside, I filled out the sheet with all of my family health history and my personal information.

A nurse called me in and asked me the usual questions then asked me why I was here today. I described what had happened to me four times in the past three years and told her about the severe pain I feel and how I couldn't figure out what was causing it. She wrote everything down so she could tell the doctor and gave me a cup to pee in. I went in the bathroom and took a deep breath. I was so scared that I was going to find out I had some sort of fatal illness or that my insides were falling out and any other crazy thing I could think of.

When I filled the cup and came back in, the doctor greeted me with a handshake. I had to have a pap smear for the first time. They'd never given me an internal exam before because I wasn't sexually active, but now it was mandatory. I squeezed my eyes shut when she inserted the speculum. It didn't hurt but it was wildly uncomfortable. I gave a huge sigh of relief when it was over.

After waiting for about a half an hour, the doctor and nurse came back in to speak with me.

"Given your family history, with your aunt, mother, grandmother, and great-grandmother having fibroids, it's no shock that you have them as well," she started. I closed my eyes and looked down. I knew I would have them eventually, but not now! The other women in my family were in their 30s before they started causing them problems.

"I know it sounds scary because you're only 22 years old, but you did good when you stopped eating beef. Beef and other red meat are some of the things fibroids feed off to grow. Now, yours are a little larger than your mother's probably were at that age, because you say they didn't start causing problems for her until a few years ago? Correct?"

"Yes, she uh…she had her uterus removed when she was 43."

"Okay. Great. Since you're so young and they're already hurting you this bad, the first thing we'll try to do is remove the tumors from your uterus. They do grow back. If they grow back again, we're going to have to remove the uterus." I suddenly look up with tears welling in my eyes.

"What? No…How will I have kids?" A tear slides down my face and the nurse rubs my back.

"We can give you some birth control pills to help regulate your period because it is rather heavy and the fibroids also feed off the blood. That should hold us off from removing the tumors for a while. I know this is hard to hear, but if everything works out the way I'm expecting, you'll have to give birth to all your children before the age of 25."

She pauses for a few seconds and gives me a sympathetic look. "Okay, honey?" I nod my head quickly and accept the Kleenex the nurse hands to me. The doctor gives my hand a pat and leaves the room. I'm in a daze. Never in a million years did I think I would ever be in this situation.

I had always wanted kids. I always wanted to give birth to my own babies. Starting a family with a man I loved who loved me was an ultimate goal for me. I equated that to eternal happiness. Giving birth…having a baby…it was a source of unconditional love for certain. I'd dreamed of that for the past seven years at least! And now that I knew my time was so limited, my heart was tearing at the seams.

I texted Dominique and told him I was ready to be picked up. I had no idea what I was going to do. The nurse gave me a prescription for the mildest birth control they had and told me I could pick it up from the CVS down the street from my house. I tried to swallow but my throat was completely dry. I managed to trudge to the car. I got in, slammed the door, and threw my face in my hands.

"Tell me what happened…" Dominique insisted, rubbing my lower back. I shook my head no.

I was practically infertile. I suddenly felt like less of a woman. Dominique would never want to be with me if he found out that I couldn't have kids past the age of 25. If I told him I had to have kids as soon as possible, I would probably scare him away. We were both still so young. I didn't even have the means to take care of a child. And who's to say Dominique would even want to have a child with me? If he didn't, then what? I didn't want to have a baby by just anybody.

I felt like I was quickly running out of options. I cried all the way home. Dominique opened his mouth to say something several times, but couldn't find the words. I knew he was probably sick of me always crying and being needy. All of the power I'd felt earlier had slipped away from me. I felt like a damsel in distress. I felt like a weakling.

I got home and cried myself to sleep. I didn't wake up until it was dark outside. I expected Dominique to be gone when I did, but he was still here and he demanded me to tell him what was wrong or he would call my mother. He was worried about me and felt that my depression had began taking over my life again. But I couldn't tell him…I didn't want him to think less of me.

He grabbed my phone and called my mother on Facetime and handed it to me. I just cried while she advised me in a soothing voice. She told me to take the birth control and that it worked for her. She told me not to cry and that she wanted me to come out to her house and stay with her so I could be surrounded by family and lift my spirits.

"I can't, the art show is tomorrow," I say through my tears.

"Well I don't want you to be upset at your show on your special day. We'll all come out and see you there, okay?" I nod my head. She tells me she loves me and to go get some fresh air before we hang up. Dominique takes my head into his chest and rubs my arm up and down.

"Oh, baby," he says.

"Yeah…oh, baby." He kisses my forehead.

"C'mon. We gonna go out." Anything to make this empty feeling subside. I needed some herb so bad. I guess tonight I would be getting some Dominique therapy.

He told me to get dressed to do something fun. That could be anything, but I took a quick shower and threw on some dark jeans that fit my shape, a tight tank, and my plaid black and red button-up. Dominique threatened to change when I saw he too was wearing his button-up, but of course he didn't. I fluffed my hair and Dominique allowed me to brush his back into a sleek, shiny puff.

"I going to drive," Dominique says as he snatches the keys out of my hand.

"I was gonna give them to you anyway, ass. I don't have a license, remember?" I say, making sure to roll my eyes extra hard in his face. He muffs my forehead and runs out the door before I can catch him. I can already see what kind of night this is about to be.

I take my time walking out to the car and Dominique beeps the horn several times. I just laugh him off and pretend that I can't see people watching us. In my mind, *I'm bloated so I'm not about to fucking run*. Every time he honks, he turns to look at me and smile. Then he does it again.

"I'm dating a damn child," I say, getting in the car. I slouch down as far as possible in my seat and look up, only to see Dominique's fat nose blocking my view. "Oh my God, I can see right up your nose." I laugh so hard that I snort a little.

"Do I have any boogies?" he asks, leaning forward and flaring his nostrils. I can't take him at all.

"No, you're good. What about me?" I lean into him and flare my nostrils too. "I got any bats in the cave?" He backs up slowly.

"Quite a few." He looks sideways at me. I punch him in his arm as he finally pulls off from the curb.

"You are such a liar!" He's making it very hard for me to stay in a bad mood. It didn't take long to get me to laugh. "I hope you're taking me somewhere that has a lot of foodddd…"

"You can eat after, fat girl. You gotta do something to lose all your energy first," says Dominique. I glance at him out the corner of my eye.

Knowing him, we could be going skydiving, talking about losing some energy. It's not like there was too much to do at this time anyway. It's about to be 8pm, everything is just about closing. We pull into a dark parking lot next to a building that was completely lit up.

You could see through the entire building from outside. I should've known. We were going go-kart racing. When we got inside, Dominique stood behind me with one arm around my waist and his chin on my shoulder. I couldn't help but think that he was letting it be known that I belonged to him. I'd just realized it was our first time being out in public together as a couple. Anyone could see that I was getting a lot of up-and-down stares. It was kind of cute that Dominique felt he had to keep a hold on me.

We got our gear and our cars and Dominique pointed his finger at me from across the way, as if to say he was coming for me.

"Boy, bye. I'm gone leave you in the dust."

I put my helmet on and sat down in my car. I blew Dominique a kiss just as we took off. I was hoping it would distract him but I failed. I stomped on the accelerator even though I was already ahead. He was gaining on me and getting dangerously close to my car. I screamed at him to back the fuck up. He just shook his head and gave me an "I warned you" smile.

He drifted to my left side and we were finally side by side after going around the course once. Dominique reached his hand out to me when we were the closest and pouted. Was he asking for forgiveness for almost knocking me off the track? I reached my hand out and smacked his. Now he gave me his "Now, it's on" smile. I giggled at his funny facial expressions.

We were on the third and final lap and I started focusing on the track and not Dominique. He yelled at me that the loser has to pay for dinner afterwards. Just knowing that we were going to get food once the race was over made me speed up. Dominique's kart was visibly slowing down and in the end, I did leave him in the dust.

I passed the finish line a whole four seconds before he did. Dominique tried to feel me up while he was helping me out of my suit but I told him losers don't get to cop feels. I, on the other hand, was not reprimanded for squeezing his ass while helping him out of his.

"So like, what was all that shit you was talking earlier? Something about paying for some food?" I smiled. The way he smiled back at me was suspicious. He was smiling like he knew something I didn't. "You didn't LET me win, did you?"

"No, I don't let you win. I just don't let *myself* win," he says, running.

"I hate you! Why would you do that!"

I run after him this time and try to jump on his back but he catches me around my thighs and throws me over his shoulder. One of the guys who was staring me down earlier was watching me now. I wondered if Dominique had caught that, but when he pulled me down in front of him and kissed me, I knew he had. He walked out holding my hand with his left and motioning at the guy that it was never going to happen with his right. I rolled my eyes.

"What are you doing, bring your ass on."

"These muthafuckas have to understand," he says, but he's smiling so I know he's not really upset.

"Where to now?" I ask while Dominique opens my door.

"Wherever you wanna eat but make sure that you order as much that you want," he answers.

"Yes, Daddy."

We end up going to Epic Burger because I've just been craving their turkey burgers so badly. They're the only turkey burgers I like and they come on real wheat bread that looks like they sprinkled oatmeal over the top. The restaurant was downtown, right down the street from my old college.

I used to stop in here when I had to work late. I'd be so hungry when my shift was over at 7pm, I'd take the train right over when the place was pretty empty. I always sat by the window eating my food and listening to my headphones. Of course, I had to take them off a few times when the male waiters would come over, tell me their names, and let me know to inform them of any issues I might have. I had a feeling none of them would be doing that tonight.

"Are you tired, yet?" I asked when we sat down in our booth. Dominique had danced in the car the whole long ride downtown. He couldn't do much while sitting down, but he managed to break out in a sweat. He sat in the farthest corner of the booth and pulled me over to lie back against his chest.

"You like a little baby," he says. "Why you never go back to school?" he asks suddenly. I shrug my shoulders.

"After three years and four different colleges, all I'd done was waste money. I had to realize that just because I'm intelligent doesn't mean I'll be successful in college. You know, every semester, I'd tell myself I was going to be way better than last time. I'm gonna study, I'm gonna go to class every day, and I'm gonna pay attention and work harder. But things always went pretty much the same. I'd always fail half my classes and pass the other half." I laugh at that. "I was just a horrible student and I have other plans for myself. You don't think less of me for not going to school, do you?" I was only half serious when I asked that because I knew he hadn't gone to college.

"Nevvvvver. Did you have a favorite class?" he asks.

"As a matter of fact, yes I did. And it was French."

"You took French? You never tell me."

"Ohhhh yes. I had a huge crush on my French teacher too," I giggle. "I loved the way he pronounced my name. I was kind of a teacher's pet. He was one of the few teachers I've ever actually formed a bond with. I'm embarrassed to say I cried on my last day of class with him."

"He look like me?" asks Dominique.

"Definitely not. He was 50 years old." Dominique can't contain his laughter when I say that.

"What is sooo amusing about that? He was a very handsome and youthful 50 year old. He had light brown skin. He was about 6'0 tall. And his smile was absolutely gorgeous. His French accent definitely didn't hurt. Had I met you back then, you would've had some real competition while you laughing." I wrap my arms tightly around myself and squeeze.

"What you doing?" Dominique asks.

"I'm just reminiscing on how it felt when my French teacher hugged me the last time I saw him," I say. Dominique pushes me away from him and I laugh. "Awww…" I squeeze his cheek between my thumb and index finger. "Don't feel bad," I say like I'm talking to a baby. "I still wuv you."

Our food comes and Dominique is acting a fool, hiding his plate from me like I'm really going to steal his food. As usual, I put away my burger in under 15 minutes and I'm munching on my fries and scrolling through Instagram on my phone. I go to Dominique's page and see the "selfie" we took on one of the rides on my birthday. I remember taking that picture and how a text from an unknown number popped up just afterwards that read *Lol you must miss me huh ;).*

At the time it stung a little because I knew it could be anybody from an ex to a groupie to, God forbid, a girl on the side. I desperately wanted to know what message Dominique had sent to make her respond that way. But it was my special day and I didn't want anything messing it up. I wanted to trust him. He doesn't know I saw it and I'd forgotten about it since then.

"Are you coming to my art show tomorrow?" I ask instead.

"Me and Damien have to leave for workshop tomorrow in Atlanta. At 2," he responds. My head drops just knowing Dominique won't be with me for much longer.

"Oh… I was hoping you could---," I stop and ask myself if it's too soon to say this, "…meet my mom." My eyes are on my plate when I blurt it out because I'm scared to see his reaction. After being silent for a few seconds, he opens his mouth to speak.

"We can come by for a little bit before we leave. It start at 12pm, right?" I look up at him in adoration and can't stop myself from pecking the side of his jaw. "Butter will miss me more than you."

"Nigga, please. He hardly sees you as it is." I reach down into my bag. "I have a little surprise…" I laugh evilly.

Slowly, I raise my hand in front of Dominique's face and reveal a small bag of green. Dominique goes cross-eyed for a second looking at it, then he side-eyes me.

"Lemme see," he says, and reaches for it. I snatch it away and put it back in my bag.

"Nope! You have to drive me home, I don't know what you're like when you're high. Fuck around and get me killed." Dominique gives me that look only he can, like he has a secret.

"I have a bigger surprise, but I tell you later," he says.

"Oh my God!" I say louder than I mean to. "I don't have any snacks at home. Let's make a run to the store. Please?"

"What store open now?" It was almost 11pm now.

"Walmart for sure. They're always open."

Dominique buys me another pomegranate soda and we head to the car. Walmart was the emptiest I've ever seen it. Only two registers were open and neither were actually occupied.

"Yes, now we won't have to wait in any lines. Come with me."

I grab Dominique's hand and run all the way to the back of the store, dragging him along the way. I stop suddenly by the electronics and he crashes into my backside, almost falling forward over me. I put my finger to my lips and signal him to be quiet. The person behind the counter was sleeping on the job.

I pick up a few DVDs and browse for a funny movie I might want to watch later. I come across Friday, Matilda, Harry Potter & the Prisoner of Azkaban, and a documentary about Whitney Houston's life. Clearly, Walmart needed to update their DVD selection.

"Ain't this some bullshit," I say to myself.

"SHH!" I hear Dominique, and turn to find him sitting on the floor pointing to a book that was upside down in his hand.

"I try to read here," he says, and rolls his eyes.

"The Cheetah Girls, huh?" I joke. He stands and almost hits his head on a half empty cart in the middle of the aisle. "Somebody leave their stuff."

"Hmm… you think they'll mind if we take it for a joyride?" I ask. Dominique holds out his hand and I grab it so he can lift me up and put me inside.

"Where you going, Queen?" he asks.

"To the toy section, please."

Dominique leans all the way forward and stretches his long legs out so he can speed to the other side of the store. I screamed at one point, forgetting where I was, but thought nothing of it. My hair flew back and Dominique accidentally got a taste of it and pretended to choke. I laughed the whole ride there, which happened to only be 10 seconds. He slowed down before he stopped so I wouldn't bust my shit, and helped me out of the cart. The first thing I saw was a skateboard. "Help me?"

I stand on it and Dominique pulls me by my arms until we reach the end of the aisle.

"Whooooooo!"

Dominique let's go and shakes his head at me. I almost lose my balance trying to dodge a little girl who's playing with a Barbie alone, no parent in sight. She looks no older than 3 years. I don't hit her, but she falls down on her bottom anyway. Dominique picks her up and places her back on her feet.

"I'm sorry, honey!" I say to her. "Are you okay?" I wipe some dust off her leg.

"Thank you," she says in the cutest little voice. Dominique has been smiling down at her the whole time and she stared right back up at him. They looked adorable together.

"You shirt is so cute," I say.

"Thank you," she says again. Her mommy walks up and scolds her for walking off by herself.

"She so cute," Dominique says to her mommy, as they walk off hand-in-hand. The little girl waved goodbye to him. I was enjoying watching them make a connection and of course it made me think about having a baby again. Seeing Dominique interact with the little girl made me daydream about having *his* baby. The girl and her mommy are long gone when I realize she left her jacket on the floor.

"It's very fashionable, I think I'm gonna try it on," I joke. I head over to the dressing room with Dominique in tow and say, "One item, please," to nobody. Dominique tries to walk in with me, but I tell him this is the ladies' fitting room and he needs to go to the mens'.

"I don't give a fuck," he says, and forces me in a room.

He makes sure the door is locked, then lifts me into our favorite position. *Up against the wall*. He kisses me hungrily and slides me up higher so he can position his groin against my pelvis. It feels so damn good but I don't want to get too hot and bothered.

"I can't wait to get you home," he says in my ear. His voice is low and sleepy. I look down between my legs and back up at him to remind him we can't do anything. "I only want to be alone with you."

"In that case, we better get my snacks and get going," I say with a wink.

He puts me down and we grab the cart we travelled in and head towards the food. I grab two pints of ice cream and some Chips Ahoy cookies and place them in the cart. I'm grabbing multiple flavors of Jarritos when two girls skip up to Dominique. They weren't screaming, but kind of shrieking under their breath, if that's possible.

"Are you one of the members of Les Gémeaux?" the less calm one asks. In my head, I'm laughing because I know how much it annoys Damien when people say that. Dominique doesn't seem to mind though. He smiles and gives her and her friend a hug. "Hiiiii," she says to me and I smile and wave.

"What's your name?" he asks.

"Angel. Can I take a picture with you?" She hands her friend her iPhone. I slide over so I can get out of their way but she says, "No, you too. Please." I look at her then at Dominique then back to her.

"C'mon girl," he says. I let Angel stand next to Dominique and I stand on the outside. We take one picture smiling and one picture making silly faces, at her request.

"Thank you so much!" she screams. She runs off telling her friend that nobody is going to believe her when she tells them she met one of the twins and his *sister* at the store. I keel over in laughter, but punch Dominique in his gut when he starts laughing.

I'm extremely tired. We did nothing but play all night. I was so ready to go home and just lay with my man. I fell asleep in the car on the way home but I regained full energy once I remembered my weed. I changed into my onesie and rolled up in the bathroom. When I came out, Dominique was on the floor in front of the bed watching TV in nothing but his boxers. He has released his hair from the scrunchie I had it in. My face beamed.

I went over and sat down in his lap, facing him and wrapped my ankles behind his lower back. I put both arms around his neck and lit my J. He stroked my waist softly and kissed my neck and shoulder affectionately. Dominique's strong shoulders with his arms wrapped around me had become one of my favorite feelings.

I inhaled quickly and closed my eyes. My entire being was high before I had even taken the first hit. I felt insanely weak and safe all at once. This right here was the high I had been floating on ever since Dominique had shared his heart with me.

"Dee...." I didn't mean to say it loud.

"What's wrong, baby?" he asks.

"Nothing. Nothing is wrong. Everything is right. I can't think of one thing that could make this night any more perfect."

"I can think of something," he says, and I remember that he told me he has a surprise for me.

He pats me so I can stand up and he reaches into his jacket pocket and pulls out some papers. I feel my heart drop immediately because I'm afraid of what I think it is. He gives them to me and I start reading them apprehensively. It's not a marriage license. But I don't breathe a sigh of relief because it's the deed to a house. I look up without moving.

"You bought yourself a house?" I ask.

"I bought *us* a house," he responds. He grabs my hand and sits on the edge of the bed. "No more coming here staying in your place with just your stuff, sharing this little place. I come back and forth and back and forth and don't have no home to go to. I want a home with you." I wince.

"But you bought the house...," I scratch my head, "...already?"

I squint my eyes trying to understand how he could possibly make such a big move without thinking about all the factors involved. There he goes being impulsive again.

"I want it now."

"Wait, wait, wait... this house is in LA," I say, reading the deed again.

"Yes well, you have to understand. Me and Damien do a lot of workshops in LA and we love it there and I know you like the warm weather so I did think about it."

"Dee! I can't just leave my apartment, I do have a lease. It hasn't even been a whole two months yet! My life is here in Chicago, did you really think I would just up and leave for LA with you?" I ask. I'm getting more and more frustrated by the second now and my voice is rising. My high is gone before it could even happen.

"Well, yes. It's simple really...you can get more ummm exposure for you art and me and Damien can get more work and you will be close to Casandra. It work out for evvvvverybody."

"Where is my joint?" I ask myself. I massage my temples. I rarely get headaches but Dominique has done it tonight. "You need to start thinking about what you're doing, like reallyyyy think about it, before you do it. What on God's green earth..." I trail off. I light my J again and sit at the kitchen table, putting my head in my hand. All I can do is look at Dominique and shake my head.

"I will take care of your lease, don't worry for that."

"Of course. Just like you take care of everything else," I say sarcastically. "What reason did you honestly think would make this happen? Tell me why. I know this is gonna be good..."

"Because... like you say. I'm your happiness." I look up at him. DID HE REALLY. "And you're my happiness and I can't do it without you and I need you."

"SHIT," I say weakly. I put my face in my hands and groan. He had done it. "Come here." He kneels in front of me like he always does and I bring his face into my chest and hug him. "This is definitely the weed talking but I will *think* about it, Dee. Just let me sleep on it, okay? I can't believe I'm saying this."

"I promise you gonna do it and you gonna like it."
"Just please hush before I change my mind."

■■■

"Do you think Dee is cheating on me?" I say into the phone. I know Casandra will tell me like it is, even if it's something I don't want to hear.

"I think…he's doing some very questionable things," she responds. I agree.

Every relationship I'd been in up until now had ended very quickly because I'm just not one to put up with bullshit. I think men really try to take advantage of me because I seem so innocent and little, but I'm quick to drop anyone in my life who tries to play me for a fool.

I am not stupid. I know that *something* was going on with Dominique and one or more females. Even if nothing physical had happened between them, he was at least thinking about it. I know Dominique is a flirt, but there's a certain line you don't cross when you're in a relationship. That text and that bitch at the concert were it.

I fumbled with the bobby pins in my hand as I looked in the mirror to see where to place them. I had decided to wear my hair in a "frohawk" for the art show. I had also made sure to get my eyebrows threaded earlier this morning. I know my art was the real focus, but I wanted everything to be perfect.

"Why do you ask? Did something else happen?" asked Casandra.

"No. We had a really good time last night. He made me feel a lot better," I said. I still hadn't told her about what the doctor said, but she knows it wasn't good. "I'm just trying to decide if it's safe to move in with him or not."

"Move in?"

"Yes." I sigh. "Dee dropped a bomb on me and said he bought a house in Cali for us."

"He went and bought a whole house?" She was even more shocked than I was when I first found out. "What's wrong with him visiting you at your place like he's been doing?"

"He wants us to have a home together, Casandra… It does sound nice."

"It sounds like he wants to play house, that's what it sounds like. I'm starting to think you should fall back from him a little. He's moving too fast."

I couldn't believe what she was saying. She was the one who suggested I speed things up a little in the first place. Stop being scared, Téa. Let that man love you, Téa. I hadn't decided I was going to move in with him yet, but I found myself defending the idea when I saw how against it she was.

"Moving too fast for who, me or you?" I ask.

"Téa, it's been two months. What are you thinking about?"

"You think I don't know how long it's been?" I'm trying not to start an argument because I don't need to be stressed on my big day. But if she only knew how Dominique and I felt about each other, it would only seem right for us to make this move.

"So you're telling me you actually want to do this," she states more than questions.

"I don't know! I'm thinking about it... Dee made a few important points about how this could be good for us personally and professionally. Right now, you're definitely pushing me in that direction."

"Don't do anything just to prove me wrong, Téa. You were just asking me if I think he's cheating. If you're questioning his loyalty to you, why would you think this is okay? Moving in with him is just gonna make the situation worse. Now he's gonna think he's got you right where he wants you and he can do anything."

Tears began welling up in my eyes because I wanted her to be happy for me. I didn't want to hear all this shit about Dominique doing things behind my back. I don't ever want to think about that.

"Tell me something. If he is cheating on you, what makes you different from that other girl? Hm?" Casandra asks. My lips are pinching together without my permission and I sniffle. I shake my head quickly as a tear slides down my cheek and whisper, "Love."

Casandra exhales loudly when she hears me crying. "I pray to God love is enough for you guys." The buzzer rings suddenly and I stand and wipe my tears with my sleeve.

"I'll call you later and tell you how the show goes," I say and hang up with Casandra. I adjust my clothes and check my face in my phone screen to make sure Dominique can't notice that I've been crying. I open the door and am face to face with Percy. I start to shut the door immediately but he puts his hand up to stop it.

"Téa, come on. I just wanna talk to you."

"We have nothing to say to each other." I start to shut the door again, but his foot is in the way. I look at the ceiling and roll my eyes.

"Just listen. I'm not here to fight or argue with you. I promise. Can't you tell when I'm telling the truth?"

I look at him and his face does seem sincere. He is noticeably doing a lot better. I can tell by his appearance. His hair and thin mustache and beard were lined up recently. He was wearing a crisp, black button-up and black jeans. He smelled of powder and musk. His eyes were slanting down and crinkling at the corners and they made his expression look genuine.

"You need to hurry up and talk before Dee gets back," I say.

"Okay, okay. It'll only take a minute." I hadn't seen this side of Percy since we were together. He was speaking very gently to me and I wasn't used to that in the past couple months since we'd broke up. "How are you doing?"

"Percy, time is ticking."

"Okay. I just wanted to come over and apologize for my behavior the last few times we've seen each other." I narrow my eyes and cross my arms to show that I don't believe him. "I know an apology sounds strange coming from me, but I really am sorry. You know… I was in a really bad place. Truth is, I knew I was fool for letting you go. I was mad at myself but I took my anger out on you. You're a good girl--- good woman, Téa. And you deserve better."

"And I have better," I say. He chuckles to himself.

"Yeah, I saw that too. I'm glad you found a man who knows how to handle you the right way. Just wanted to let you know that I didn't mean any of those things I said to you and that I'm growing and learning from it. I'm not quite there yet, but I'm becoming a better version of myself and I just wanted to show you." He held both his arms out as if to show me all of him. "The new Percy will never intentionally disrespect a woman again."

"Well, that's great. I really mean it, Percy. I'm glad you're bettering yourself."

"Thank you," he smiled. "I heard about you being in that art show too." I look confused because I don't see how he could hear about that. "Your grandma," he says, reading my mind. Of course. She has no idea the things that have gone on between us. "This is my way of saying good luck in that and in the future." Percy hands me an envelope that was hidden in his back jeans pocket.

"What is this, anthrax?"

"C'mon, Téa," he says with a laugh, "Just open it when you get inside. And know that it comes from the heart." He points to his chest and starts to back down the steps. "I'll see ya around. Oh…tell umm… *Dee* I said no hard feelings." He turned around and made his way down the street. I definitely would not be telling Dominique he said that.

■■

My sister and I have slowly been hanging all my canvases up on the wall in my little area for the past 30 minutes since Dominique dropped me off. He and Damien were off picking up some things they would need before leaving for their trip later. He told me he would swing by around 12:30. I was just hoping he didn't flake out on me. It was already 11:30 now and the show would be starting in another half hour. Trini kept getting distracted by all the fruit and finger sandwiches that had been set out.

"Do you know how many smoothies I could make with all this fruit? Oh my God," she said.

"Stay focused." I could see my mami heading our way out the corner of my eye.

As she walked through the room, she glanced around at everyone's artwork with big eyes and a wide gap-toothed smile. My mami stood five feet even and had a dark caramel complexion. Her weave was the same shade as her skin and she wore a lime green sundress around her chunky little frame. She slid her shades back onto her face even though she was inside now and waved to me. I hugged her tightly when she finally reached me.

"Hi, baby." I could see the excitement on her face. "Look at this. This is nothing like I expected. This is very classy."

She made the A-OK symbol with her fingers and continued to admire the building. I wished my brother could be here but he didn't come back from Texas this summer. He wished me luck over the phone last night though, and I knew he was supporting me from afar.

"Where's Davon?" I ask about my stepdad.

"Tryna find parking. You know how this parking be downtown. It's a mess out there."

"Mami, I'm hungry," says Trini. She pouts with her lips and lays her head on my mami's chest. She was 14 years old and still the biggest baby. My mami and stepdad treated her as one too. I pointed out all the food laid out for us but Trini insisted on pizza.

Once my stepdad got inside and we'd finished setting everything out for display, my mami got us all together to take some pictures. Her pictures came out shaky every single time, but she was the main one always trying to be a photographer. I smiled at our blurry pics and got ready for the show to start.

"We're proud of you, young lady," my stepdad says. I beam with pride.

Trini stood by me the whole time and smiled at everyone who came by to look at anything. A few people had inquiries about the meaning of some of my art, even things as simple as an eye. I tried not to look at anyone funny and just answer their questions. A really tall White man ended up purchasing my "Almost Famous" colored pencil drawing.

It was a picture of a man standing behind a topless woman with his hands covering her breast and her reaching up to rest her hands behind his head. They were faceless, but you didn't need to see their expressions to understand that they were a power couple. I also sold a few prints. Me and Trini jumped with excitement as I counted up how much money I had made so far.

My mami was away looking at other people's art when Damien and Dominique walked in. Dominique had his hair twisted up underneath a snapback and was also wearing shades. They were so dark, I couldn't tell what he was looking at. I knew he was dressed like this so he wouldn't draw attention or be recognized. The man thought he was Michael Jackson himself. He leaned down so I could kiss his jaw and Damien playfully picked Trini up, giggling, for a hug.

"Did you have trouble finding parking?" I asked.

"I got all my bags in the car." Dominique's answer has no relevance to my question, but I look confused and let it go. "I don't know they give you food to go with the art," he says, biting into a sandwich.

"Art and food, it's good together," says Damien, laughing. My mami comes up behind me suddenly and asks, "Is this your friend?" Dominique is towering over her of course and points down at the top of her head.

"Is this your mom?" he giggles. I'm not the best at introductions and I hate giving them, but here goes.

"Dee, this is my mami. Mami, this is my Dee. I mean...my boyfriend." I'm blushing with embarrassment. But Dominique just laughs and caresses my face.

"Aww, she call me her Dee," he says to cover my embarrassment.

"Hi, how you doing, I'm Sonya." My mami holds out her hand.

"My name is Dominique," he responds, and holds his arms out for a hug instead. My mami is slightly surprised at how tightly he hugs her, as if she is a close friend. But that's Dominique...

"I'm so glad we're finally meeting," she says once he loosens his grip.

"I know, I thought I never meet you." My mami is smiling from ear to ear and I know she's listening to the adorable way he speaks. "You have to understand, Téa never wanna bring me around."

"That is not true. Just eat your sandwich," I say. "Oh, this is Damien. Dominique's brother, if you can't tell."

"No, we not brothers," Damien says sarcastically. He's flashing his little kid smile when he hugs her, showing off his bunny teeth. I'm sure on the inside, my mami's heart is about to burst out of her chest at how cute the twins are.

"We're gonna have to have some kind of family day so you guys can come and hang out with us and have fun," she suggests. She has done this with all of my ex-boyfriends. She can't help it.

"Ohhhhh, yes," Damien replies.

"Gonna have to get Dominique out the house when he's in Chicago, right?" she asks, playfully.

"Yes, well we sleep *a lot*. When we don't sleep, we eat. All I wanna do when I get there is relax and I just think about fun later, you know?" He is starting to ramble and says too much, as he always does. I can tell by the look my mami gives me that she has some questions about what he's saying.

"Wow, you two just sleep and eat huh?" she repeats. Her eyes are wide again and she gives a fake smile. I already know what she's thinking.

When Dominique finishes his sandwich, he hugs my mami again and shakes my stepdad's hand, and I walk him and Damien back to the entrance. He is now snacking on some baked chips and tea.

"You better let all of that digest and don't eat again before you get on the plane. You know how you get, babe." I stand on my tip-toes and give him a small kiss on the mouth. I was going to miss that so much while he was gone.

"I never get sick on a plane til I meet you. You rubbing off on me," he says, referring to the motion sickness I get when I look out the window while the plane is ascending.

"Whatever. See you, baby. Have fun, okay?"

"Always." I watch him walk all the way out the door before I walk back to my area. My mami is waiting for me with a funny look on her face.

"That's some kinda relationship, just sleeping and eating," she says.

"I already know what you're about to say. That is not all we do, Mami. He only said that because he's been on tour this whole time and he gets tired. When he comes to my place, it's like his only time to rest."

"Téa. Dominique seems like a very sweet guy, but why would you want a man that just wants to lay up with you." I got angry as soon as she said this.

"HE DOESN'T JUST LAY UP WITH ME," I say quietly but fiercely. I look around to make sure nobody is paying attention. "Just because we like to relax together? We can't chill sometimes? Dang…" I wanted to say *shit*, but I wasn't even about to go there with her. I was just so fed up with all her assumptions. She always takes one little detail and runs with it.

"You want a man that's gonna take you out to nice places and show you things." Here she goes, telling me what I want again. "And I know if he working with Beyoncé, he has the means to."

"We go out, okay. We just went out last night. I am very happy with how me and Dee spend our time, thank you very much." I try to end the conversation, but she keeps talking.

"Okay, Téa. I'ma let you make your own decisions. Like I said, Dominique seems very nice. But he's at that age where he needs to be settling down and preparing to start a family."

"So you think that me and Dominique should be working towards that?" I ask.

"If you all claim to have all these feelings for each other, he should be taking care of you and yes, you all should be thinking about the future."

"Okay then. It's settled. You are absolutely right and I will talk to him about it."

I plaster a smile on my face and get back to the art show. Later that day, after replaying all the successes I had today in my head over and over and getting home, I call Dominique. He doesn't answer, but I leave a short voicemail on his phone.

"I know we haven't been together long and this has been somewhat of a whirlwind romance, but I have faith in it. Like you said, we're gonna grow together. If we can advance to the next level by making a home together, I'm willing to do that with you. So let's do it…I hope you're being safe and staying out of trouble. I love you. Call me back."

FIVE "WHERE I WANNA BE"

Two months later

The large curtains on the floor-to-ceiling windows in the family room were drawn, allowing sunlight to flow anywhere and everywhere. That was how I liked it. Now the inside of the house matched my mood perfectly. I had Damian Marley blasting on the surround sound speakers; his rhythms always seemed to give things a summertime feel.

I had been dancing and singing around the house while cleaning since I woke up at 8am this morning. Like I said before, this kind of weather is what made me want to get up and do something. It was a far cry from the frigid 16 degree weather we'd left back in Chicago when we moved 3 days ago.

Dominique hadn't moved a finger since we got here. Right now, he was relaxing on one of the white sofas with his feet up, Jordans and all. *Didn't I just get on him about that earlier*, I thought to myself. I didn't want him to dirty that perfect white furniture but I was so happy, I decided to just forget about it. I just tried not to cringe at the greasy slice of pizza in his hand and hoped it didn't drip. Dominique laughed at me as I dropped my broom and shook my ass to "The Master Has Come Back."

"Why you twerk in you dress?" he asks.

It felt lovely just to be able to wear a dress again! I was wearing a white and orange striped skirt that started at my belly and ended just before my toes. I even wore my sandals with the four inch heel on them. It takes a lot to get me in a pair of heels. Don't get me wrong, I love them and I can definitely work some. But at 5'1, I just hated feeling taller. I'd probably be going out to buy a lot more dresses and skirts. The doorbell rang and I opened it for Casandra. I had invited her to come over as soon as we got situated so I could show off our beautiful place.

"Damn girl, it is looking Bohemian as fuck up in here!" she exclaimed as we hugged and kissed hello. I was smiling so hard, my cheeks were starting to ache.

"I know, you know I chose all the furniture and color patterns," I say, smirking and pulling on Dominique's black bowtie. His gaze was stuck on the television, so I went and turned down my music for him.

She loves my culture, herbs, and my locks
Silky smooth way I flow my words on my tracks
She's hoping we can spend a night at
Somewhere that's warm and cozy, why not?

"Listening to your boo, huh?" asked Casandra.

"Girl, yes. Now that we live out here, I can finally go to one of his shows. He stay having shows in Cali. Come on, let me show you something." I grab her hand and lead her to the second floor. We walk through the master bedroom and Casandra is in awe at how huge it is. She dives onto our King-sized bed.

"I'm moving in," she says with her eyes closed, savoring the fluffy pillows.

"Come here, I wanna show you something in the bathroom." Our bathroom is the size of three of my bathrooms back at my old studio apartment. There was a large, circular Jacuzzi tub on one end of the room and a shower on the other end. In the middle was a sink so long, Dominique could lay his entire body across it. In fact, he did that when he first saw it. But what I wanted to show Casandra was the best part. I pulled the shower curtains back and revealed the window inside, surrounded by beautiful light brown tiles.

"That's what you wanted to show me? Not this amazing Jacuzzi? But a damn window?" she asked.

"You don't understand. I have always wanted a shower with a window inside. Look, when I take my shower in the morning, the sun coming through the window makes my skin absolutely glow. It lets you see everything, there's nothing to hide. Seeing your naked body in the sun really makes you admire yourself more. It's beautiful." Casandra gave me a blank stare for a few seconds, then patted me on my shoulder.

"Whatever you say, Téa. I'm glad you have your sun in the shower." I laugh.

"You just don't get it. I have a very deep connection with the sun. Man, I feel like I'm on vacation."

"But you've done nothing but clean and fix the house up."

"Yes, but just escaping my old life in Chicago makes me feel so free. This change has been so…liberating."

"Can you and all your liberation show me to the food?"

When I led Casandra back to the kitchen, I couldn't help but notice the imprint I saw through the grey drop-crotch sweatpants Dominique was wearing. I silently daydreamed about feeling on it later while Casandra helped herself to a few slices of pizza.

"I'm surprised you're eating this, Téa. No green vegetables, no nuts and oats and milk that doesn't come from cows because that kinda milk isn't good enough? What happened?" I roll my eyes at her.

"I just haven't had any time to go grocery shopping or cook, that's all. I'm not eating this pizza, it makes me feel lazy. That's all Dominique's." Just as I speak his name, he comes up behind me to get more. When he reaches over me, I can feel the cloth from his pants graze my behind and it takes everything in me not to throw my head back and grind into him. But I had to remind myself that I had company and bide my time until Casandra left.

■■■

I leaned back in the tub until my head was touching the wall and allowed all the bubbles to cover up my body completely. God, I hadn't taken a real bubble bath like this since I was probably three years old, still taking baths with my brother. I even had incense burning, and it reminded me of good days at home as a child, when my mami was in a good mood.

The tub was so huge, I was like a small fish in a pond. I stretched my legs out and turned the volume up a little on the dock. Donnell Jones crooned into my ear. Dominique stuck his head in the door and peeped at me.

"You have fun with the tub already?" he asks. I know he's just upset that I'm having fun without him.

"You're welcome to join me..." I splash a little water on him and wink. He immediately comes in and starts undressing. I watch him strip out of those beautiful sweatpants and his black briefs until he is hanging before me. The man really was a masterpiece. When he reached for the bowtie, I stopped him. "No, no, no. Keep that on...please." I smile.

"One second," he says, and turns to walk to the light switch and dim the room.

"Dat assss," I yell.

"Don't be looking at my ass, girl."

"How can I not?" I pinch it playfully as he reaches one leg over to hop in with me. "It's so beautiful." I slide over so that he can lie where I was and I climb on top of him. I felt those strong arms tighten around my waist as I rested my head against his chest; I never get tired of this.

"Hmmm." Dominique rubs his fuzzy head against mine. "My baaayyyybeeee." I kiss the muscle popping out of his left arm before kissing his soft, pink lips.

"You love me?" he asks.

"No, no..." I shake my head quickly, splashing water in his face. He grabs my hair in his fist and forces me to look up at him.

"Say that again," he threatens. I come closer to his face until our noses are touching and look him directly in his eyes.

"NO." Dominique moves faster than the speed of light and had both of my hands pulled behind my back quicker than I could say, "Just joking."

"So you don't love me?" I now fully understand the pleasure in being man-handled sexually because even though it hurt my wrists to be pushed together the way they were, it made me hornier than ever to see the look in Dominique's eyes. He had hunger in them and his gaze was fixated on me like I was the piece of meat he's been looking for. I hesitate…

"What are you gonna do if I say no?" I ask.

"I'm gonna *make* you say you love me," he responds, with a straight face.

"You think you can?" He doesn't answer, he just lifts me up with my arms still behind my back and pulls me out of the tub. I know I'm tiny but the way he just grabbed me and had me in the air…I was so turned on. The whole moment was so intense; he was staring me down and his bottom lip was trembling.

I wanted him to *fuck* me. The same thought seemed to be clicking in his head but when he turned to leave the bathroom, Butter came trotting in. He looked at us with his head cocked and for a second, I forgot about all of the sexual tension in the room.

"Butter, do you see how your daddy is abusing me?" I say. He runs to Dominique's ankles and taps them, then backs up. Then taps them again. "Look at him defending me!"

"Daddy gotta go fuck Mommy, then I come back and feed you. Oki?" I want to punch Dominique in his chest but I remember that he still has my hands stuck behind my back.

"Don't say that to him! He's just a baby!" Dominique bites the tip of my nose, knowing I can't do anything about it.

"How about---," he kisses me, "I make you fat---," he kisses me again, "with *my* baby?"

He bites my bottom lip before I can answer and takes it in his mouth, sucking gently. Then he licks the side of my face and I shudder. It's killing me that I can't move a muscle. My legs wrapped around his waist is the only way I'm holding myself up.

"C'mon, Dee. Let me go…" I whisper.

"I let you go when you come." He presses my back against the entrance of our bedroom door. His tongue is tracing the outline of my tattoo that sits just under my right shoulder and above my breast. It gradually made its way to my boob and Dominique feasted with his eyes locked on mine the entire time.

He was so sexy… being in lust with the person you're in love with makes the sex so much more satisfying. Satisfying in a dangerous way. I couldn't take it anymore, I was ready to feel him pounding into me. I was usually all for foreplay, but damnit, my pussy was pulsating so bad, it hurt.

"Dee…I want you…" I could barely say.

"Uh uh," he said through a mouthful of me.

"NOW!" His eyes shot upwards at me and he raised his eyebrows. Releasing my breast, he rose until we were face to face.

"If you wish for something, you gonna get it," he said. He finally let go of my arms and I wrapped one around his broad neck and the other hand reached out for his dick. He smacked it away. I looked at him with a confused look on my face but he ignored it and threw me on the bed.

"What are you doing?"

"Turn around."

There was no hint of a smile on his face at all, so I knew he wasn't playing around. I just did as I was told. I turned over on my stomach and waited for whatever was next. Dominique grabbed my arms again and put them together behind my back.

"Arch you back and open your motherfucking legs." The way he was talking had me giddy with excitement. He was always a little arrogant when he was horny but this was a new level. I was almost scared he would pull out a whip or something and hurt me for real.

When I lifted my ass in the air and arched my back like he told me to, he slid underneath me while still holding my wrists together. He lowered my waist until my *lips* were touching his lips and started eating my pussy like it was his last meal. My knees instinctively squeezed together as soon as I felt his warm, wet tongue on me. Dominique didn't seem to mind though, because his tongue only went deeper.

I had nowhere to go. My arms were stuck and my face was in the pillow. I groaned and whimpered like a little puppy. I really wanted to scream. It was scaring me how good it felt and how openly I was reacting to it. My eyes were closed so tightly, I was squeezing tears out.

I came so hard, it felt like all the strength and energy left in my body had been released into Dominique's mouth. But he wasn't done. When I fell over on my side from exhaustion, he gripped my hips tighter and pulled me back on top of him.

"Noooooooo," I moaned. I couldn't breathe. My breaths were coming in tiny pants. Every lick, every time I felt those lips close around my labia, my breath was literally taken away. "No moreeee…." I had been trying to run away for three minutes and he finally let me go.

"Where you going?"

He bit his lip and smiled seductively. Dominique pulled me by my ankles until I was laying underneath him and kissed me deeply. I felt so weak, but I couldn't resist kissing him. It was getting me worked up all over again. He knew exactly how to touch me to satisfy my yearning. He knew just how to press his thumb into my clit to open me up. He knew exactly just how to kiss and breathe into my neck while he entered me. He knew exactly how to roll his body and grind his pelvis into me to make real tears stream down my face. At the moment, I felt 100% fulfilled in every aspect. I felt his love filling me entirely and I let out a shriek full of pleasure and satisfaction.

He finished and swung my sweaty body around to lay on top of him. I felt his thighs lock around my legs, keeping me close to him. "Ohhhhhhh...." I exhaled. "I love you, baby. I love you so much. I don't ever wanna be without you."

■■■

I woke up the next afternoon under the covers, still naked with Dominique's bowtie wrapped around my ponytail. I don't recall putting my hair in a ponytail before falling asleep. I don't even recall falling asleep. This was definitely the work of Dominique. I forgot everything that went down last night too until I tried to get out bed.

My thighs were extremely sore and my nipples stung as a breeze came through the window. I hopped over to the window and shut it. I had to sit down on the sill for a while to get myself together. The one thing that hadn't left my mind all night was Dominique telling me he was going to make me fat with his baby.

Although I didn't react to it at the moment, I had thought about it every second after the words left his mouth. I know that guys say things they don't mean when they get caught up in the moment, but Dominique knows what this means to me.

He wouldn't play around about something like that, I hope. I didn't want to seem pushy, but I knew I would have to ask him about it. I found my way into the kitchen and pulled a couple strawberries and a banana out for a fruit smoothie. Dominique didn't seem to be home, so I wanted to try to get a little workout in. That is, if I could even get my legs to rise.

I plugged my iPhone up to the speakers and searched for my workout playlist. I could feel the bass from Higher Ground by TNGHT rumbling inside my chest as I clenched my ab muscles for my jack-knives. When I first started to exercise regularly, it was because I wanted to tone my belly and thicken my thighs.

Now that I know exercise is such a stress reliever and a pain reliever for my fibroids, I was even more motivated to do it. Four days a week, I would do crunches, leg raises, squats, side sculptors and more for an hour. I was beginning to work up a real sweat when I heard Dominique's key in the door.

"Hey, baby." I bent down and grabbed my water bottle off the floor.

"What you doing up?" he asked.

I guess he expected me to be knocked out for the whole day after what he did to me. Trust me, there was nothing more I wanted than to be in bed relaxing, but I don't like to waste my day. He snatched my bottle out of my mouth and drunk the rest of it.

"I'm minding my own business, why you always messing with me?"

"Wait, wait, wait." His hand glides up and down my ass. "What is THIS? Look at youuuu," he grins. "It wasn't like this last night." He turns me around so he can get a better view.

"Is it bigger?" I ask, with my eyebrow raised.

"Yeah, it's sexy." He palms it with both hands and lifts me a little to plant a kiss on my forehead. Then he motions his head to the right, towards the stairs. "C'mon."

"Wha? Uh-uh," I push him away and turn back around. "You got me fucked up," I laugh. But he just wraps his arms around me from behind and puts his face in my neck.

"Why not?"

"Because!" I turn to look up at him. "*AGAIN?*" Damn, last night seemed like enough to hold him off until at least tomorrow. What was he trying to do to me? I enjoyed our lovemaking as well, but a woman could only handle so much at a time.

"Yes...*c'est trop bon*," he whispers into my neck and I feel him reach down and grab my pussy. It felt good but it was not about to happen.

"No, I'm all hot and sweaty. I'm hurting, baby."

"I like you sweaty." His tongue flickers across my neck. "Please, just a quickie. Before Damien finish parking and he find us in here."

"What!" I push him off and walk away. "Damien is right outside and you tryna have sex. You are so silly."

"We still got a lil time," he responds, smiling from ear to ear. Then I remember what I wanted to talk to him about.

"Actually, now that I think about it, I wanted to ask you about last---." I'm interrupted when Damien comes in and greets us. He kisses me hello and then wipes my own sweat off on me. "Whatever," I say.

"It's love, it's love," he says with a giggle.

"Yeah, I bet." I manage to lift myself up into one of the high stools at our dining room table. "I'm glad you're here though. I wanted to ask you two what are you planning on doing for your birthday?" Their 25th birthday was coming up in less than two weeks and I know they're not into simple get-togethers like me. They were going to do something huge.

"We justtttt come from check out this club on Hill Street. I like it. We gonna shut down the VIP and everything like that. Some family fly out too."

"Mann, I miss da club life so much. I never go out since we been here," Dominique replies. "I can't wait to get back out, man."

"I thought you and Damien would be all partied out by now since the tour just ended and everything. Ya'll just don't know how to stop moving." Damien laughs in agreement and shakes his head.

"We gotta keep moving, man. This nothing compared to like how we gonna feel after dis South America leg, Beyoncé tour, is over." I put my drink down.

"South America leg?" I asked. I didn't know anything about a South America leg. I thought the tour had ended for good. What the fuck was he talking about? I looked at Dominique and the expression on his face was that of someone who had been caught.

"Yeah, Monster extend tour til May next year," says Dominique.

He's obviously avoiding making eye contact with me. I don't blame him, because there is fire in my eyes right now. He just got back. We just got ourselves situated and now he's about to go on the road again? It was bad enough when we didn't live together, but I'm already accustomed to lying next to him every night and I can't stand to be away from him for too long. Skype calls will not suffice anymore.

"You didn't tell me that," I say plainly.

"I know, I forget. You know I wouldn't keep it from you, I'm sorry, baby." I ignore his apology.

"When does it start?" He doesn't answer immediately. Damien is nervously scrolling through his phone and clearly doesn't want to be a part of the conversation anymore. "Well?"

"It start in February...I leave the 15th."

I stare at him for a few seconds, just thinking about how cold and lonely every night would be for me from February to May. He knows how it was just being alone for a month. He saw what shape I was in when he got back. I couldn't even sleep without him. I was a walking zombie. How dare he leave me in this big ass house by myself for three months?

I feel like I'm being extremely selfish for even thinking he should stay here with me instead of doing what he loves. But then I think about the fact that he probably wasn't even going to tell me if Damien didn't say something about it. Why is that?

"Well that's great," I say.

I'm done with the conversation. I pick up my towel and my water bottle and make my way towards the stairs. I already know he's going to follow me, and he does. He tries to pull at my arm before I get to the top of the steps but I pull away from him and turn to look him in his eye. I almost giggle when I see that he is three steps down but we are still eye to eye. It's kind of funny that I had my finger pointed in his face getting ready to chew him out when I was so tiny compared to him.

"I feel like I'm in a fucking long-distance relationship!" I yell.

"Baby, why you screaming, just stop," he says, and grabs my arms to stop me from shoving him away. "I don't do it on purpose, this my job, what you want me to do? I wanna be here with you but I wanna be there too."

"Well, I just want you to be happy." My remark is full of sarcasm. I turn to go up the stairs again and he grabs me tightly around my hips and swings me around.

"Why you actin up?" he asks. "Huh? Why you actin like that? You gone miss me?" A smile is forming on his face and I almost fall for his charm, but my anger is too real.

"Just worry about what *you* gonna be missing. And I'ma tell you one more thing." I raise my finger again. "I'm not stupid. You're keeping things from me on purpose and one day I'm gonna get fed up and I'm gonna walk away." I grabbed my shit, stomped to our room and slammed the door.

I knew I was being a little more over the top than I usually was, but I didn't need any more upset in my life. I had enough of that. I knew Dominique wasn't going to come in after me. He had to get his pride in check. I surprised myself when I went off on him like that too. But Dominique wasn't just some guy that was interested in me anymore. He was the love of my life and he was my everything. And I would NOT allow him to fuck this up.

■■■

Dominique didn't slip into bed next to me that night until after 4am. He woke me when he came in and drowsily wrapped his arm around my belly from behind and pulled me in closer. I was a little surprised that he did that since I snapped on him so hard earlier. It made me feel a little immature. I turned over and tried to apologize for my behavior earlier, but he was fast asleep. His nose was doing that thing when it puffs up a little and I kissed the tip of it. It was hard to get back to sleep after that. I threw the covers off of me and was greeted by Butter.

"What you doing up, Boo Boo?" I pick him up and cuddle him in my arms. "You looking out for Mommy? Hmm?" I stroke his fur and we make our way downstairs and into the kitchen to get him some food. "Ooh, you stink Butter. We gonna have to give you a bath in the morning, huh?"

I pull out the huge bag of dog feed and pour some into his little bowl, then fill his other bowl with water. Before I met Dominique, when I couldn't sleep, I'd use that time to get some work done. So while Butter lapped up his water, I grabbed my laptop and hopped on Photoshop in hopes that a new shirt design would come to me.

Two hours passed and I had finished editing a Michael Jackson design for a crewneck. I turned my head to check on Butter, who had stopped making his little whimpering noises a while ago. His chest went up and down as he snored. I frowned when I noticed that he'd finished his water but only nibbled at his food a little. The lights flickered on and I looked up to see Dominique standing at the bottom of the stairs. He wasn't wearing a shirt and his hair was smushed, but his face was freshly washed and he had on shoes.

"Where you going so early?" I ask.

"Me and Damien have workshop in Bronx at 7pm," he replied, rubbing his eyes. "4pm our time."

"Why would you come in so late if you knew you had to get up so early?" I scold.

"Come on, baby, I don't feel like this right now today oki?"

I admit he looked very stressed out and sleep-deprived. I knew I added a lot to his stress. It wasn't intentional at all. Sometimes I just forget how much he does for me and where I would probably be if I wasn't here with him. I go over to the counter where he's leaning and hug his waist tightly. When I rest my head against his chest, I can feel how fast his heart is beating.

"You okay?" I ask.

"Yes, I love you." He kisses my forehead firmly and runs his fingers through my hair, softly massaging my scalp. "You can come with me if you want." I consider rushing to get my bags packed for a second, but decide to decline.

"No, today's the day I have to go shopping for groceries and toiletries and cleaning supplies and all that good stuff," I remind him. "Besides, we both know I can turn into a jealous bitch real quick. Soon as I see one of those fangirls try to caress you..." Dominique throws his head back in laughter. I chuckle a little too but I am half serious. "I have a new design up for sale on my shop. I'm ready to start making shirts and shipping. I have all my materials."

"That's so good, baby. I'm proud of you. You on you shit right now. I wanna see them."

When he puts his head down again and gazes back at me, I observe the way his philtrum curves up into two points underneath his nostrils. I had to taste those raspberry lips. And he had to get a good grip on my ass and lift me up on the counter for easier access. And I had to fumble with pulling my hoodie over my head so he could get to my breasts. And he had to tongue me down repeatedly until I was ready for all of him. And we had to have morning sex on the kitchen counter because nothing beats morning sex. And I'd have to remember to wipe the kitchen down later before I cooked dinner.

∙∙

A whole week goes by with no problems. My mom had been at my throat about leaving Chicago so abruptly for the first few days we were here, but she has finally let up. I haven't heard about any nonsense with my dad. My man is good. My best friend is good. I'm…okay.

I've been putting off the follow-up appointment I'm supposed to have with my doctor. I picked up my birth control from the pharmacy here two days ago and I've been taking it, unwillingly. But I was still taking it. My Michael Jackson shirts were selling at a nice pace. Dominique and I had even discussed possibly starting a Les Gémeaux collection for my line. I knew for sure money would start rolling in if I did that.

But right now, my work was not the focus. Getting Damien and Dominique's birthday plans together was. Their birthday fell on a Monday, but they wanted to invite their fans to celebrate with them, so they decided to hold the party on the 3rd, a Friday. The twins had already chosen the venue and time and my job was just to help promote.

I'd created the party fliers that were plastered all over twitter, facebook, and instagram. Not that the twins even needed all of that to get people to come out and see them. Casandra stopped by to help me decide what I would be wearing. I didn't know if I should be casual or not. After all, it was at a club. Clubs weren't my scene, but I did know women got all done up just to shake their ass in some heels. I didn't want any woman at my man's event looking better than me.

Casandra sat down on my bed while I took out the new heels I'd bought the day I went grocery shopping.

"Wow, I didn't even know you knew how to walk in heels," she said, as I strutted across the room.

"I know. I hate wearing them, I feel like a giant." I slid them off and showed her a very tight black dress that ended just beneath my ass and showed my back.

"Hmm...what is Dee gonna wear?" she asked.

"Probably jeans and a beater. Why does that matter?"

"I don't know. I think it'd be cute if you matched your man's swag instead of feeling like you have to go out of your way to be so sexy for him. That's what fangirls do, Téa. Women who think they're about to get chose, but in reality, he's gonna be taking you home that night."

She paused, waiting for my reaction. I didn't quite understand.

"Dominique already knows you're sexy. To him, you'll look sexy in anything. You can be sexy wearing a pair of jeans and a tank too. If you dress up like these other thirsty hoes, you're gonna look just like one of them. It's a party anyway, you don't wanna be in that bitch struggling to walk around. You wanna have fun."

"You think you know everything, don't you?" I ask, playfully. Honestly, I was glad she said all that. I didn't want to dress up, I wanted to be comfortable.

"Girl, just do your hair, throw on a chain, some cute earrings, and put all those rings all over your fingers like Dee does so it looks like you got brass knuckles and you'll be good," says Casandra, making me laugh. "So how's business? It seems good, but you look tired."

"Oh, I'm definitely tired. But it has nothing to do with work." I look up at her and raise my eyebrows. "It's Dee."

She touches my hand softly and looks compassionate before saying quietly, "Is he keeping you up all night with his talking again?" She cracks up at her own joke.

"That's hilarious, but no. It's worse." I look around the room, as if there was even someone there to listen, and whisper, "When he's here, he's fucking me twice a day. I can't take it anymore."

"Twice a day?"

"For hours each time."

"Where does he get so much energy?" She says, taken aback.

"I don't fucking know but it's getting to the point where I can barely walk. Thank God I work from home. I told him I'm gonna stay with you for a few days to "help you and your roommate clean up". It was bullshit but if I stay here, he's gonna tear me apart." I pause. "You know what he said to me the other day when we were about to have sex?"

"Don't tell me he said he was gonna marry you."

"Well, no... but he said he was gonna give me a baby."

"He said that?"

"In so many words."

"Niggas always talking shit, Téa."

"I know, but you think he would say that to me when he knows my condition if he didn't really mean it?" I ask.

"Honestly, I don't know about that. But what I do know is fucking you so much all of a sudden is not a good sign." Now I'm lost.

"It's not a good sign that he desires me?"
"No, he's gotta be cheating." I throw my head back. Not this shit again...

"How the hell does he find time to cheat when he's always in bed with me?" I question her.

"*When he's here*, he's in bed with you. Just like you said. But when he's not here, he could be doing anything. Listen, men do one of two things when they're cheating on you. Either they stop fucking you because they're too busy fucking the other woman or just don't wanna risk catching something and passing it on to you. *Or*, they fuck you twice as much so you won't even suspect that they're cheating."

I kind of slid down my wall and crumpled on the floor at this news. It made too much sense and it never even crossed my mind that that could be the reason he'd changed so suddenly.

"I don't know what I would do, Casandra," I mumble.

■■■

Finally, I had a reason to show off all the progress I had made from doing my ab workouts. The white crop top I was wearing slid up even higher when I raised one arm in the air and held on to the mechanical bull moving in slow motion with my other. Usually this is not something I would do, especially with so many people recording with their phones. I don't like when the spotlight is on me, but Dominique challenged me so I had no choice.

He rode the bull a few minutes before me while almost every girl in the club heckled and egged him on. Even though Dominique had to help lift me up there and the bull went slower for me, the crowd at the club still screamed louder for me and I won. I got off the bull laughing and cheering for myself and I was honestly having the best time of my life. I couldn't remember the last time I'd actually been out at night for fun. Oh right, September.

I won a free drink and even though I don't drink, I boasted in Dominique's face as he smirked. Just then, "Wait For a Minute" blasted throughout the club and the twins dropped everything they were doing to dance. The way the crowd of people just immediately formed a circle around them and the twins commanded all their attention was so amazing. Besides the workshop I attended the day I met them, I have never watched this unfold right in front of me. And the crowd at the workshop was nothing compared to this one.

I stood on top of the bar so I could see without getting trampled and cheered for them as I sipped my apple juice from a straw with no shame. A couple girls hopped on top of the bar to join me and danced like their lives depended on it. I could tell they were trying to get noticed by the twins, but Damien and Dominique were focused on their own dancing. I didn't mind the girls though, I just let them do their thing.

When I tired of being on the bar, the twins were still entertaining. I hopped down and was instantly greeted by a guy only a few inches taller than me. He put his hand on my waist and said, "How you doing?" The way he said it was just to get my attention, not to really find out how I was doing. I smiled faintly and tried to scoot past him, but he grabbed my hand.

"Where you going so fast?" he asked.

"Hey! Hey!" I, the guy, and several people around us turned to see Dominique yelling in our direction from inside the crowd. "Don't do that!" he yelled at the guy, who promptly dropped my hand.

Everyone was laughing because they thought Dominique was joking, but I knew he wasn't. They all turned their attention back to Damien's dancing but after a few seconds, Dominique noticed that the guy was still following behind me trying to talk. He left the circle and brushed past a bunch of people to get to me. "Baby," he said, completely ignoring the guy.

"My bad man, I was just tryna talk," he explained to Dominique.

"No, it's oki, it's oki," Dominique said, turning to him and patting his head like a dog.

It was bad enough he towered over the man, making him look puny, but then he had to go and do something like that to emasculate him even more. I tried to hide my laughter. Dominique turned back to me and the guy finally walked away. "I want you to come over here oki, we about to do something," he says to me.

He takes me by the hand over to the crowd where Damien is holding a microphone, explaining how unprofessional Dominique is. Even though he's holding my hand, he turns around to make sure I didn't get lost.

"I'm here, babe." Dominique takes the microphone from Damien.

"This is my birthday, bro. This is not work. Just one nigga try to talk to my girl, you know. You know how *that* go," he says.

Once again, everybody laughs at his words and I'm blushing with embarrassment because they're all looking at me. At the same time, I don't mind because a lot of women who handed Dominique gifts earlier that night and were all over him were staring me down right now, envious. The DJ drops a hard beat and the twins are lost in their dancing again.

Seeing how different Dominique was when he was putting on a show was incredible to me. I had never seen him like this up close and personal, and it had me thinking maybe I don't know as much about him as I think I do. He looked *so passionate* and while I knew he was happy when he was alone with me, this was another kind of happiness.

When it was time to sing Happy Birthday to the twins, they were both pouring sweat and trying to catch their breath. I don't know anyone else who celebrates their birthday by entertaining others. But it's what they loved to do, so who am I to stop them? The twins shook hands and hugged each other, causing half the club to orgasm.

I rolled my eyes and started slicing the giant cake we bought, which was simply shaped like a treble clef. I caught a woman who looked familiar eyeing me from a few feet away as I fed Dominique a piece of cake. She didn't even stop staring when I caught her. She just kept giving me the evil eye. I took my eyes off her and went on about my business. Some of these bitches were crazy.

Dominique asked someone to bring him a chair and he set it down in the middle of the crowd.

"Come here, baby," he spoke into the microphone. Everyone turned to me and I looked at him with a face full of confusion. "Yes, *you*, motherfucker." They laugh. Dominique was just a comedian tonight. "I don't mean it, baby," he says, laughing.

I slowly walk over to the chair and mouth the words, "What the fuck are you about to do?" He only smiles and motions for me to sit down. I know exactly what's about to happen as soon as I hear Pony start playing. The whole club screams and I cover my face so nobody can see me blushing.

I peek through the spaces between my fingers. Dominique has pulled his shirt off and is strutting over to me with a knowing look on his face. He slides on his knees until he's between my legs and the girls' screams get louder. I can't believe he's doing this. Especially on his own birthday. How am I getting a lap dance from the birthday boy?

Dominique grips the side of my waist to balance himself while he grinds in and out between my legs. A drop of sweat falls from his forehead onto my wrist, and it reminds me of our lovemaking. For a second I forget where I am and that so many people are watching us, until Dominique lowers his head and imitates eating my pussy in front of everyone.

I try to pull him up by his hair and stop him but that only turns him on. Everyone has a phone out by now. He's staring directly into my eyes very intensely for what feels like minutes, then suddenly laughs and kisses my cheek. An "Awwww" resonates through the crowd. He rises up and pulls me out of my chair also, then bows. He holds his arm out as if to present me to the crowd.

"Thank you, baby for do this for me and my brother. She is the best," he says into the mic. Everybody is clapping for me so I have no choice but to bow too. Even though he's always doing things like this without permission, I had to love him for it. I laughed at it and I couldn't stop laughing because I wanted to kill him when he first started and now I realized this is the most excitement I've experienced in my whole life.

Dominique walked me back out the circle and the rest of the night consisted of everyone dancing, Damien singing on the mic, and meeting and taking pictures with fans. I figured tonight I wouldn't mind if Dominique wanted to keep me up.

January

Five months. It has been five months. It has been five whole months since I woke up and thanked Jah for allowing me to live for another day. How could I forget to do that? He has given me so much over this short period of time and I knew I didn't deserve them. Yet I had completely forgotten about praising Him for it.

It has been five months since I thanked Jah for my talents, blessings, and my health. But this morning, I would have to beg Him for strength and patience. I needed the strength to stay focused and help myself move past whatever was about to happen. I needed the patience so I wouldn't catch a case and have Dominique end up in the hospital when I was through with him.

I don't know how I didn't see it last night. I don't know why I didn't think to check the house for things like this after leaving him there alone for the weekend to visit my family back in Chicago. Oh, that's right. I trust him. That's why I didn't think to do it. When I first laid eyes on it, I felt an ache in my heart and my cheeks warmed.

The adrenaline was pumping through me but I wanted to be calm about the situation. I didn't want to jump to conclusions. I sat up in bed and shoved Dominique's shoulder as hard as I could. Then I did it again a second later. Then I did it two more times even though he was already waking up.

"*Que voulez-vous!*" he demanded.

"I don't wanna hear that bullshit, what is this?" I hold up the long, thin strand of hair I found under my pillow.

It takes a little time for his eyes to focus, but when they do, he can't even hide the surprise on his face. Then his face changes and I can see him about to lie. He turns away and rubs his eyes and yawns and messes with his hair and does whatever he can to delay his answer to me. I'm not moving an inch until I get it. I watch a lopsided grin slowly make its way onto his face.

"Téa, come on, man," is all he says. I shove him again.

"Come on, nothing! Be a man and be honest with me!"

"So what you think, I cheat on you? Did you put that there?"

I can't believe he even had the nerve to suggest I had planted evidence of him cheating on me just to find a reason to argue with him. I laugh a little to myself to keep from getting angrier.

"Look. All I know is I have kinky hair. You have kinky hair. So what the *fuck* is this fine, straight shit?" I muff him upside the forehead to put influence on the *fuck*.

"Don't hit me. Stop that shit right now," he warns. I don't even pick fights with men, so I took his advice. I wasn't afraid he would put his hands on me, but I wasn't about to make him angry to the point he would just walk away from me.

"You better tell me something right now, Dee cause this is not looking good."

I was honestly so hurt, despite how tough I was acting in front of him. I pretended I wanted to just go upside his head when really, I just wanted to ball myself up and cry. That's what the thought of another woman getting even a piece of what he gives me does to me. What happened to belonging to each other?

"What not looking good? Us?" he asked. I say nothing. "I would nevvvvvver have another woman in you bed," he responds.

"But would you have another woman?" I look him in his eyes and I can feel my bottom lip trembling and tears welling in my eyes. Dominique turns away from me and puts his head down.

"Don't cry. Okay?" He squeezed my thigh but was this supposed to be some kind of comfort?

"You didn't ANSWER me," I say calmly.

"No. I would not."

"But you did." Dominique kisses his teeth and throws the covers back. The way he got out of bed and didn't look at me while he put his clothes on and made up his side told me he was done with the conversation. "So you're just gonna walk away huh?"

"I don't know what I have to say to you!" he yelled back at me for the first time, making me jump a little. "I don't know what I have to do for you! I do everything and it's nothing! I'm tired of try and prove myself."

I didn't know what to say at first because I was still surprised he'd talked to me that way. Out of all the times I've gotten loud with him or angry at him, this was the first time he had argued back.

"So what are you saying, I don't appreciate what you do for me?" I ask.

Dominique was in the closet with his back turned to me. I really didn't want him to just grab his things and leave. That would solve nothing. I should know because I watched my daddy do it for years. I prayed to God I'd never experience a relationship like that and end up beaten down and broken the way my mother was for years.

"Fine, don't answer me. You still not off the hook until you tell me which *bitch* you had over here while I was gone. Was it Leslie? Hmm?"

Nothing. He continues to get dressed.

"You know, I do believe I saw her at your party a month ago. She was watching me like a hawk too. What's funny is she doesn't even live here. Does she? No...so did you fly her out again, Dee?"

Still nothing. He's lacing his shoes up.

"I mean, that is your bitch right? That's your little shit on the side right? Is she in LA right now? It's funny how you have time for another bitch but you don't have time to go to a doctor's appointment with me or ask me if I'm making any progress with my condition or *anything*."
He finally looks at me and speaks.

"I care about what happen to you, but you keep try and push me to the edge. I don't deserve shit like that. I work hard try and take care of you. I be there for you, I buy you shit, I make love to you, I travel place with you, I'm your best friend. What you gonna do if I'm not here? Be miserable." Be miserable?

"So you really feeling yourself right now? Newsflash, Dominique. You are *not* God's gift to the world. And doing all that shit means nothing if you fuck it up in the end. Right?"

"Whatever, talk to me later." He slams the bedroom door on his way out and I burn holes into it with my eyes until I hear him leave the house and start his car.

"OH MY GODDDDDD!!!!!!!!!!!!!!!" I scream at the top of my lungs.

I wasn't about to let him just drop the whole argument like that. I texted him saying, *I won't argue with you while you're driving but this isn't over*. He read the message and said nothing. I fought the urge to violently throw my phone at a wall. Instead, I breathed in and out several times and closed my eyes. *Count to ten, Téa.* I leaned down and picked up Butter, who was whimpering at my feet.

"I know, baby," I say. "I wanna cry too."

I hold him close to my chest and rub his fur. I feel a small lump between my fingers when I stroke his ear. I examine it, and there is definitely a red lump that has grown on his ear. I immediately get scared because I don't know if he just hurt himself running in the house or if it's something serious.

I pull out my laptop and start searching google for 'red lumps growing on dog's ear'. Several similar questions popped up and all the answers suggested that it was a cyst or a hematoma. I didn't know the details about either of these, but when I reached to touch Butter's ear again, he squirmed. I could tell it was hurting him, whatever it was.

I instantly dialed the number for the vet they had referred Dominique to when he first picked Butter up and made an appointment. I was a little relieved when he said he could see us in three days. At least Butter wouldn't have to hurt for too long. I held him in the air and let him give me a wet, doggy kiss. Now that Dominique was angry with me, Butter was all I had to cuddle with.

■■■

Dominique didn't come home that night or the next night. I stayed up past 4am waiting for him both nights, hoping he would come home and just get in bed, rub up against me, and all would be forgotten. But I guess he had other plans. Once I got done making myself some breakfast, I called Damien's phone. I wouldn't be surprised if he had gotten a smaller place nearby and Dominique was over there hiding out. There was a lot of noise in the background when he picked up, but I distinctly heard more than one female voice.

"Hey, Damien," I say in a voice that would suggest nothing had changed. I'd be a fool if I thought he didn't know though.

"I don't talk to Dee in two days," he lies automatically.

"I don't believe you."

"Well, deal with it." He hangs up.

I am speechless. My entire world had turned upside down in a matter of 24 hours. What have I done? Never in the past six months had Damien talked to me that way. First Dominique and now him. I could feel my heart sink down into my stomach. My pulse was louder than my thoughts and it was moving at a frighteningly quick pace. I set my phone down and tried not to tear up but it was already happening.

My face scrunched up and three tears slid down my cheeks. I sniffled and told myself to suck it up. Dominique loved me more than anybody ever did, and this was nothing compared to what we could be going through. Everything would be fine again soon. When I wake up tomorrow, he'll be in bed with me. He'll tell me how crazy he was to ever treat me like this and I will forgive him and we will make love until we're too tired to make love anymore.

But he wasn't in bed with me when I woke up the next morning. I was having a groggy, gray morning for the first time since I'd left Chicago. Even with the sun beaming and the birds chirping and the beautiful green trees swaying in the wind, I couldn't be cheerful today. I dragged my feet around the house all morning getting dressed to take Butter to the vet.

It wasn't far away and I was halfway looking forward to walking there. I think Butter and I could both stand to be surrounded by nature and people. So we hustled the six blocks to the vet and struggled through a few tests and blood work that Butter was not happy about. I didn't like to see him so sad, but I knew it had to be done to ensure that he was healthy.

The vet said I should be expecting a call from him in less than a week with Butter's results.

"Say bye-bye, Butter."

I wave his little paw at the doctor and all the pets in the waiting room and we make our way back to the house. Dominique's car is in the driveway. I'm hoping he wasn't waiting until I left the house to come over and planning to sneak out before I got back. I unlocked the door and he was in the kitchen making himself a turkey sandwich. I watched him and waited for him to look up or acknowledge my presence at all, but he never did.

"Good afternoon, Dominique," I speak.

"I just come to eat, that's all. I don't wanna talk."

"You and Damien don't waste any time getting to the point, do you?" I joke. I giggle a little but he ignores me. I just want to lighten the mood. He didn't have to laugh with me. He could scowl at me if he wanted to. I didn't mind. I just wanted *some* kind of reaction from him. "When are you coming home?"

He looks up at me but doesn't answer. I open my mouth to say something else, but ultimately I just stand there with my keys in my hand, my eyes burning. I look away because the insincerity on his face is choking me. When I look back at him, I can almost see him feeling bad for me. That quickly disappears. He doesn't stay to eat. He picks his food up and brushes past me and out the door. I feel like he won't be satisfied until he has completely broken me.

■■

I rise the next day with an entirely different attitude. It dawned on me that Dominique is continuing to act out towards me because I'm not trying hard enough. I'm not showing him that I care enough to get him to come back home. Home is where I want him, so I devised a plan to get him there.

I would do something nice to my hair, assemble my sexiest outfit, put on his favorite shade of lipstick. Then I would call him up and invite him over for dinner. I would cook all his favorite things. I would have his favorite music playing. Then I would apologize for accusing him of doing something I always knew he wasn't capable of doing to me. He would sit me in his lap and kiss me so softly…

I was walking down the street wearing a tight, red maxi dress that hugged my curves and showed off my assets. I had just come from getting my nails done, something I hadn't done since my high school senior prom. My hair fell in flawless curls that surrounded my entire face and blew in the light breeze. My lipstick matched my dress and made my already full lips appear more voluptuous.

I smiled at the male passersby who couldn't help but show me attention, and declined offers for a ride home. They knew I looked good. I knew I looked good. Dominique would think I looked good too. He'd be back home with wifey in no time.

This time, I wasn't surprised to see his car in the driveway when I got close to the house. He was definitely watching me somehow to make sure he only stopped by when I wasn't home. It didn't bother me. I was a woman on a mission. I was feeling good about myself again and I was confident that Dominique would forgive me and everything would be back to normal.

It never entered my mind at all that anything could go wrong. I knew in my heart that God had placed Dominique in my life because he was the one. When I met Dominique, my life changed drastically. Unbeknownst to me, it was about to change drastically again.

The second I put my key in the door, I heard muffled noises coming from upstairs. Lord, please don't let him have company over. If anything was going to ruin my plan, that would be it. I put my finger to my lips when Butter reacted to me entering the house, even though I knew he couldn't understand me. I needed him to be quiet so I could surprise Dominique.

I whispered to him that we would play later. Pulling my long dress up over my feet, I silently tip-toed up our carpeted staircase. I could see from the third step that our bedroom door was cracked. I could see from the top step that Dominique wasn't alone. I could see, from a few feet away, the naked body of a woman.

My eyes widened and time seemed to move in slow motion as I watched her ass bounce up and down on his dick. I was only there for a few seconds, but it felt like minutes. Her back was facing me and he pulled tightly on her long, black hair. His face was buried in her breast; sweat dripped from his shrunken afro. A short moan escaped his lips...

At that moment, I felt my knees give in. I leaned against the wall to hold myself up, but it didn't help, considering my eyes had glazed over and blurred my vision temporarily. I held my hand to my heart in an attempt to stop it from shattering. But I could feel it breaking apart, piece by piece. I had to get out of here.

I managed to slink down the stairs without being heard, almost falling and breaking my neck. I couldn't seem to walk straight. I stumbled out the door and ran until I felt I was far away enough from the house. My brain wasn't controlling my movements anymore. I don't know what was driving me, but I just kept picking up my feet and telling myself to go.

There was not a single thought in my mind as I ran. I had panicked. I saw blurred faces pass me on the street and a few spoke to me, but I couldn't understand their words. They probably thought I was being chased or had been attacked. They were right. The image of Dominique pleasing another woman in our bed was chasing me. The finality of his decisions and what was yet to come had viciously attacked me.

When I stopped, I was on a busy street. The sounds of car horns and ambulance sirens deafened me. I glanced around and around but nothing looked familiar. Beads of sweat had formed on my forehead and my hair was a mess. I broke four nails in my hurry to get out the door. I didn't feel the pain or the tears on my face until I took a minute to breathe. Then all of my thoughts suddenly came rushing into my head.

You really thought you could win him over by wearing a nice dress? What made you think you were good enough for him in the first place. Wipe your tears, you're too good for him. If he can't see that, you don't need him. So you're just gonna let him fuck another bitch right in the spot where you lay your head? Did you see her body? You could never compete with that. Don't cry, babygirl. Somebody will want you. Suck it up. You look pitiful. You are an embarrassment.

I hiccupped loudly as I cried on the corner in front of several people. I leaned against a brick wall and hid my face. I can't believe that I am doing this right here right now. I can't believe what Dominique has done to me. He knew I would be coming home. He intentionally did this to hurt me. And it hurt so bad.

My heart was literally aching. My chest was burning. I needed someone. But Dominique was the person I called when I was hurting. Who would've thought he would ever turn on me this way. I am in so much shock that my body is shivering in the 77 degree weather. I open my eyes briefly to pull out my phone and wipe the dirt from the bottom of my dress.

I dial Casandra's number but the phone keeps ringing.

"Please…please…not when I need you," I moan.

I'm sniffling uncontrollably and it feels as if everyone's eyes are on me. She doesn't pick up. I want to scream but instead I cry some more. I have no idea what to do. How does one become prepared for a situation like this? I could feel a piece of my soul dying.

"Excuse me miss…miss?" I turn to see an older man, not much taller than me. He's pointing towards the street. "That's my cab right there. Is there somewhere I can take you? You don't need to be out here like this." He looks sympathetic, but I decline. I have absolutely nowhere to go. "At least let me take you somewhere you can get something to eat and clear your mind. It'll make you feel better." I pause to ask myself if I have money and I remember my purse is hanging from my shoulder. I nod my head slowly.

The entire ride there, I'm telling myself what has to be done now. There was no doubt that I still loved Dominique. There was a lot of doubt that he still loved me. But either way, I couldn't allow myself to be with a cheater. He knew from the beginning that I don't put up with cheating whatsoever, and he had done that and then some. He had completely betrayed me.

I don't even think betrayal is the word. It was something far worse. I honestly don't think I can ever stand to look at him again. I feel so disgusting right now just knowing that he was the man I had decided to give my heart to. I was disgusted thinking about all the cheating he'd probably done already. I was disgusted thinking about him touching another female and then coming home and relieving himself inside of me.

The cab driver stayed with me to "make sure nobody would take advantage of me in my vulnerable state". I ate quickly and bought more food. I was already feeling that motivation I get after being knocked down. I'm ready to get back up. Dominique had given me plenty of happiness, but that doesn't mean he gets to take it back. I hope he had a great time not being with me temporarily, because I was about to make it permanent.

When I finished my meal, I went to the bathroom and cleaned myself up. I wiped off what was left of my lipstick and applied gloss. I wet a paper towel and washed the tear stains from my cheeks, then massaged olive oil into them. I wet my fingers and fluffed my hair a little and I looked like the confident Téa I was before I walked in on that disaster.

I gave the cab driver my address. It had only been two hours, but I didn't care if I had to walk in and beat Dominique's ass *and* his hoe's ass. Luckily for them, they were gone by the time I got to the house. That didn't change a gotdamn thing. I paid the cab driver and walked in my damn house and changed my damn clothes and got comfortable.

I rolled myself a couple spliffs to blow afterwards. I wasn't going to burn or cut up or pour bleach on any of Dominique's belongings. No. I wasn't going to smash any of his game systems with a hammer. No. I could do all of these things. But instead, I'm just going to chill, call him up, and tell him to come over. I wasn't going to end this over the phone. I wanted to see the look on his face when finds out he's never going to see me again.

I pick up my phone, but before I can dial out, he's already calling me. I smile to myself. Perfect.

"Yo," I answer.

"Whassup. Are you home right now?" he asks. As if he didn't know.

"Yeah, I'm here."

"Cool, cool. I come in a few minutes, oki? I have something to tell you, but I wanna see you." This is laughable. If he thinks he's about to "inform" me that he's been going behind my back, he has another thing coming.

"Sounds good," I say, and hang up.

I wait patiently for him to get here, shaking my head and laughing to myself. It's funny, you know. Two people meet and grow together. They grow until they become one another. And you think to yourself, this is it. I've got it. I've found the one God made for me and I'm set for life. But in the end, it's just another bullshitter. I changed my life for this man. I moved thousands of miles away from my family to be with him. We all do crazy things like this for love. I just want to know when is it going to be real?

I hear Dominique's key in the door and hop off the couch quickly. I'm right there, meeting him face to face when he opens the door. My arms are crossed over my chest and my nostrils are flared. He can tell that I'm about to go the fuck in on him.

"So, before you even start "confessing" all your dirty ass secrets, I just wanna let you know that I know about you fucking that hoe here earlier." I pause to let the confusion set in on his face. "Yeah, THAT'S RIGHT. I know. I saw all of it with my own eyes. It was disgusting. So, what the fuck do you have to say to me now?" There's nothing he can say to me. We both know I have the upper hand now, and he's the one left looking stupid.

"You really are crazy, ain't you?" he asks calmly. "I don't know what you talk about but I just wanna let you know that I'm gone. I'm leaving, go back to Paris. And me and you, we're done."

When he says done, he motions his hand over his throat and smirks. What he just said doesn't quite register and I don't know what to say except to repeat what he said to me.

"You're leaving."

"Yeah, I'm outta here mami. I think about it a long time and I'm finally done with your shit. Finally. So… you know. That's it. The house is paid for. You can stay here if that's what you want. Or you can take your ass back to Chicago. It really don't matter to me. I just can't be with you anymore. I just try and do everything and you just wanna be sad all the time. You just wanna be angry at me. You just wanna tell me what I do when you not there. So I'm not gonna be there. It's over, baby. *Fini.*"

The smile on his face is confusing me. I stand there staring up at him with my arms still crossed over my chest and I don't move. I don't even know what's happening.

"You're breaking up with *me*," I say.

"Listen, mami. *We are done.*" Now he's talking to me in slow motion like I'm stupid. "*Me and Damien go back to Paris for a while. We no stay here.* Well, we might come back for a little bit just to hit some clubs and some parties. Shit like that."

All of his words are going in one ear and going out the other. I don't understand. I caught him cheating on me and he is the one breaking up with me. He is leaving me. It's just now dawning on me that we are actually about to end the life we have made together. He doesn't want me anymore. He doesn't love me anymore. When he turns to leave, I finally move.

"Dominique, stop," I say as I grab his arm. The way he pulls away from me would make you think my touch had burned him. I'm beginning to plead with him because I don't know what else to do. "Please don't." I try to stand in front of the door. I try to do anything to keep him from leaving.

"There is nothing you can do now, Téa."

"No. No..no..no..no..no... Why are you treating me like this?" I don't want to, but I start to cry.

"Why you treat me the way you do? Huh? Since we been together, you don't support me not one time. How many workshop you go to? How many battle, how many performance you go to? How many time you encourage me and tell me I can do better? How many time you take *me* out or come to me and wanna spend time together? I come home and my body hurt and I'm tired. You don't even ask if I want a massage or nothing. You don't go out with me. It feel like we not even together. All you do is cry and whine now. You make it impossible to love you. You just no make me happy no more, girl." The truth in his words hurt me to my core.

"I can do that now, Dominique. I didn't realize I wasn't loving you enough, but now I know!"

My hands are on his chest, forcing him to look down into my eyes and hear what I was saying. I knew the way he had loved me could never happen again with another man. But he wasn't trying to hear any of it. His hand was already on the doorknob.

"Deeeeeeeee….." I squeak.

"I'm sorry. It's not enough. I think about this for a long time. Even before all this." He stretches his arms out, referring to the house. "I start feeling like maybe we not right for each other."

"So you show me how you feel by telling me you wanna give me a baby and buying me a home?"

"I just have to go. Don't worry about my clothes, my guy come get them later." He tries to close the door behind him, but I'm pulling at his waist.

"Please don't do this!"

He forcefully removes my hands and tosses them out of his way. The door slams. I fall to my knees. My tears are accompanied by loud moans so eerie, I don't even recognize them as my own voice. I just sit on the floor and cry and scream. Suddenly I feel sick to my stomach.

I run to the kitchen sink and vomit all of the food I'd eaten at the restaurant. Then I cried some more until I choked up more vomit. I tried to comfort myself by rocking side to side, but the tears wouldn't stop forming. My head felt like it was about to burst. I bang my palm hard into the countertop repeatedly and cry out.

"SHIIIIIIIIIITTTTTTTTTTTTTT!!!!!" I couldn't seem to pull myself together.

Everything had hit me at once. I didn't need time to think it over or analyze what was going on. I knew. It didn't matter how terribly Dominique treated me over the past week. I knew I had just lost the best thing that would ever happen to me. My crying had become hiccups and I figured now that I could talk a little, I should call Casandra. Dominique wasn't my superman anymore. He couldn't help me now. But Casandra's phone just kept ringing and ringing and ringing.

What could I do now? I took a chance and dialed Damien's number. To my surprise, he actually picked up.

"Hello?" he said. I was silent, thinking of what I could say. Why did I call him? I say the first thing that comes to my head.

"Damien….." I moan. "Why….." I hear him let out a sigh. I know I appeared very weak right now but I didn't care. I was hurting so bad, nothing could feel worse.

"Téa, I am not the one you should talk to right now."

"Do you love me, Damien?" I asked. He was supposed to be my brother and a confidante. What happened? Did that all change suddenly because Dominique didn't think of me the same way? Wasn't he his own person?

"I love you, Téa. But you have to understand, nobody come before my brudda. That's it. I'm sorry for how I treat you, but it is better this way. To just let it go. Okay? I'll see you around." He hangs up the phone.

I wrap my arms around my knees and curl up on the floor in front of the sink. Rocking. Back and forth…back and forth…back and forth. The numbness is beginning to set in. I can no longer feel my red-rimmed eyes burning or my chest aching. I can, however, feel my phone vibrating on the floor. I don't recognize the number, so I don't pick up. They leave a voicemail. Something told me that Casandra's phone died and she's trying to contact me from someone else's.

I call my voicemail and enter my password. I know she's worried about me. I never call her back to back like this. I don't even know how I'm going to tell her what's happening. I don't feel like I can face anyone right now. I feel like such a fool. I'm not ready to hear "I told you so".

"Good evening. I hope you are well. This is Dr. Harper from the vet on Washington Boulevard. We've gone over Butter Scotch's tests several times and I'm calling to inform you that he does, in fact, have cancer. I'm prepared to schedule some dates to start the chemotherapy whenever you're ready. Just call the clinic and speak to my receptionist. Have a good night."

Butter. Butter, where are you?

I forget about my own pain for a minute and search for him. I call out his name. I whistle. I blow kisses. I don't even get a bark in return. I look in both the bathrooms because I know he likes to dip into the toilet. Nothing. He's not in the laundry room. He's not in the family room.

Suddenly, I hear his faint cries coming from the bedroom Dominique and I...used to share. I hesitantly made my way up the stairs and found Butter in his tiny bed in the corner. He was sniffling and shivering. I felt his pain and then some. I picked him up and rocked him in my arms.

"Oh, Butter..." I cried. "I'm sorry. I'm so, so sorry." We cried together for a few minutes. Then I decided to close the curtains and turn off the light. "We won't sleep in here anymore." I grabbed his bed and closed the door behind us.

I fix Butter's food and water and sit down to eat something myself. It was hard. It all felt so dry in my mouth, I couldn't swallow any of it. I tried to drink some water but it didn't help. I just didn't have an appetite. I knew my blood pressure had probably risen from all the "excitement" I experienced today, and I needed to eat. But it just wouldn't happen.

I couldn't believe how sick Butter was. Never in a million years would I have thought he had cancer. I couldn't take anymore. Today had completely destroyed me. How do you come back from this? How do you start over fresh? How do you become happy again?

I didn't want to go upstairs at all. I put Butter's bed on the floor next to the sofa and I would sleep there tonight. I planned on calling the vet in the morning. I needed to get some sleep now. But I didn't sleep. I tossed and turned for the first few hours. I finally knocked out around 3, but I had multiple nightmares.

When I woke up and looked at the clock, it had only been half an hour. My mouth was so dry, it hurt to swallow. I shuffled into the kitchen to make myself a glass of milk. I couldn't tell if my body was sore from lying on the couch or if it was because of everything I had been through. Whatever the reason, it prevented me from getting anymore rest that night. So I did what I always do. I put myself to work.

I went into the room we'd designated as my creative area. It housed all my watercolor paints, colored pencils, graphite pencils, charcoal pencils, paint brushes, drawing pads, sketchbooks, frames, and miscellaneous junk I couldn't place when we moved in. You would think the way I'm feeling right now would inspire me to create masterpieces, but my pencil wouldn't move.

I had this huge, blank piece of paper in front of me and all of these thoughts, but I didn't know what to do with them. A single tear drop fell on the paper and dried. He had even stripped me of my talent. In an angry attempt to somehow lash out at Dominique, I shoved everything off the table. I don't care about the mess I'm going to have to clean up later.

I just couldn't focus. Memories and little details about our relationship that I held close to my heart kept haunting me. Memories like me pulling a Whitley and waking up early so I can brush my teeth before Dominique gives me a good morning kiss. Memories like Dominique teasing me about my bottom lip being so curvy that my drink almost always dribbled down my chin. Memories like Dominique always kneeling in front of me when I sat down so that we could be eye to eye.

Little memories like that are the ones I treasured the most. I held those on a pedestal above all the outings, the things he bought for me, and the mind-blowing sex. I don't have those kinds of things to hold on to from any of my other past relationships.

A white envelope catches my eye and I pick it up. It's blank. Then I remember it's the envelope Percy had given me when I last saw him. I never opened it. I stuck my finger in the corner and ripped it open. It was a simple letter. It read

Thank you for helping me change my life. Without you, I couldn't have become a better me. I had to change my surroundings and be around different things in order to grow. So I'm leaving and starting my new life in another place. I love you and I hope your talent takes you far. If you ever need me in the future, just know that I got you.

He left his new phone number and address on the bottom. He was living in San Francisco now, only a few hours away. I didn't hesitate to give him a call.

SIX
"OUT MY MIND"

When I was 15, my grandfather passed away and it would be my first time viewing the dead body of someone I saw and hugged and spoke to regularly. Before the wake, my mami told me that if I couldn't handle it then she wouldn't let me go to the funeral. Back then, I wasn't so against attending funerals. I really wanted to go so I tried to toughen up before walking in and seeing my grandfather lying lifeless in a casket.

We all stood around him and I reached out and touched his skin. The only thing that could prevent me from bursting into tears was talking a mile a minute. I just kept my mouth open, saying anything so the tears wouldn't come, no matter how shaky my voice became. Later, my mami would tell me that some of the things I said were rude and that you don't talk about the dead like that. But I was only saying the first thing that came to my head.

I was using the same technique now to get through this phone call with Percy without crying. I wanted him to know what happened without him knowing what happened. I also didn't want to have to go into all the dreadful details. I was already feeling pathetic enough. I fully expected to hear him tell me "I told you so" even though he hadn't. I and everyone around me were so sure that I was set for life. Even he thought I had found the one for me.

"So you gonna tell me why you're calling me at four in the morning?" he asked. "I know you not calling out of nowhere just to make small talk with me."

"No…" I hesitate.

"So what is it?" I close my eyes tightly and feel warm tears squeeze out of them. My face scrunches up and I'm unable to fake it anymore.

"I need your help," I say in a barely audible voice.

"Damn, baby, what's wrong? What happened?" Hearing him call me that and immediately feel sympathetic only made me cry more. I was starting to think I had nobody. "Who hurt you?" I wipe my nose so my voice will stop coming out so nasally.

"Dominique. It's over… it's all the way over. I'm all alone again. What the fuck was I thinking Percy? Usually I know when shit is too good to be true but I just kept eating all the shit Dominique fed me. Why?"

"That nigga left you, huh?" he asked. He kissed his teeth. "You stayed cause you had real love for him. You not the first female to do that."

"But I've always been smarter than that. I promised myself to never stay in a relationship if I was being hurt…I just…I don't know how this could happen."

"I know that nigga wasn't putting his hands on you," Percy responded.

"No… he wouldn't hurt me that way." *He would just stomp on my heart and shit on my life.* "I just don't know where to go from here. Where do I go from here, Percy?"

"Well, I'm not at home right now." My heart dropped for about the 15th time tonight. I was hoping that somehow I could see him. "Me and my bros are out in Atlanta right now but I could stop there on my way back and you can ride with me to the crib." I feel a little glimmer of life in my soul when he says this.

"That sounds perfect. When are you coming back?" I ask eagerly.

"Morning after tomorrow. Just be ready before 10am, okay?" I give him my address and he writes it down.

"Percy…"

"Whassup?"

"I don't usually ask people for things. I don't like to put my burdens on them. Especially something this big. And I know our past isn't the greatest, so thank you. I appreciate this more than you know. You know… dropping everything and just coming to my rescue like this." The way Dominique used to do…

"It's nothing, Téa. I told you a long time ago that I got you. You might not be ready to say it yet, but I still love you."

"You're right, I'm not ready… but thank you for loving me."

"Yup."

"I'll see you." We hang up and I release a sigh of relief. I can finally sleep knowing that I have something to look forward to.

Soon as I get off the phone with Butter's doctor in the morning, the doorbell rings. Low and behold, it's Casandra. As much as I want to be angry that she took so long to come to me, I didn't exactly have anybody else to physically cling to. I was just happy she was finally here.

"I'm so sorry. My phone was off all day yesterday and I didn't see any of your calls from last night until this morning, but I just ran into your man like 20 minutes ago and he gave me the cold shoulder. What the fuck is going on?"

"You saw Dee?" I glance up at her, my eyes big.

"Yeah, I spoke to him but he didn't speak back. Did I do something?"

"What did he look like?" Did he look like he was torn up inside? Was he doing as bad as I am?

"Ahhh... he looked pissed. What happened?" I sit down in a stool at the counter, but she stays standing.

"So you're gonna make me tell this story while you stare down at me?" I ask. She pulls out a stool.

"You better tell me *something* quick, before I go confront that nigga myself. I know that much."

"Long story short, he's not my man anymore."

I turn away because my eyes are already stinging. I didn't want to cry again today. I couldn't take anymore crying. My head was killing me. Casandra stood up and shook her head. She paced a little with one hand on her hip and just shook her head until I thought it might fall off.

"Oh my goodness... look at this!" She held her arms out wide. "Look at all of this. Look at this home you two made. And ya'll just end it? What could have possibly happened that would make you give everything up?" I hear her mumbling *I knew this would happen* to herself before I answer.

"Well he apparently was thinking about it for a while. I guess I became too needy for him. But ultimately, it was going to happen anyway. Because…I caught him cheating on me…so…"

"Is this real life?" I can see stress lines forming in her forehead. You would have thought Casandra was my mother the way she was behaving. Her voice rises with every word she utters. "What in God's name are you supposed to do now, Téa."

"I don't know, Casandra! I wasn't exactly planning on this happening either! Shit…"

I put my head in my hands. It's pounding. For a moment, we're both quiet and I can hear my pulse thumping loudly in my wrist. Then her hand is on the back of neck, rubbing it slowly.

"I didn't mean to yell at you like that, Téa. But damn… this is just so fucked up." She just sits there and hugs me for a while before I'm ready to talk again. "So you caught him?"

"Yeah. I would much rather have found out from seeing it in his phone like other women do, trust me. That image is gonna hurt me forever."

"Wait, no. He wasn't *here*," she says in shock. I nod my head to confirm that he was.

"Right upstairs in our bed."

"That dirty bastard." From the look on her face, I can tell she has a lot of questions. "You didn't recognize the girl?" I shake my head.

"I was down the hall by the stairs. The only reason I saw anything is because our bedroom door was wide open." Like he didn't even care who saw him. "Besides, her back was turned to me. But I definitely found out where that hair I found came from, huh…"

"And this all happened…yesterday?" she asks. I nod my head.

The look on her face turned to shock and confusion. I was feeling the exact same way. She stood back up and starting biting one of her fingernails. I could tell she was already plotting on a way to get back at Dominique, but that just wasn't in me.

"Look everything's cool… I mean, it is fucked up but that's alright. I actually talked to umm…," I hesitated because I knew she might not be happy about this either, "Percy." I pause for a reaction. She is still lost in her thoughts. "And he's gonna come get me so I can just get away for a while, you know?" She has been absentmindedly nodding her head the whole time, her eyes wide.

"Right. Percy. That's good."

"It is?"

"Yeah, get away. Get some rest. Do you think you'll be okay for the rest of the day? I'm gonna go…" Her eyebrows furrow and she's not looking at me. She's looking off into space still.

"Casandra, you're not thinking of doing anything stupid, are you? Cause I don't need no more drama." I snap my fingers to try and bring her back to reality.

"Nah, I'm just gonna head out and take care of some business. Call me when Percy gets here." She's already on her way to the door, but I walk her out.

"Okay then…bye," I say to her back.

Percy made it to my house at 10am just as he said he would. Seeing him in the opening of my door was both a relief and also heartbreaking. It kind of cemented the fact that me and Dominique were no more. The whole thing felt so strange. Over the past six months, I'd grown accustomed to Dominique's smell and voice and body. So much so, that hugging Percy felt like I was doing something wrong. I was with him before Dominique, yet he felt so unfamiliar. I didn't feel the safety that I felt when Dominique's arms were squeezing me tight. But I told myself that I would get used to his touch again.

I felt Percy's eyes on me when I turned to the fridge and grabbed a can of Dominique's Sprite for him. I was wearing a pair of ripped denim shorts that hung low on my hips and a white and red top that showed off my belly. I leaned down to lace up my gray high-tops and asked, "You ready?"

"Damn, girl. Your skin looks like it's been kissed by the sun. So fucking beautiful."

He grabs me by my wrist and quickly pulls me into a kiss before I can object. I immediately feel guilty even though I know me and Dominique are broken up. This just doesn't feel right. I'm not even positive that this is what I want. I allow the kiss to happen at first, then put my hands against his chest and pull back.

"Too soon…" I say, and look down at my fingers. I'm preparing myself for the attitude I'm sure to get from him. But he just nods his understanding.

"True. My bad," he replies. "Is it too soon for this?"

I feel his hand slide down and cup my ass. He has a sexy smirk on his face but it disappears when he sees my lip tremble. I don't understand why I'm feeling this way. Shit, Dominique wanted to leave so I clearly don't belong to him anymore. I'm free to do whatever I want. But I just wasn't ready to be free…

"Can we go?" I remove Percy's hands from my body and grab Butter and my bag. "I'm gonna have to ride that long train back in a few days so we won't miss Butter's appointment."

"Don't even sweat that, I'll drive you. I don't want you on that train by yourself at night. It's dangerous."

"Really? You would do that?" I ask. It was asking a lot and he was already doing so much. Percy had really surprised me the way he was stepping up like this. I was starting to believe he really did go through a serious change and he really did love me.

"I don't want nothing happening to you. Don't worry. I'll take you and Butter. C'mon, we need to get on the road ASAP."

I purposely have my laptop with me through the entire ride so Percy wouldn't feel the need to badger me with questions. I knew he wanted to know more about how everything went down with me and Dominique, which was perfectly understandable. But I'd had a long night full of tears again by myself and I honestly just wanted to erase everything from my mind.

Whenever I go through a breakup, I remind myself that one day I will wake up and I won't care anymore. But I feel like this time, that day is centuries from now. What if I *never* get over it? I close my eyes and say a silent prayer when Percy isn't paying attention.

I ask God why he had to be so blunt with me. Why did he have to do all that he did to get his point across? Nothing ever hurt as bad as it did to see Dominique in bed with that other woman. I think about the time when I was a child and my daddy would let me use his email account to play Dominoes online.

A Yahoo! Messenger IM popped up in the middle of my game from a woman with a very explicit screen name. She asked my daddy something about her *pussy*. I could see that she was one of his friends and they spoke frequently.

I was so angry, I wanted to tell her that my daddy is married and he doesn't want anything to do with her. But I just told her that I was his daughter, not him. She was extremely embarrassed and apologized several times and called me "baby". I was disgusted. But I knew my mami had no clue that he even talked with women on the internet. Just like her, I had been completely clueless about my man's actions. Was it our fault? Were we not paying them enough attention? Why did men always have to stray…

I knew I shouldn't be blaming myself but I couldn't help it. By the time we made it to Percy's place, he had me feeling like I had every reason to blame myself. I still hadn't told him one detail of what happened, but he was talking as if he knew everything.

"I can tell that nigga wasn't a gentleman to you. You tryna carry your own bags in and shit," he remarks as we enter the house. I stare him down because I can't figure out why he would even assume something like that. I was just doing me and this had nothing to do with Dominique. *I can't believe I'm still defending him in my head…*

"I don't wanna make it a habit to bring up his name, if that's okay with you." I don't say it with any attitude. I don't want to start anything. I really just want to pretend I'm on vacation, away from all the mess.

"You know it's okay with me. I'm just glad you finally opened your eyes and realized that nigga wasn't right for you. I know I fucked up or whatever, but you shoulda never let him make you fall for him so quick. He knew what he was doing. He knew you was vulnerable. You can't just show the first nigga you meet some attention."

I close my eyes and tell myself to count to ten. Not now. Not now was he suddenly showing his old side when I was already at this man's house.

"Is that what you think I did, Percy?" He can see the flare in my nostrils and eases up a bit.

"I'm not tryna make you mad. I'm sorry. All that matters is that you came to your senses and decided to give me another try." He grabs my hand and pulls me closer. *Another try? Is that what we were doing? Were we back together?* "I think you knew from the beginning of ya'll relationship that I was the one for you. You just wanted to give me a hard time. But you can stop all that now, I learned my lesson. Stop playing hard-to-get, baby."

I stood there in shock at the fact he actually believed I started a relationship with Dominique, fell in love, and built a home with him simply to make him jealous. My mouth was wide open but I couldn't even speak.

"You can stay here as long as you want, until you got your mind right. By then, you'll probably be wanting to move in with a nigga permanently." He laughs to himself. "It's been a long, hot day. I'm gonna go shower and you can unpack your bags and put everything in the guest room."

He kisses me suddenly and I feel like his lips might swallow mine. I don't kiss back, but I don't stop him. I can barely move at all, to be honest. I am in too much disbelief. He smacks my ass before walking towards his bedroom and I'm left there asking myself why I'm here and what have I gotten myself into?

■■■

Three days later, I open my eyes and glance to the right side of my bed quickly. Relieved, I slid the covers off my body and got up to shower. I'd been checking every morning to make sure Percy wasn't laying next to me. The first night I got here was very hard for me and

I lied awake for a while crying and thinking about Dominique. Percy heard me weeping and came in to comfort me.

I allowed it, but I was surprised to wake up with his arm around my waist, snoring loudly in my ear. I had given him permission to console me, not spoon me. To be honest, it kind of creeped me out and I didn't know how to handle it. I politely asked him if we could sleep in separate rooms from now on and he apologized and agreed. But I still felt the need to check.

As I brushed my teeth, I stared at my reflection in the mirror. My cheeks were dry from the stains my tears left behind. I still had a headache from my fit. I really didn't want to go anywhere or do anything right now. But I knew I had to make sure Butter was taken care of. I decided to use his health as my motivation.

I called Percy's number to make sure he was awake and getting ready to take this six hour drive back to LA. I couldn't thank him enough for this. I knew how tiring it was to be on the road like that, especially with the current traffic.

"Whassup, baby?" he answered. I brushed off his "baby" comment. Maybe if I kept doing that, he would eventually get a clue.

"Good morning," I say, cheering up a little because he was actually up and sounded ready to go. I look up at the clock on the wall and see that it's already 5:20am. Butter's appointment is at 1:30pm. "What time should we leave, maybe 6?" I ask.

"Where we going?" he asks. I think he's joking around until I realize I can hear the sound of a car speeding up in the background.

"Butter's chemo appointment…?" I say helplessly. There's a long pause and I know he's reprimanding himself.

"FUCK. Don't be mad at me but I'm already halfway to the studio."

"Oh, that's no big deal. Just turn around. We still have 40 minutes before we have to leave."

"Yeahhhhh, but this is kind of important."

"Please tell me it's more important than my dog's cancer."

I am quickly losing my patience with this man. He can't be serious right now. He knew all about the appointment and Butter's condition. It was his idea to drive me in the first place. I would've been fine taking the train. Even if I had to spend my last money to afford that expensive ass train, I wouldn't mind if it meant help for Butter. I'll be damned if he didn't get to his appointment today. Percy better stop fucking around right now.

"Look, I forgot about the dog's appointment. I'm a busy man. That's what happens when you making so many moves. When you start making moves, maybe you'll understand."

So now he's insulting my work. True, my shop hadn't been doing as well for the past month. The only reason for that is I haven't created anything. Percy is making so many power moves, yet him and his brothers haven't released another single in almost a year.

"When you said you were gonna take me, you should've done what real businessmen do and made a note of it in your calendar or your appointment book or whatever the fuck you use so that you wouldn't overbook yourself."

"Who you cussing at?"

"Out of everything I just said, 'fuck' is all you heard, right?" My frustration was building and the corners of my eyes started to sting. If he made me miss this appointment, I don't know what I'm going to do. "Even if I leave right now on the train, I will miss Butter's appointment by hours! Why would you do this to me?"

"I promise I will make it up to you when I get back, baby. This is nothing a good back rub won't cure or a lit---." I hung up before he could finish his sentence.

I screamed and fought the urge to throw my phone at the mirror. I was screaming a lot these days. I knew there was absolutely no way we would make it back to LA in time today. Sure, I could reschedule the appointment. But the longer it took us to get to the doctor, the longer Butter had to go without treatment. And the sicker he would get. I felt a huge weight on my shoulders for putting him through this. It was completely my fault. What in the hell made me think it was okay to come to San Francisco anyway? I need to stop making such big decisions while I'm upset.

I called the doctor to tell him of my situation and he recommended me to another vet closer to me. He even offered to fax over all of Butter's paperwork so the new vet would be up to speed on his condition. I thanked him graciously and felt a little better. This still didn't excuse what Percy did at all.

How could he be so heartless about it? It was like he didn't take the cancer seriously at all. I was beginning to see his selfish, self-centered ways again. If it had been his pet with cancer, he would lose his mind at the idea that someone could simply *not care*. I rolled my eyes and went looking for Butter so we could go for a walk and get some fresh air.

We got back to the house only 15 minutes later because Butter just didn't have the energy to walk much today. Dealing with the pain of my heartbreak and then seeing Butter in such a weak state made me so upset, I just sat at the kitchen table and cried. God, please make it better. I'm so sick of crying, it's crazy. You would think I'd be out of tears by now.

■■■

It has been almost two weeks and I can't believe I am still here. Percy was angry with me when he got home because I had hung up on him, so the two of us have been walking around the house avoiding each other. Well, I was avoiding him. He got in my face the other day and I wasn't for it. I walked away from him like I didn't care, but on the inside I was scared he might try to force himself on me again.

I was scared I might wake up and find him in my bed, uninvited, again. I was scared I would be pressured into doing something I didn't want to do. So I quietly kept my distance. I knew I should just go back home. I looked up the train schedule online just in case I would have to suddenly leave.

I haven't had a real conversation with Casandra since the day she left my house so abruptly, and I was feeling very much alone. Every time we talked, I sensed a coldness in her voice. She no longer spoke to me with emotion like a friend would. Our encounters lately were very short. It wasn't bad enough that I lost the love of my life? Was I going to have to lose my best friend as well? I didn't understand what was going on right now, but I just hoped it ended in my favor. I *still* have hope. My phone vibrated against my thigh and my adrenaline rushed when I saw Damien's name appear on my screen. I didn't hesitate to answer.

"Hi, Damien," I said.

"Hello, how are you?" he asks.

"Terrible," I admit.

"Are you home? Me and my friend about to come over and get Dominique's stuff. Is that okay?"

"Yeah… you can go ahead. I'm not home. I won't be home for a long time. You don't have to worry about running into me."

"We don't worry about that, just wanna make sure we can come. Me and Dominique leave tomorrow for Beyoncé tour in South America."

"Oh my God, is tomorrow February 15th already?" The memory of Dominique informing me of the tour plays vividly in my mind. I also remember how foolishly angry I was at him about it. Boy, do I wish I could take that back.

"Yeah, so we gonna be gone until first of May," says Damien.

I hesitate a little before asking, "Has Dominique said anything…about me?"

"He don't tell me a lot about it, Téa. He just say it's over and that's all I need to know. Why don't you ever just call him if you wanna know how he feel so bad?" I shake my head, even though he can't see me.

"No. I can't…"

I was halfway hoping that Dominique would contact me before he leaves, to be honest. I needed him to say *something*. I was a woman in need of closure. You would think I got enough of that already, right? But it wasn't enough to diminish the hope I still had…

When I got off the phone with Damien, I made a promise to myself. I promised that if I didn't hear anything from Dominique by midnight, I would know for sure that I was cut out of his heart completely and I would give up all hope for us. I kept my phone in my hand hour after hour to be sure I didn't miss even a text. I told myself that if I kept thinking about it and wanting it to happen, it never would. But if I acted like I didn't care whether he called or not, my phone would ring.

So I kept myself busy by washing my hair. Doing this only frustrated me more. After I shampooed, my hair was dry and unmanageable. This never happens, so I knew something was wrong. I figured it would be fine after deep conditioning. But when I rinsed the conditioner from my hair, it was still too unmanageable to finger-detangle. I used a comb for the first time in months, and couldn't help but notice how much of my hair was coming out. The stress from me and Dominique's breakup was taking its toll on me.

I cried silently as I twisted my hair and wrapped it up in a satin scarf. It was now after 7 and Percy was home from being at the studio all morning and afternoon. He didn't greet me when he came in. Nothing new. I couldn't care less about that, I was focused on getting my phone to ring. I had a weak moment where I was tempted to contact Dominique myself, but I told myself that would defeat the purpose. He had to contact me. That's the only way I will know he cares, even if he only cares a little bit.

But I don't have to tell you how this ends. I never received a call or a message from Dominique. Not even a simple "Goodbye". Not even to say "Fuck you, I'm gone". I lay in bed, rubbing Butter until he fell asleep. It was hard for him to fall asleep now that the chemo had started. I put him in his own bed and returned to mine to cry.

My chest heaved as I tried to force myself to stop, but it only made me louder. I couldn't continue to live like this. I would never be happy! When would the hurting be over? I guess it was my job to end it. Now I had to fulfill the promise I made to myself earlier. It's done, Téa. There is not one bit of love left in Dominique's heart for you.

Percy must have heard me, because he entered my room a short while later and closed the door behind himself.

"Come on, Téa," he said, as he sat down next to me.

He helped me sit up against my headboard and pulled me in so my face rested against his chest. I cried until his entire shirt was covered in my tears. He didn't get upset about me "ruining a $120 t-shirt" like I expected him to. He just rubbed my arm up and down until I became quiet. When I did, he pushed my chin up with his finger until I was looking into his eyes. Then his lips were on mine.

I let it happen. I didn't stop his tongue from entering my mouth or his hand from going up my shirt. I didn't fight it this time. Why should I? I could never have Dominique again. That was a dream I had to finally give up on. But I refused to be by myself because of him. I needed someone to love me again. I needed someone to *need* me again. If that someone had to be Percy, then so be it.

SEVEN
"SOMETIMES I CRY"

2 Months Later
April 5, 2014

I cry out in the wee hours of the morning as I feel a spasm go through my lower back. It feels like it started in my back, then circulated through my entire body and ended up in my belly. I remind myself to be quiet as I look to my side at Percy's sleeping body.

The stress pains I've been getting are becoming unbearable. I never wanted to eat now because my stomach was always hurting. But I didn't know how to stop it. I got out of bed and tried to go to the bathroom, but nothing happened. I might as well take Butter out for some fresh air since I'm up and about now.

I slip on some sweatpants and my sneakers and walk out the door with Butter cradled in my arms. He has become too exhausted to walk on his own anymore. I no longer prayed for myself in the morning. I only prayed for him. He was becoming weaker and weaker and I couldn't stand to watch him deteriorate before my eyes anymore.

I was still taking him to treatment but the vet said if nothing changed after this week, there was nothing else they could do for him. I just don't understand why it had to happen to him. He is the most loving, obedient dog and he's so young! I've been trying to prepare myself for the day his time comes.

It was starting to dawn on me that once he was gone, I would have no friends left. Sure, I would have Percy. But I needed more than him. We've only been back together for two months and he had already started lying to me and hiding things from me. I didn't even have the energy to fight him on it anymore. I just let things be.

When he called me a bitch last week, it was the final straw. I started packing my bags and ordering tickets to leave on the next train, but he stopped me. He begged me for forgiveness and pleaded with me to stay. He hugged and kissed me. He also reminded me that without him, I was completely alone. I didn't want to be that weak, but I knew he was right.

Percy was still knocked out in bed when Butter and I returned. I put some food out for him and wrapped him in a warm blanket. Then I fixed myself some breakfast. This has been the routine every day. Wake up. Walk Butter. Eat breakfast. Clean the house. Watch court on television. Eat lunch. Cook dinner. Fuck Percy. Fuck Percy again. Shower. Go to sleep. Wake up all over again. This had become my life.

My heart skipped a beat when I heard my phone vibrate against the kitchen counter. The only person I'd spoken to in the past week was my sister. I had grown accustomed to having no interaction with the outside world. I picked up the unknown number.

"Hello?"

"Hey girl, it's Casandra."

"Oh…hi," I respond. She sounded like she was in a good mood, a big change from the last time I heard her voice. I wish I could say the same for myself.

"What's wrong? You sound sick," she says.

"I'm not sick. How is everything?"

"Well, first thing's first. I'm sorry, Téa. I really am. I know I've been missing in action for a while, but I honestly didn't mean to distance myself from you. I just been going through a lot that I wasn't able to talk about but I'm here now. I promise I'm here now. I wanted to stop by and see you if that's okay."

"Sure, come on by. We just have to be quiet cause Percy is resting." I make sure I close our bedroom door before Casandra gets there. She arrives a few hours later and I'm not surprised at how shocked she is when she sees me.

"TÉA….," she exclaims. I smile to hide how self-conscious I am.

"I know, I dropped a few pounds," I respond. It wasn't intentional. I haven't been eating the way I should because my appetite is almost nonexistent now. But I would never admit that to her. "Aren't you gonna hug me?" I reach my arms out to her and she comes forward, hesitantly. But she doesn't hug me. Her hand grazes my face gently.

"What happened?" she asks, her voice filled with emotion. Her eyes are starting to crinkle at the corners as they fill with pain. I don't want her to cry for me. I don't need anybody feeling sorry for me. I was just going through a hard time, but it will all pass. I know it.

"Don't worry about me," I say, smiling to reassure her. "I'm gonna be okay. What about you, wha---?"

"Is it Percy? Is he the reason you're this way?" she interrupts me. "Téa, he's destroying your soul."

"Percy isn't destroying anything, okay. If anything, I did this to myself. You know, I haven't been eating right or exercising and I lost weight because of that."

"NO." Casandra's intense eyes lock on mine. "HE is the reason. You need to get away from him, you don't need him."

"Well I don't need a cheater either, do I!" I spit, angrily.

My eyes burn as the tears come and fall to my feet. Casandra is crying too now and I know she hates to see me like this, but I didn't want to talk about this. I don't want to go through this again! I wish I could just figure things out on my own without people interfering. I sit down at the kitchen table and put my head in my hands. Once again, Casandra is behind me, holding me. Consoling me. We cry together until my head hurts.

"You don't have to---," she stops speaking suddenly when we hear Percy's feet enter the kitchen. I jump up from my seat and hurry to wipe my tears, but he can already see that I've been crying.

"What ya'll in here talking about?" he asks. He looks at Casandra, but she says nothing.

"We're just catching up on all the time we've been apart, baby. We missed each other," I explain. Casandra nods her head in confirmation.

"Oh, is that right? You've never missed me *that* damn much," he laughs to himself. His laughter ends as quickly as it started. "We don't have any secrets in this house, Casandra."

"Cool, I'll just leave," she replies. She looks at me with sympathetic eyes as she grabs her purse. "You wanna come with me?" she asks. I look at Percy, then open my mouth to respond.

"We're busy today," he answers for me. "Remember, baby, we got that thing to go to." I nod my head and look at the floor.

"Yeah, I forgot. We do have something to do today." Casandra shakes her head and walks toward the door. "I'm sorry you had to come all this way," I add. She doesn't respond. When he's sure she's gone, Percy gets in my face for the thousandth time.

"Why the fuck am I being put in the position where I gotta defend myself in my own house?" he questions.

"What exactly are you defending yourself against, Percy?" He laughs angrily, the same way my father used to do when he was drunk with a belt in his hand.

"You think I don't know you talk shit about me to your friends? I don't want that bitch here again." He puts his index finger to my nose. "And keep talking shit and you gone find yourself alone."

His hand flies across the counter and knocks my breakfast to the floor. When he exits the kitchen, I realize that I'd unknowingly picked up the knife I cut my pancakes with, and I'm squeezing it so tight that I've started to bleed. I drop it and rinse my hand off. Then I sit on the floor and bask in my own sorrow.

■■

"I'm happy to hear from you, baby," I hear my mother's voice come through the phone. The sound of it is like angels harmonizing in my ear. It's been so long since I've known that familiar voice. "How are you?"

She doesn't know about anything that has happened. To her knowledge, me and Dominique are still living together, blissfully in love. I couldn't bear to tell her what was really going on with me. But I knew I didn't have to. I began to cry and she didn't ask questions.

"Whatever you're going through, baby, you just need to pray. God is very busy, there's no doubt about it and the devil has been working hard these days. But He knows how you feel and He is going to make it right in due time. I know it hurts but now is the time for healing. Open your heart up to God and allow him to heal you and you will open your eyes one day and realize you got through it. You're gonna be okay, baby. Just like we enjoy the sunshine, we have to stand the rain." I nodded my head and wiped my face with my sleeve.

"I miss you, Mami. I'm gonna come out to Chicago and see you guys real soon." Surprisingly, my cash flow had increased recently due to Dominique. Everyone was ordering clothing from the Les Gémeaux collection so that they could wear it to the concerts. I'd saved up more than enough money to book a flight.

"Ohhh, I can't wait to see my baby," she responds.

I smile for what feels like the first time in years. Percy nudges me with his foot. I look up at him and he's smirking and nodding towards the bed. I look at the clock. I'm scheduled to fuck Percy in two minutes.

"I can't wait to see you either, Mami. I love you."

"I love you too, Téa." Before I can say goodbye, Percy takes my phone from me and hangs up.

"I'm fucking talking to my mother, Percy!" I yell, and climb to my feet.

"Come onnnn," he grabs my hand and kisses it, "I want you." His lips are on my neck before I can object. I push him away.

"I had a really long day, I just wanna go to sleep." He doesn't stop.

"I'm gonna put you to sleep, baby, don't even worry about that."

His lips are back on my skin as we fall back onto the bed. He's breathing hard and moaning and making a bunch of noise while I just lie there and take it. After barely any foreplay, he slides a condom on and begins to pump into me. It hurts because of my lack of lubrication, but I know if I stop him, it'll just take longer. I just wait for it to be over with.

His clammy hands run up and down my body with every thrust. I close my eyes and imagine how slow and gentle and passionate Dominique used to make love to me. There was love in his hands and emotion in his kisses and he meant every second of it. He believed in it. It was his way of expressing his love for me.

Percy was only looking to bust a nut. This didn't mean anything to either of us. Is this what I had lowered myself to? To being Percy's fuck toy? I didn't feel any pleasure, nor did I climax. A tear slipped from my eye as I remembered what it felt like to have Dominique inside of me.

Percy relieved himself quickly and fell on top of me. He either misinterpreted my tear or just tried to convince himself that it meant something else, because he kissed it away and said, "I know. It was good for me too." He slid off of me and was snoring within minutes. I got up to go wash his disgusting scent off my skin.

I played with the thought of sneaking out in the middle of the night and leaving Percy over and over again, but I didn't think I was brave enough to do it. I couldn't risk him waking up and possibly becoming more violent than he ever was with me...and hitting me. He never took it there but if he did, I knew I wouldn't be able to fight back. Just the tone in his voice made me flinch. And when he's angry, he's unpredictable. But one glance over at him lying in bed peacefully gave me the motivation to get up and get my ass out of there. I was finally taking the time to open my eyes a little.

Percy was living his life. He came and went as he pleased. I'm positive he was out doing his own thing with other women when he couldn't get me to do what he wanted at home. He controlled every aspect of my life. I can't even create the art I want to because he only wants me to make things for his group, which we all know has gone to hell.

I wasn't receiving any affection or emotion that I needed in a relationship from him. Shit, all I received was a hard dick in me every night and it wasn't even pleasurable. He was enjoying his life while I was allowing him to keep me miserable. How could I forget my self-worth? I got out of bed and looked in the mirror. I didn't recognize myself. And that shit was going to have to change.

I ran downstairs to the kitchen and fixed a bowl of food for Butter. I quickly placed it beside his bed and rushed back to the bedroom to slip on some clothes. I tried to hold my breath so he wouldn't hear me in my hurry to pack a bag and all my toiletries. The clock read 2:32am. I knew if I kept up this pace, I could make it onto the 3:00 train headed to LA. I flipped through the bills in my wallet. I had exactly enough money to make the trip. Lord knows He was looking out for me right now. I said a silent prayer, threw on a hat and my jacket, and silently shut the bedroom door behind me.

I had to stock up on some snacks since I didn't have any money for food. I piled anything I could find in the cabinets into my duffel bag. My heart was racing and I could hear it beating loud and clear. I just prayed that Percy couldn't hear it. I pulled open the refrigerator door and grabbed a couple water bottles. When I closed it and turned to put them in my bag, Percy's footsteps were already on their way towards me. I panicked.

He was almost down the stairs and I didn't have anywhere to go. I looked at the stairs then at the front door, measuring the distance. I could make it. If I ran for the front door, that would mean leaving Butter there with him. I couldn't do that. I backed up until my back was against the refrigerator and waited for my punishment.

Percy seemed surprised when he turned the kitchen light on, blinding us both. He looked me up and down, examining my clothing. It registered in his brain that I was leaving and I had no intention of telling him beforehand. He placed his hand on the counter and let out a sigh. My eyes were wide, waiting for him to tear into me.

"I want us to work, Téa." I was shocked by his words. His voice was so calm, I almost didn't recognize it. "I knew this day would come. I knew you would get sick of me and want to leave."

"Percy…I just need to breathe," I say, hoping to keep him calm. Telling him the truth would undeniably set him off. "I'm just leaving for a little while," I lie.

"What can I do to make you stay?" His words reminded me of the night Dominique walked out our door. I knew that pain. But this was something completely different.

"You shouldn't try to do anything. Just…let me experience a change of scenery so I can see how I feel…about us…" He nods his head slowly.

"I understand. I do. But maybe this will change your mind."

I half expect him to pull out a gun when he reaches into his back pocket. When he opens his hand, it is much more frightening. He's holding a small diamond ring between his index finger and thumb. Getting down on one knee, he grabs my left hand. I pull away slightly, but he doesn't seem to notice.

"Percy…"

"Stop. Don't talk. I wanna be the only one talking right now." I obey him because I don't want to make him upset. "I know I haven't been treating you fairly for the last few days." *The last few days?* "I know it hasn't been easy for you to live here with me. I know I been hard on you but it's just because I see the potential we have and I know we could be perfect. You know I mean well." *I do?* "We both have some things we need to work on." *Oh really?* "But I'm willing to put time in for you. I'm willing to spend the rest of my life with you until we get it right." He looks up at me. "Will you be my wife?"

"Percy, this is crazy." I can't even lie to him about this one. He had to be out of his mind if he honestly thought I would be okay with being treated like this for years to come.

"Is it?" He stands up and I cower against the refrigerator again. "You don't know what I go through every day for you!" He covers his face with his hands and I know he's trying to control his temper. But when he removes his hands, there are tears in his eyes. "I love you man…I just. I love you so much and I thought everything was going good but you leaving me man. I never ask for nothing from you. I never ask for nothing. The least you can do is do this one thing for me." Percy had officially lost all of his marbles.

"Okay Percy, I'll do it." You better believe I was going to say anything I had to say to get the fuck out of his house. "Will you let me go now?"

"Wait. I need you to wear it." He slides the ring onto my finger. "If you have to go, you have to wear it. It doesn't mean anything if you don't wear it. You better keep it on." His hand tightens around my wrist.

"I promise I won't take it off. Just let….me go. Before you cut off my circulation." He releases my wrist and places his palms on either side of my face. He pulls me in and kisses me hard.

"I'm gonna miss you. When will you be back?"

"When the time is right…"

"I get it. You just need some time. You can take all the time you need but you better be back here in time for our wedding."

"I will be. My train is leaving soon. I have to go get Butter and leave now, okay?"

He nods his head and moves aside so I can run upstairs. I only have 10 minutes now. I throw all of Butter's stuff in a bag and grab a blanket to wrap around him. He's sleeping peacefully in the corner of his little bed. I almost don't want to wake him because I know how tired he is. But we have to go. I nudge him a little and whisper his name.

"Come on, baby," I coo. But he doesn't move. It is then that I notice how stiff and cold his body is. I stare at him in disbelief. "No…"

I back away from him because I don't want to disturb his lifeless body. But it hurts and I can't help but let out a cry. I weep on the floor next to his bed. I knew this would happen eventually, but not like this. I wasn't prepared. And the timing couldn't be any more terrible. Percy came in to see what was wrong, but it didn't take long for him to realize it. I cried inaudibly for minutes with my mouth wide open and shook my head because I didn't understand.

"It wasn't supposed to happen like this. We were supposed to put him to sleep when the time came. I was supposed to say goodbye to him on my own terms. But this isn't on my own terms…I couldn't say goodbye to him. He died with nobody by his side because of me!" Percy bent down to rub my shoulders.

"Come on, we gotta call somebody before he starts to smell." But I am stuck in my position on the floor.

It's almost as if I've been petrified. Percy calls the pet crematorium to come and pick up Butter's remains. He assures me that he'll pay to have Butter's body transported out to LA so that I could put him away the way I want to. Of course I don't believe him. He's promised me plenty of things that never came true. It was partly his fault that Butter went so long without being treated. But he handed the money over to the vet right in front of me. He held my hand while I watched them put Butter inside a bag and haul him off. I felt myself getting sick. I keeled over, but Percy caught me before I could fall.

He left the room and came back with a water bottle and told me to drink. I did as I was told. I just wanted the strange feeling in my stomach to go away. I had never been in the same room as death before. I thought about death all the time. In fact, there was rarely a moment in my day when it wasn't on my mind. Being so close to it made me realize that I was living my life completely wrong. I couldn't get out of this house fast enough.

As if he could read my mind, Percy said, "I'll drive you to the train. If we leave now, you can still make the 4:15." I gathered my things. I was suspicious because, once again, Percy was being extremely caring. This was a complete 180 from the confused, teary-eyed Percy I was standing next to in the kitchen. I'd been in this predicament before. I didn't want to fall for it again. But he was the only one there for me…

He helped me gather my things and we headed out. We didn't exchange any words on the ride over. There was a somber vibe throughout the car. Percy got out to walk me to the car I would be riding in and pulled me into a long, meaningful hug. It was the first time I felt anything at all while he embraced me. I didn't know why. I felt a different energy than I usually did when he touched me.

"This probably isn't the best thing to say right now, but just look at this as the end of one good thing and the beginning of another." He kisses the ring on my finger to indicate what he's talking about. "Be safe, okay?"

The way his whole attitude had changed so drastically and so quickly was making me think I was losing my mind. But I let it go and hopped on the train. I found a seat where I could be away from people, which wasn't hard because of how early it was. I stuck my arms inside of my jacket and cried for Butter.

▪▪▪

When I open the door to my home, I'm so happy I want to bend down and kiss the floor. As soon as I got back to LA, it was like I was breathing a different air. It was so refreshing to be back in familiar surroundings. It had been two months since I'd last seen this place, but it felt like a lifetime. I couldn't wait to spray down, wipe, mop, dust, and polish every inch of this place. I needed to breathe some life into it. But this was home.

I did just what I set out to do. I took the sheets off all the beds and threw them in the washer. I sprayed Windex on all the mirrors and wiped them until they sparkled. I scrubbed every sink and tub clean. I polished the wooden dining room table and mopped the dining room floor. I vacuumed in the family room and bedroom. I dusted all the TVs and washed every dirty dish in the sink. When I finally finished cleaning and sprayed some air freshener, I stopped to stare at the walls and realized I didn't like the color. I could go for something a lot more cheerful than this olive green.

I called Casandra and without explaining anything, I asked her to pick me up several buckets of canary yellow paint and to join me back at the house. When she arrived an hour and a half later, I still didn't explain anything about our last encounter or why I was here. I just asked her to paint with me. And she did. We stayed silent and painted for a long time, exchanging smiles at random.

"This is very therapeutic, isn't it?" I finally speak.

"Are you gonna talk to me about it?" she asks.

"Not now. But I think you should know that Butter passed away this morning." Casandra stops painting and I am suddenly engulfed in her scent as the hugs me.

"I'm sorry, Téa. I loved him too."

"I know. But I think I am at peace with it. I think… a lot of things are going to have to change around here."

"I don't wanna speak too soon, but I do believe the old you is beginning to come back." She smiles warmly.

"Hmm…" I sit for a moment and ponder what she just said. "I don't wanna be the old me. I wanna be a better me." And I leave it at that. "Will you stay with me tonight? I don't wanna be alone."

■■■

Casandra ended up staying for the next couple of weeks. We finish our painting project together. Every single wall in the house, with the exception of my bedroom, has been covered in canary yellow. In the time it took to complete, I had managed to gain 15 pounds of my weight back. I feel accomplished knowing that I did it through diet and exercise. Plastered on the family room wall was a list of things I planned to do every day in order to get my life back on track:

1. **Pray**: Thank Jah every morning for waking you up. Thank him for your blessings, talent, and health and your family's health. Ask for strength, happiness, and patience.
2. **Eat clean**: Consume plenty of fruit and leafy greens. Drink lots of water. No caffeine, no added sugar, no preservatives.
3. **Draw a picture**: It doesn't matter what it is or how small,

just draw. Stay creative. Don't be hard on yourself if the finished product isn't what you wanted.
4. **Exercise**: Don't get lazy. Remember that it will help you with your stress and make you feel better. Keep pushing for thicker thighs and a toned belly. And don't forget to warm up and cool down!
5. **Study French**: Do it for at least 30 minutes. Don't get lazy! You want to be fluent don't you? Use Duolingo or listen to your audio tapes.
6. **Read or Write**: If you can do both, try that. Keep your mind at work. Go ahead and lose yourself in a good story.
7. **Write down every good thing that happens this week and reminisce about it on the weekend**: Even if it happened in a dream, write it down.
8. **Stay positive**: Don't respond to negativity, on the internet or off the internet. Think of the brighter side of every situation.

It was my own form of self-motivation, but Casandra had decided to join me. I was proud to say we were both on the road to living a healthier life, physically, emotionally, and mentally. My rebirth had begun. My spirituality was heightening more and more each day. I felt amazing. It was unbelievable how far I'd come in such a short time.

My sleep was no longer restless. I had pleasant dreams about my beloved Butter. Just as Percy promised, his body was transported here and we held a small ceremony and burial for him. I thanked him many times over, but told him I would still be staying in LA. He still believed we were engaged and just taking a little break from each other. I was still trying to figure out how to get out of this one without causing more damage.

This morning, I'm waking up to an empty house. Casandra is off at school finishing exams, so I take this time by myself to roll a joint and become one with Jah.

Minutes later, my lighter flickers over the end of my spliff and I take a hit. I lay back on the sofa as the house fills with the aroma of tree smoke. I try my hardest not to doze off, but I do. I'm awakened to the sound of Casandra entering the house. I'm still lifted and I greet her happily. She shakes her head at me.

"Guess who I ran into today? Just guess," she says, pulling turkey out of the refrigerator to make a sandwich.

"My weed man? Look, whatever he told you is a lie. I don't even blow anymore," I joke. I add a little cough at the end of my statement and smile mischievously.

"I ran into Dominique. Can you believe that nigga actually had the nerve to come back here?" she asks, and my high vanishes instantly.

Something he said the night he left came to my mind immediately. He told me that he was going back home to France. He said that he and Damien were leaving, so why was he back here? I didn't plan on ever seeing him again and I had finally started to be happy again.

But everything would be different if he was back in LA. I wouldn't be able to handle seeing him around. I wasn't at all over him, I had only learned to block him out. Why the fuck did he have to come back? I'm not ready for this. Casandra must see the worry in my eyes because she sits down next to me.

"Look, we're not about to start backtracking, Téa." She's holding my hand but I'm looking off into space. "You've been doing so great. You turned your life around. Hell, you turned my life around. Look at me! I even stopped eating red meat. We're getting better, don't let him get inside your head and tear you down again."

"I'm not…I just…I'm just surprised, that's all. You know. Wow. Dominique is back," I chuckle, but it isn't funny to me in the least. "This means nothing, Casandra." I look her in her eyes to show her I'm serious. "I'm not gonna let him affect me."

"DO NOT TALK TO HIM," she warns.

"I'm not!" I stand up and start walking to my room. "I would be the last person he wants to talk to, I'm sure." I skip up the stairs two at a time and close my bedroom door behind me.

Once inside, I sit on the edge of my bed and put my head in my hands. I tell myself it's nothing to stress over, but in all honesty, I'm going crazy. Just thinking about possibly running into Dominique has me losing my mind. What would I say? What would *he* say? Would he pretend that he didn't know me and nothing ever went on between us? Would he still be pissed and have an attitude towards me? I'm not the best with confrontation. If we came face-to-face on the street, I'd probably scurry off before any words can be exchanged.

It was frightening to think about. Emotions I'd suppressed were already returning just thinking about his tall, strong figure standing in front of me again. I didn't know how I could still feel this way about him. I told myself to remember all the hateful things he said to me that day. *All you do is cry and whine now. You make it impossible to love you.* I was impossible to love. Yeah, that did the trick.

"Téa!" Casandra knocks at my door and I tell her to come in. "Let's order pizza. I think we deserve a little treat. I'll pay."

"What happened to not backtracking?" I ask with a smirk.

"I can let it slide if it's gonna make you feel better. And me," she laughs.

I allow her to spoil me for the rest of the night, only because she'll try to force me to talk about my feelings if I don't. We turn on Perks of Being a Wallflower and stuff slice after slice into our mouths. It's been a while since either of us had any greasy food. I knew we'd both feel terrible afterwards.

"I was actually thinking about Damien the other day," I spoke up out of the blue. Casandra looked up then turned back to her plate, pretending to be focused on her food.

"What made you think of him?" she asks, with her head still down.

"Well, I was looking through the drawers in my room trying to find some damn bobby pins for my hair... and I came across one of Dee's rings."

"What? Wow..." she says, almost uninterested.

"Yeah, and it obviously made me think of when Damien came to pick up all of his stuff. And suddenly I thought to myself... how did he even get in the house that day? Because I wasn't home."

"Hmm...maybe he had Dee's key."

"I thought of that too, but nope... Dee left his key here the night he left. I remember that clearly." I shudder as I remember how terrible it was to go to bed alone that night. "I don't know why I didn't think about it when I was on the phone with Damien that day. I probably left the door unlocked since I was losing my mind at that time. Gotta make sure I never do that again. People are crazy."

"I think my phone is ringing," says Casandra. She hops up quickly.

"No, I think it was just the..." I say, but she's already running to her room. "....TV." I was left sitting on the couch by myself, eating pizza alone.

■■

Casandra didn't speak much to me over the next few weeks. She stayed in her room whenever she wasn't at school and only came out to eat. She told me she thinks she got food poisoning from the pizza because she wasn't feeling well. I didn't badger her, but I wasn't stupid. I noticed how strange she acted when I mentioned Damien. I just wished she would feel okay talking to me about it.

I could hardly understand her still feeling rejected by him after all this time, but she should know that I wouldn't judge her for it. How could I? Look at my situation. I'm still head over heels for a guy that turned my life upside down then dropped out of it. If anyone knew how confusing emotions were, it was me.

I was packing my bags for my trip back to Chicago to celebrate my sister's birthday when she came in my room and told me she was leaving for the day and she would be back tomorrow.

"Where are you going?"

"To a friend's house." She cleared her throat and looked at the floor.

"Okay… are you okay? What the fuck is going on with you because you're starting to scare me. You helped me when I was in need, why won't you let me help you?"

"I am fine…"

"You're fucking tearing up, you're not fine."

"I just need some time to think about some terrible decisions I've made." She wipes a tear before it can fall from her eye. "I just… I don't wanna regret anything. I think about that shit. It's important to me…"

"Okay." I nod my head. I don't quite understand what it is she's going through, but I completely understood needing time away from life to think. "Well… if you're gonna go, you should go now. Beat the storm."

"Yeah," she whispers.

"Feel better. I love you."

I give her a hug that she pulls away from immediately. We'd both expected me to be the one to go through an emotional breakdown, but it turned out to be her. It seems like things always start going bad just as they're getting better. I had no clue what the fuck was going on in my best friend's life and she lives five feet away from me.

Not soon after she leaves, the rain starts pouring. I wasn't a huge fan of being alone when it was raining but I had no choice. I cooked and showered before the weather really got bad. I was just about ready to knock out when the doorbell rang. I stood on my tiptoes to see through the peephole.

I saw Dominique's broad shoulders and long neck and to my surprise, my heartbeat didn't speed up. I opened the door and looked him in his eyes. I'd thought about this moment several times. What would it be like when we saw each other again? I thought I would cry. I thought I would be overcome with emotion, but on the contrary, I was emotionless. I didn't have the urge to lash out at him. I was actually quite calm.

He used his hand to hood his eyes while the rain glistened against his thick eyelashes. I had never seen him look so pretty. That thought made me recall my mother's voice in my ear. It was a childhood memory that made me cut my eyes at her at the time, but now almost made me laugh out loud. It was a conversation about the beautiful Michael Jackson, may he rest in peace.

My mother had tried to explain to me that men are not supposed to be pretty. But it fit Michael just as it fits Dominique. In fact, Dominique really reminds me of the 1977 version of Michael with his tall, lean figure & his full, curly fro. Dominique licked the rain from his lips and snapped me out of my daydream.

"You gonna let me come in?" he asked with big eyes.

I couldn't just leave him out in the rain, although I'm sure his hair would catch all of it. I stepped aside and he walked in as if he was right at home. Technically, this had been his home for a significant period of time. I guess I expected him to act unfamiliar with it like one does with an old friend they haven't seen in a long time. Why did he come here? What does he want from me?

"Why did you come here …?" I spoke loudly. "What do you want from me?" He chuckled like he was sharing a private joke with himself.

"I guess you not too happy to see me then," he responded, still smiling. "I bet Butter will be happy to see me. Where is he anyway?" I look down, trying to think of the best way to explain to him. I never even thought that he'd ask me that.

"Butter……….died. A little over a month ago, actually." I watched Dominique's face fall and his eyebrows furrowed. His bottom lip got tight. I could tell he was about to be angry with me. "It really did happen so unexpectedly ---"

"He died and you don't even tell me? I mean, you hate me THAT much. You could not even come to me and speak to me even to tell me ---"

"How dare you!" I said, louder than I expected. "How dare you try to tell me how I'm feeling! I swear, you are so condescending. You think you know everything, sometimes it really makes me sick to my stomach."

I was suddenly feeling vulnerable again and I didn't want to be around him like that. I was bound to let tears fall at any minute. I couldn't give him the satisfaction.

"Now who's telling people how they feel?" I could see his anger fading as he said this. He looked down at the floor and kind of half smiled. "You almost sound like your mother just then, you know." I rolled my eyes.

This is the part where Dominique changes the subject so that he doesn't have to deal with confrontation. I remember when we first met, he'd told me he doesn't get into arguments. I couldn't understand how any human being could prevent that from happening. How could he let someone make him so angry and not say anything about it? But I witnessed it for myself throughout our entire relationship. It wasn't until the end when he blew up that I knew he'd been holding it in the whole time. I've come to know his technique very well. I can even see it coming sometimes.

"Please, don't start," I said.

"I run into her the other day," he ignored me, "and she seem like she doing good. She was really surprised to see me cause I don't come to Chicago for a long time. Of course, she would not let something like this stop her from hugging me so tight." He laughed again, it seemed, to himself.

Dominique always did joke about how my mother would've had him if I hadn't roped him in myself. As if he was some gift to women. Sometimes I think I'm crazy to think such harsh things about the man I love, but then I think about what he's done to me. Unforgivable things…

"Are you going to tell me why you came or not?" I asked rudely.

"I love you." I looked up. It's nothing I've never heard before. "I……..I love you, Téa. I don't hear myself say this to you in a long time. Too long. Don't you think?" I didn't answer. "I want you to know that I been thinking about you every day I been away from you. But I'm back now. I'm back and ---"

"And you expect me to be waiting here for you so that we can pick up where we left off like nothing happened?" I could feel the tears forming in my eyes. I sighed loudly. "Let me guess. You went away and had some time to think and you came to your senses, right? I think you should just go, Dee." He shook his head at me like I was a child.

"That's the thing you keep doing," he said, still shaking his head. "You keep pushing me away. You keep acting like you don't want any things to do with me and you want me to leave you alone forever, when really all you want is for me to stay!"

I knew it was true as he said it. I felt it in my heart, but I couldn't let him do that to me again. I wouldn't. I refused to let him pull me in and make me believe that everything was all good and it wasn't.

He came to where I sat on the couch and grabbed my hand in his. I fought the urge to pull it away. "Stop it. Stop letting you foolish pride get in the way of what we both want. I want you. Swear of God, you're all I ever wanted."

"You left me!" I cried.

I snatched my hand away from him and used it to hide my tears. I couldn't help but sob right in front of him. It hurt so bad just thinking of when he abandoned me. Everything was so perfect. That alone should have been a sign that things wouldn't turn out good for me.

Dominique had me feeling like I was the only woman in the world. I never even THOUGHT of love until Dominique. Ultimately, I found love in him. It created a new me. I thanked him for the love he gave me and all I wanted to do was give him the same in return. And I did. Mind, body, and soul. I gave him all of me. By the time I realized it was over, there was nothing left.

"I know I left you, but evvvvery body deserve a second chance. Don't they?"

"I was done giving out second chances by the time I met you, Dee. How much hurt can one's heart take?"

"I never meant to hurt your heart. When I hurt you, I hurt myself. I try to stop both of us from hurting ever again. You see?" He came closer to me. "Let me make this right. Let me make you feel happy again…"

The tip of his nose grazed mine. He stared directly into my eyes before he let his lips fall on mine. It was the softest kiss I've never felt. I knew I was being a fool, but all of a sudden my feelings for him came surging and I allowed myself to be kissed.

Our hands entwined as he kissed me once more. I could feel his heavy breathing on my neck. It whispered a song to me with every exhalation. Dominique's hands slid slowly up and down my thighs, and I allowed his tongue passage into my mouth. He still tasted the same. Like raspberries and vanilla. I felt my body warm up immediately from his touch. My juices began to flow and I know what I wanted and Dominique knew too. I was ready to feel and remember him again.

In the back of my mind, I knew this was the reason Casandra told me not to talk to him. She knew this is where it would lead. She knew he would get inside my head and persuade me to think whatever he wanted me to think. I had to be strong. But I couldn't.

The way he was touching me felt a million times better than being touched by any other man, and that was something I would never be able to forget. Then I thought about the hundreds of other women he's undoubtedly touched the same way and I know I have to think of a way to convince him that we can never work. No matter how bad I want us to. And God, I want us to…

His large hands slid down and cupped my ass, as he picked me up. His lips never left mine. We were both breathing heavily now, knowing what was about to come. He led us into the kitchen and sat me down on the counter where we had made love many times before. Every time felt like the first time. A new, wonderful experience. I just wanted to experience it one last time...

I threw my head back and rested it against the wall while Dominique slid my sleeveless top down to my belly button. His mouth grabbed at my nipples with hunger. He massaged my other breast while he devoured the left one. His slim waist was pressing in between my legs. I wanted nothing but this, and all of a sudden I came to my senses. At this very moment, I realized that what I was doing was wrong. I yelled at Dominique to stop but he couldn't resist.

"Shhhh...." he whispered into my neck, trailing kisses down to my chest.

I felt the warm tears brimming my eyes. I tried to cover my face with my hands... I didn't want to do this to myself again. I knew what Dominique was capable of and I could not allow him to break me. I made sure to place my left hand over my mouth. Just as I'd hoped, he discovered the diamond ring on my finger.

Grabbing my hand with so much force I almost fell to the floor, he lifted it to my face and spat, "What is this!" I could see the flare in his nostrils... I knew this wouldn't end well.

"I tried to tell you, Dee, you wouldn't give me a chance!"

The tears were beginning to roll because I couldn't believe it had come to this. I couldn't believe what I was about to do, but it seemed to be the only way to keep him out of my life for good. Dominique began backing away, his head in his hands.

"Please... don't say this is happening," he said, more to himself than me. "Is this what I think it is?" I tried to swallow the lump in my throat but it was completely dry.

"Yes, Dee. I'm engaged now..." I managed to say.

"To who, Téa."

His head was down and I couldn't imagine how he must be feeling right now. But he left me! He left without saying anything and took my entire world with him. I was lonely, cold. I couldn't eat. I couldn't sleep. I couldn't even see color anymore. Everything was black and white. I fell into the deepest depression of my life. It was worse than what I went through after all the issues I dealt with concerning my family. It wasn't my life anymore. I would have to explain to him about how I'd carried on a relationship with the person he hated the most.

"WHO THE FUCK ARE YOU ENGAGED TO, TÉA!" he yelled suddenly, and punched the wall. I didn't want to do this to him, but I knew I had no other choice.

"Percy!" I screamed. "He… He was there for me! Percy came into my life and he made me feel beautiful again. He made me feel like I meant something, after feeling like dirt for so long," I lied. "I never expected that you would come back into my life. He knew how I felt and he said I deserved better! And I did, Dee… I did. So…when he proposed, it wasn't even a question for me," I continued to lie through my teeth.

"Percy?"

Dominique stood and snatched his coat up. I could now see that he was holding back tears. I expected him to be pissed off, but I had never seen him cry before. I didn't mean for it to go this far. It never crossed my mind that it would actually hit him like this.

"Wait! Where are you going?" I ran after him and stood in front of the door so he couldn't get past, but he simply pushed me out of the way. "Wait, please don't leave me, Dee," I tried one more time.

It seemed our arguments always ended this way. He continued to walk to his car without a word. It wasn't until he slammed the door and started the ignition that I could see the tears flowing down his cheeks. His eyes were red-rimmed.

"This. Is TOO MUCH. FOR ME. Téa... I should not have come back..." he almost whispered. I felt a pang of guilt in my heart as I watched him cry. I couldn't believe that Dominique LeBeau was crying over me. I wanted to hurt him, but I didn't want to destroy him. I know how that feels...

"You're upset. Stay here for the night... please. You shouldn't drive," I tried to reason with him. I would do anything to get him to stay at this point. "Damnit, Dominique, do you want to get into a car accident!"

"It would not matter if I did. The pain would feel nothing compare to what I feel right now."

He stared ahead as his words registered and burned my heart to its core. He abruptly pulled off and left me standing there with nothing but my tears. For all I know, he was driving towards his death and it was all because of me. It's funny how you plan things out and don't think twice about the consequences. I wasn't normally a vengeful person, and for good reason. I couldn't handle knowing that a human being was feeling pain because of something I'd done. What have I done?

EIGHT
"EX- FACTOR"

Dominique

Dominique's eyes flew open when he felt himself falling in his sleep. He was having a nightmare for the 3rd time this week. It seemed to be all in his head though, as he realized he was positioned awkwardly on the floor already. A feeling of light-headedness came over him as he tried to sit up.

His head was pounding and he stroked his temples with his thumb and index fingers. He felt absolutely terrible and didn't know why. Wiping the sleep from his eyes, he leaned up against the sofa beside him and checked his surroundings. Nothing looked familiar.

"Fuck!" he exclaimed in frustration. At the sound of his voice, a woman appeared in the hall across from him. He didn't recognize her until she spoke.

"Well, look who finally decided to wake up," she snarled.

She was tall for a woman, at least 5'9 in her bare feet. Her hair was blonde and she was Latina, with a distinct New York accent. Suddenly, he remembered meeting her at a bar last night. He remembered purchasing a few bottles and throwing them back quickly. The blonde was in his ear all night and brought him home with her, undoubtedly expecting a good fuck. But Dominique had passed out on the floor not long after getting there.

"I'm sorry, I don't drink," he apologized. He picked up an empty bottle next to him that read 1800. "What?" he mumbled to himself.

"Hmph. Coulda fooled me."

Dominique's phone went off and he hurried to silence it before his head could explode. So this is what it feels like to be hung over. He had several missed calls and texts from a few women he met on tour. Most of the missed calls were from Téa though. She had been trying to contact him for a week now, but he didn't want to talk. But he *did* want to talk. He just wanted everything to be right again. Why did it take so long to make things perfect, but so little time to fuck it all up?

Despite how he felt, it was high time that they did talk. He knew for sure that he had taken the wrong approach when he went to go see her, but his ego was in the way. He probably shouldn't have pretended everything was sweet, but it wasn't usual for Dominique LeBeau to be running back to a woman. Then again, it wasn't usual for Dominique LeBeau to be in love. He knew he'd left his car at the bar, so he decided to call Damien and ask him to take him to it. Trying to stand was a mistake. His knees gave in and he fell back down almost instantly

"What the fuck, man..." he whimpered.

"That's my fault. I may have accidentally kicked you a few times while you were sleeping," said the blonde with pride. "I hope you have a ride and shit because I gotta work."

"What time is it?"

"A little after 9am." Dominique groaned. What he wouldn't give for a few more hours of sleep. He called Damien and the phone rang 7 times before he finally picked up. He was probably knee-deep in some pussy.

"Bro, I need you come get me man." Damien kisses his teeth.

"Right now? Where are you?"

Dominique texts the address to him and waits patiently for him to get there. The blonde stood and stared at him while tapping her foot the whole time. Dominique would've broken her off a little but he just didn't have it in him. There was nothing wrong with her, it was all him. Something had changed while he was overseas.

"You're welcome!" she shouted when he walked out the door. But not *that* much had changed, and he gave her an asshole look and left without a word. After all, the bitch did beat his ass while he was passed out. Dominique hopped in the passenger seat and waited for his bro to start questioning him. He didn't have to wait long.

"Who was that?" he asks.

Dominique observes Damien's wife beater and Nike flip-flops and can tell he was "busy" when Dominique called him. He was appreciative that his brother came to get him anyway. He was very appreciative of a lot of things lately. Losing his woman taught him to stop taking advantage of the people he loves. And there was always more room for kind gestures in his life right about now.

"I don't know. I don't know anything. I was drunk last night," Dominique explains. Damien shakes his head.

"You look like shit too," he remarks. Dominique's phone goes off again and Damien is reminded of what he wanted to talk to him about. "You talk to Téa?" he asks.

"No. She been calling me though."

"Yeah and you know she been fucking calling me too. Evvvvvvery time I look at my phone, it's her. Every time. I love her but I will fight her," he says, only half jokingly. "For real bro, say something to her so she can stop."

"I go see her after I get my car, man."

"Good then. I don't know why you deal with that anyway. You could have any girl that come after you and you wanna be with one girl."

"And why not? Just cause you don't find the right girl, you want for everybody to be miserable. Just stop, Damien."

"I'm not miserable. I'm happy every night. No matter who bed I go to sleep in," Damien laughs.

"Yeah, well everybody don't wanna do that shit for life," Dominique responds, not amused in the least.

His brows are furrowed and Damien is starting to piss him off. They were twins, but they never did anything the same. Damien wanted one thing for the both of them while Dominique wanted another. He disagreed with his brother often, but feared losing the close bond that they shared if he acted on it. But he wasn't about to let Damien make him lose out on something important again.

"I'm just saying bro, she got you acting crazy. You get mad all the time and I nevvvver see you go out and drink. Now look at you."

"It's not her fault! I do this to myself, Damien!" he yells. "I try not to snap on you but it is enough, Damien! Leave it alone!"

"How I am supposed to know it's not what she did, you never tell me nothing about it," Damien claims, intimidated by the rise in Dominique's voice. The car is filled with awkward silence for a while before Dominique speaks up again.

"I don't tell you nothing about it because it hurt, man." That is the end of the conversation and they don't speak again until they pull into the bar's parking lot.

"You good, bro?" asks Damien.

Dominique nods his head and Damien drives off. His head is still pulsating with pain every second, but he didn't want to hold off any longer. There were some things Téa needed to know about, and he was the only person who could tell her. For all he knew, it was his last chance to get her back in his life.

He was prepared for whatever steps he had to take to convince her that she was making a huge mistake by marrying Percy. Just thinking about her walking down the aisle and smiling at that bum nigga made his eyes sting. He would never admit it to anyone, but crying was becoming an everyday thing for him.

When he turns onto Téa's block, he calls her to inform her that he will be at the door soon and they have a lot to discuss. She sounds apprehensive on the phone, but he isn't going to take no for an answer. This has to happen. Téa opens the door and hides herself behind it, as if Dominique is a stranger. He doesn't ask to come in like he did the first time. He pushes the door open and walks right past her. That's when he sees Percy sitting on the couch with a dumbfounded look on his face. Dominique doesn't skip a beat.

"Why is he--- you know what, it doesn't matter to me." Dominique grabs Téa by both hands. "Téa, I have some shit I just gotta get out."

Percy doesn't allow him to say another word. He walks toward Téa and questions her as if Dominique isn't standing right there.

"What the fuck is this nigga doing here?" Téa is clearly at a loss of words. Of course she is, she wasn't expecting Dominique. So he speaks up for her.

"Look, I don't know you gonna be here but I tell her that I'm coming to talk. It doesn't have nothing to do with you, so just shut your mouth and stay over there."

"I know you see that ring on her finger, right?" asks Percy. "I know you see that shit with those big ass eyes. So my fiancé has everything to do with me. So whatever you gotta say not important, my nigga."

Percy knew exactly what Dominique was capable of and Dominique laughed internally at his boldness. He wasn't above knocking Percy's teeth out again.

"First of all, Percy," Téa finally speaks, "You *did* come over here unannounced."

"So, the fuck does that mean? This nigga announced hisself before he came? Ya'll made plans or some shit for him to come over?"

"I didn't say that, and you need to calm down." Dominique could see the fear on Téa's face and he didn't like it one bit. What was this nigga doing to her to make her look so afraid of him?

"No, I don't need to fucking calm down. I'M the man you getting married to. I'm the one that got your little finger all iced out. Don't forget, Téa." Percy starts pacing, angrily and Dominique almost can't hold back his laughter. He was looking like a true psycho right now. "Don't forget what you promised me," he points at her.

"One second," Dominique says to Percy, then turns to Téa. "Fuck him, okay? Please just come with me so we can talk alone."

"She not going nowhere with you!" Percy approaches Dominique with such speed that Téa feels the need to step in front of him and face Percy herself.

"STOP."

"Wait, wait, wait. So you protecting this nigga now?" asks Percy, an evil grin forming on his already devilish face. "Ain't this some shit. I lost to this nigga the first time, I'm not about to lose to him again. You can believe that."

"Percy, you need to just chill out for a second and let me figure out what the fuck is going on. God…"

"Nah, what you need to do is check this nigga for disrespecting the man in your life and stop acting like a little bitch."

"Oh hell naw," Dominique shoves Téa out of the way. He'd had enough. He couldn't believe this is the guy Téa had chosen to be with over him. He would never talk to her that way. Dominique got a grip on Percy's collar and was ready to toss him across the room, but Téa kept putting herself in between them.

"Just stop! Stop! This is not even anything to fight about! Stop fighting all the time!" Téa screamed. They were separated from each other now, but Dominique was shocked at Téa's reaction to Percy's words. It's like she wasn't even upset.

"What the fuck, Téa? You just gonna let him talk to you like that? This is how this nigga talk to you? He just talk down to you like that? He call you a bitch? This is crazy!"

Téa covered her face with her hands. He could see that she was overwhelmed with everything that was occurring all at once, but so was he. He couldn't believe his eyes or his ears.

Téa had talked all this shit about how great of a person Percy was and how he was so sweet and always there for her, but he seemed to be the same dickhead he was when he first came across him almost a year ago. This nigga was nuts.

He was behaving like he belonged in the crazy house. And he'd be damned if he let him disrespect Téa like that again. Dominique didn't care if she wasn't affected by it, he was. After all, she belonged to him. At the end of the day, Percy and Téa would both know and believe that she belonged to him and him only.

"It's fine, Dominique. I can handle it." Téa slowly turns to Percy. "Percy, I think you should leave. I asked you to leave days ago. I don't wanna see you here anymore. Now, can you please go. I'm asking you nicely. I'm only gonna do that once."

"So I have to leave and this nigga gets to stay?" he asks.

"YES!" Téa exclaims. Dominique stands by her side and he can feel her trembling with anger. He lifts his hand to rub her arm softly and comfort her.

"He always did get to touch on you when I couldn't. You're such a proud hoe, aren't you."

Unexpectedly, Téa charges into Percy. She screams at the top of her lungs as she shoves him into the nearby fireplace, knocking over a few of her framed artworks. Dominique watches on as the glass shatters over them. He is pleasantly surprised at Téa's sudden act of physical violence.

She doesn't even give Percy a chance to recover from the blow to his back. As soon as he looks up, she punches him directly in the nose. Dominique foresees what is about to happen next. Percy lunges towards Téa, but Dominique's fist connects with his eye before he can lay a finger on her. He is knocked out cold and lands with a giant thud on the living room floor.

Dominique is so overcome with anger at the fact that Percy would even attempt to put his hands on Téa, that he doesn't stop. He punches him twice more before Téa can pull him away.

"Don't! He's out cold, it's enough! Just leave him there!" Téa yells at him. Dominique has a second mind to spit on him as he laid there, but he went to the kitchen and filled a bowl with cold water instead. He threw it on Percy's face and it splattered all over the hardwood floor. Percy woke up, sputtering and choking on the water. Téa stood behind Dominique, afraid that Percy would try something again. But he looked up at them in a daze. Dominique pointed at the front door.

"Get out." He said simply.

Percy struggled to his feet and stood on shaky legs. Blood poured from his nose and his eyelid was swollen shut. Téa pulled the ring off her finger and threw it at him. It took him another minute to find and pick it up and he stumbled out the door without another word.

When he was finally gone, Téa breathed a sigh of relief and hugged Dominique. She clung to him and he held her and stroked her hair. He missed doing that so much. He missed consoling and being the person she ran to when things were all bad. He was going to take advantage of the opportunity he had now to be that person for her again.

"It's becoming a tradition for you and him to fight in my home," she said. *Our home*, Dominique thought to himself.

"You did a number on him, girl. You see his nose? It was turned to the side like this," Dominique showed her with a laugh. But there were tears in her eyes. She cried into his chest.

"I wanted you to come. I wanted you to walk in and make him leave. I've been calling you!" she exclaimed.

"I know… I was not ready to talk to you yet…" He looked away from her because she had the power to look in his eyes and see right through him. "What happened? I thought you was so happy."

"I… HATE him…" she said with so much anger. "I'm sorry. I lied to you… I just didn't know how to deal. I didn't know how to handle you being back here in this house with me like how we were before.

I still don't." She released herself from Dominique's grip and he looked at her, confused. "Thank you for coming, but this day has been a little much for me and I just wanna relax. I don't wanna think anymore today."

Dominique was a little discouraged because he never even got to do what he planned on doing. The whole reason for him coming over was to sit her down and explain things to her so that maybe she could understand why he needed her back. He just needed a chance to plead his case.

"Lemme stay here with you. In case he try and come back," he adds at the end, hoping it will increase her chances of saying yes. But she shakes her head slowly.

"I don't know... I'm not ready for that, Dee."

"I won't try anything with you, I promise. I just don't want you to get hurt. I'll sleep on the floor," he tries to convince her. She looks up at him with sorrow in her eyes and he already knows what her answer is. He was sorry too.

"Just give me some time. I need to breathe a little bit..." she explains.

Dominique nods his head and accepts that he's just going to have to wait a little bit longer before he can have her back for himself. He doesn't want to badger her with everything he has to say because that will only make her upset and push her away. That doesn't stop him from sitting outside in his car, watching the house until the sun started to set.

NINE
"THE AIR THAT I BREATHE"

"Knock, knock!" yells Casandra from downstairs.

I'm in the master bathroom doing my hair, but I put it on hold to go down and greet her. There is a huge smile plastered on her face and it makes me smile. I'm guessing things have gotten better and I couldn't be happier for her. It was nice to have my friend back.

"You are grinning from ear to ear," I mention.

"Do you notice anything else?" she hints, as she turns slowly in a circle.

"Uhhh, yes honey. I noticed your fire engine red hair all the way from the top of the stairs. Nobody missed that," I laugh. "So what made you do *that*?" She grabs my hand and leads me over to the couch so we can sit down. And she takes a deep breath…

"Téa, you are my absolute best friend. I go off about all my problems with school and work and my love life to you and you just sit there and listen to everything and offer me your wisdom. To you, it's something small, but for me it's huge. I want you to know just how much I appreciate that."

I sit with wide eyes, waiting for her to get to what she really needed to say.

"You know me better than anybody else. So you know that I would never intentionally hurt you or anyone I love." She looks down at her hands. "I've made a lot of mistakes in the past and I've hurt other people, but I would never hurt you. Anything I do is to help you. And I just hope that no matter what happens, you can remember that. And remember that you've helped me so much too."

"Girl, you wouldn't hurt a fly," I try to lighten the mood and I succeed as she giggles.

"That's not the point. The point is that I was feeling low. Really low. And you were my motivation to get better. I watched a man break you completely. Then I watched another man tear you all the way down to the point where you felt like nothing. But you made a plan to get better and you did. So I knew I had to do the same. You were my inspiration."

"You always getting deep on me when we're supposed to be happy," I laugh. I lean away from her and narrow my eyes. "You sure a new man didn't enter your life and have this effect on you? You kinda have that 'I just got some good dick' look going on." Casandra bursts into laughter and playfully slaps me on the shoulder.

"NO girl. It's time we realize that we don't need men to be happy." My phone vibrates in my hand and I look down to see Dominique's name. Casandra sees it too.

"I know that," I say. She looks back up at me.

"And also, I want you to know you've made a lot of progress since he's been gone. You should keep it that way. You shouldn't talk to him."

"Talking to him won't change that. Have a little faith in me. Geez…"

I stand up because I fully intend on having this conversation in private. The truth is that I don't want Casandra judging me for still feeling emotional when I hear Dominique's voice. I know she wants me to keep progressing and I do too, but it's hard when you had a love like mine and his. I almost have to wean myself off of him because it's too difficult to drop him all at once. She just doesn't understand that…

"I do have faith that you'll do the right thing," she smiles. I smile back, but it quickly disappears as I answer the phone and hurry up the stairs to get to my room.

"Hey, Dee."

"I almost think you not gonna answer the phone," he responds. His voice still sends a shiver up my spine. I shake it off.

"Well… I did… what's up?" I ask.

"I wanted to come over but I know it's hard for you to talk about things face to face and I don't want you running away from me again." I swallow. I have no idea what to expect, but he was right. He knew me so well. "So I call you because I have to get my feelings out. I don't want you to say nothing until I finish, okay?"

I stupidly nod my head then realize he can't see me. I barely whisper, "Okay," and he continues.

"Being in a relationship with you put a lot of stress on me." I don't like the way this is going already. "When we first get together, we didn't care about anything. It was so easy. When I meet you, I have some things to look forward to when I get off stage. Being on tour makes me happy but it make me so tired and homesick too. But coming home to you make it better for me. I don't know when it change. But one day, it feel like you become a different person. You start to get so angry at me and I feel like I'm always at war with you. I didn't feel like you love me anymore. And then you call me a cheater and that was it for me."

"Well, technically, you are---," I start.

"I'm not finished yet," he interrupts me. "Listen. I was so happy to leave by the time me and Damien have to go. Being home with you make me so depressed. It make me feel like a stranger in my own house. I feel like I do all these things for you and it don't matter. In South America, so many women want to be around me. They want to buy me things, they want to give me anything I ask for. When I see that, I just knew I was wasting my time being with one woman."

I understood that Dominique had to get his feelings out, but stepping all over mine wouldn't help anything. It was becoming very hard not to hang up the phone on him.

"I went out every night," he goes on, "me and Damien both do. Every night I wake up with a different girl in my bed. It was the same every day. The night would be great and the morning would be lonely. Every new woman took more out of me than the last one. They never make me better. They always make me less. It was nothing like waking up and having you on top of me. It was nothing like falling asleep inside you…"

I close my eyes at these words and automatically begin reminiscing. Of course it was nothing like that. Absolutely nothing could compare to that feeling. I shiver.

"And then one I day I think to myself…you never ask me for anything. But I still just want to give you everything. All these bitches take and take from me. They feed off me like a… I don't know the word." *Parasite*, I think to myself. "But you nevvvvvver ask me for ANYTHING!" I can hear him getting upset with himself.

"And I know then that I was stupid and scared. I was quick to leave you because I was scared of how close I got to you so soon. I was afraid of how much I love you. It was too much for me. I never go through that before. I didn't know what was happening." He pauses for a few seconds, and I hear him sniffle. But his voice is unshaken when he speaks again.

"I think about you every night after that. I don't allow no more bitches in my bed. You know... when we were walking around in Spain, I actually jumped to protect you from all the pigeons out of habit," he laughs at himself. I laugh at this too, but soon my laughter turns to tears. "I don't say this to make you sad. I just want you to know that I messed up and I know I did. I know I made a big mistake and I wanna fix it. I mean it, Téa. I'm sorry for all the hurt that I make you feel. I been feeling it even worse. You don't know what I been going through without you."

"What's that?" I ask through my tears.

"I just can't go anywhere without seeing something that remind me of you. And thinking about you with Percy...it just make me sick to my stomach. And when I find out how he treat you, it hurt me so much. I act tough when he there, but I went home and cried for you. You don't deserve that shit. It never would happen if I didn't leave like I did. I fuck up so bad, I didn't think God would ever let me have you again. So I jump at the chance."

"Well, I forgave you a long time ago for all the pain I went through because of you. I had to if I ever wanted to move forward. But...since we're apologizing, I'm sorry too. I'm sorry for not putting you first like you did for me when everything with us was good. I mean, you were right... I never even thought to do anything as small as rubbing your shoulders after a long day.

"I never listened to how you were feeling or comforted you when you were sad. I was very much disconnected from you in that sense. Who knows, maybe if I had been more loving, all the craziness never would've happened. But I won't dwell on it. Thank you for acknowledging that I was a good woman. I needed that reassurance because for the longest, I felt like such a shitty person."

"You not shitty. You so beautiful...I never met nobody beautiful as you. I still want another chance to show you how beautiful you are," he says, and I know this is his way of asking me if that's possible. But it hasn't been long enough for me to think about this. I had a lot of things to consider. It wasn't this easy...

"Just let me sleep on it. I don't wanna be impulsive like I have in the past when my feelings are involved. You understand that, right?"

"Yes, I get it."

The frustration in his voice is evident. I didn't want to prolong his pain, but I had gone through pain too. I don't ever want to make decisions as stupid as I did in this relationship ever again. And if this is something he truly wants, he'll be willing to go through a little pain to get to it.

"Cool...so I'll talk to you tomorrow. I'm gonna try to get out the house and enjoy myself," I say as I wipe the tears from my cheeks.

"Well, be safe. Watch your back for that nigga Percy. You know he trying to press charges on me for beating his ass."

"Are you serious?" That was the worst thing that could happen right now. It seemed like no matter what I did, I couldn't get Percy to leave my life. He was just so persistent to stay in it, whether he could have me or not. I wasn't about to run from this nigga for the rest of my life. I'd never be happy. "Don't worry about it. I'll take care of it."

"I don't want you to take care of it," says Dominique. "I don't want you nowhere near him."

"Look, don't worry about it. I won't be anywhere near him. Just trust me."

"I do trust you." I wish that I could trust *him* again.

"Talk to you tomorrow."

"Bye."

When we hang up, I sit down at the kitchen table and write a letter to Percy:

Dear Dipshit,

I am writing this letter to you to let you know just how much I despise you. I want you to know exactly how sickening it was to stare into your face every night while you pumped away at me for 4 minutes. The hideous look on your face as you climaxed was a face not even a mother could love. I wanted to scrub every inch of my body with bleach after lying next to you in bed. You disgust me.

I imagined being with Dominique every second we spent together. Every time you snarled at me, I envisioned Dominique's beautiful smile beaming at me. Every time your hairy legs rubbed up against me at night, I daydreamed about Dominique's leg caressing me to sleep. I know you wished you could be him. You were so angered by the fact that you couldn't be him, you decided to take it out on me. But I'm free now and I'm not going to let you do it any longer.

For the first time in your life, be a man and own up to all the things you did to me. You deserved what you got back from Dee. No other man, especially not you, will ever be able to tongue me down or lick my pussy the way Dee does. And pressing charges against him because your ego is hurt is not going to change that. So drop them, you pathetic son of a bitch. And move the fuck on. I don't ever wanna see you or hear from you again.

I write Percy's address on the envelope and add a stamp before walking back downstairs to join Casandra.

"Hey, do you wanna go out to eat today?" I ask.

"Girl, yes. That's exactly what we need."

"Cool, I just gotta make a quick stop at the post office first." I grab my coat and wait for Casandra to ask questions, which can only be expected.

"So I guess everything went okay on the phone," she says.

"Yeah, we had a good talk. He said some things…that I've been waiting forever to hear him say. So it was good." Casandra gives me a look.

"He said some things to try to pull you back in, huh?" I kiss my teeth and roll my eyes. She just doesn't get it. "I can see it in your face that you're actually considering taking him back. Aren't you!"

"I don't know how you could get all that from one look, but okay. I haven't decided anything. I just still love him, that's all. That kind of love doesn't just go away because he hurt me, okay? It's something I can't do nothing about. Doesn't mean he's getting me back just like that."

"Well I would hope NOT. Just remember this. You don't want a man that will stick his thing in any and everything. You can find much better than that, girl."

"Yes, I know that." I'm getting tired of discussing this with her, so I change the subject. "Turkey burgers at Epic?" I ask.

"Lead the way," she says with excitement.

■■■

We get back home just as the sun is setting. I can tell that Dominique has been over the house before we even walk through the door. I can just sense that his presence was there. I'm sure he was just keeping an eye out for me. He was rightfully worried about something happening to me when he's not around. The change in the house was evident as soon as we stepped in.

The wall with the highest ceiling in the family room had been painted completely white. All of the furniture had been neatly moved to the side, with the exception of a small table. On the table were sets of acrylic paints and various different sizes of brushes. They weren't the cheap kind either. Next to the paint was a small note that read

Now you can paint your mural.

I felt my hand fly up to my mouth in shock. He had designated this wall to be the wall I paint my mural that I told him about on our very first date. The date I didn't know was a date. That fateful evening at the restaurant that started this whole whirlwind romance. I was speechless. Mostly because I knew I had to call him. He didn't have to do all of this because I had already made my decision about us. Casandra looked on as I waited for him to answer the phone. He didn't say hello.

"Do you like it?" he asks, immediately.

"I love it, Dee." My voice is shaking.

"I knew it would make you happy." I could hear him smiling

through the phone, but I was not.

"I appreciate the fact that you remembered this. And that you realized how important it was to me. It really does make me happy. I'm sorry you had to go through all this trouble." I start to cry. "And I'm sorry that it's not enough..."

"I know it don't make up for everything, but there's so much more where that came from, baby."

"No... you don't need to do anything else. I can't be with you. I thought about it long and hard and... I just cannot be with someone who, for all I know, is out with other women and coming home to me. I can't be constantly worried about you bringing something home and getting me sick. I can't do it, Dee. I can't live my life like that." He stays quiet, knowing he has no defense for what I just said. "I love you and I'm gonna always love you. But I'm not gonna take that chance. Okay?" He says nothing. I wait for what seems like minutes before begging him to say *something*.

"I...I used the spare key to get in and I accidentally took it with me. I will come over tomorrow and give it to you." I knew he was taking this final opportunity to try to see me. But I would not face him.

"No. Just drop it in the mailbox. Please," I say.

He hangs up. Casandra doesn't console me or hold me this time as I cry. She just watches me let it all out until I don't have the energy anymore and my head and throat are aching. It was the hardest thing I've ever had to do. But I knew it had to be done.

One week later

Casandra knocks on my bedroom door just as I'm tying my gym shoes, preparing for our 2-mile walk. It was her idea to start waking up at 6am to do this, but it has become a very relaxing ritual for me. I grew to look forward to it every morning. I was hoping that maybe it would get my mind off the baby thoughts I was having.

"Come in!" I yell.

"Hey…what's wrong?" she asks. I guess she noticed the solemn look on my face. I never was good at hiding what was on my mind. There was no point in pretending everything was all good.

"Hey. I'm fine…I just…" I exhale sharply. "My doctor called and it was just kind of a reminder that this thing is still happening to me. And now of course there's no solution for it." Casandra's eyes crinkled in the corners as she felt my pain. "It just sucks cause I felt like I was so close but now that Dee is gone, what are my chances? You know…"

"I know it sucks, Téa," Casandra says, "But I have faith that you will make me a little niece one day." I laugh at that because I'm actually hoping my first child will be a boy.

"Look at me. I just keep finding reasons to bring up Dee in conversation. My bad, I know you're sick of me." Casandra waves my comment off as if to say she's cool with it, but I know she's scared I'm going to change my mind and go back to him. "Why aren't you dressed?" I ask, noticing the onesie she has on.

"Oh, I decided I'm gonna sit this one out cause I was up all night."

"Can't sleep?" I ask, concerned.

"I don't know what it is, I'm probably just stressing about the upcoming semester. I'm good though."

"Okay well, I need this so lemme go outside before I try to change my mind." I grab my jacket in case it's too cool outside and check my face in the mirror.

"Enjoyyyy..." Casandra says sarcastically.

Usually we jog the four blocks it takes to get to the nearby high school, then jog back. I decided to head in the direction of the nearest gas station so I could stop in for a snack and also dodge the pervertic old men who sit on the corner down the street. It was nothing to ignore them when Casandra and I were together, but I didn't want them to see my little ass alone and try to follow me. I made my way down the street at a steady pace, the sound of Destiny's Child's "Free" in my ear.

There was no need to bring my jacket because it was clearly going to be a scorcher today. I was so hot and sweaty by the time I made it to the gas station, I decided to get a cold drink to go with my snack. Casandra would scoff if she saw me in here buying these greasy Super Donuts, but we all have our vices.

I go towards the counter to pay for my food, but I feel someone tap me on my shoulder. I turn to my left and see no one. Then I feel a tap on my right shoulder. I turn to the left again, praying that I don't see Dominique in front of me, and I don't. I see Damien's giggling face.

"Damien...hi. Hi!" I pause before hugging him as I realize it's been five whole months since I've seen his face.

"How are you?" he asks, still beaming down at me.

"I'm good! Aww...it's so great to see you. I missed those little bunny teeth smiling at me," I gush. It's true that all our phone calls haven't been exactly peachy, but that didn't change the love I had for him and how much I missed him being here. "Where are you staying?" I asked, remembering he doesn't even have a place in LA.

"At my girl house," he says, with a mischievous look on his face. He pushes me forward a little to let me know I'm next in line.

"What girl?" I ask.

"Whatever girl I feel like," he responds. I roll my eyes, remembering how much of a player he was. But then, I guess I could say both of the LeBeau twins had those player ways. "You need a ride home?"

"Nah, I'm tryna get my walk on," I giggle. After I pay for my snacks, I follow Damien outside so we can sit in his air-conditioned car to talk. His music starts blasting as soon as he starts the car, but he turns it down to hear me ask, "How is Dee?"

"I know you never beleef me, but he don't talk to me about what happened," he answers. "He just... don't wanna talk about it."

"No, it's okay, I believe you... I just wanted to make sure he's good. I guess he's not." I become lost in my thoughts until I notice Damien staring at me out the corner of my eye.

"You chew for so long," he says.

"I know," I laugh, "I was thinking..."

"Dominique don't have to talk to me for me to know he is hurting. He really do care."

"Yeah, you say that but his actions said something else. I could see that he was really trying *after* the fact, but that doesn't change what he did. I mean, that alone made it clear to me that he doesn't love me."

Damien rolled his eyes and groaned, "He *does* love you."

"How, Damien? Let's be real. How could he love me?" I ask.

"BECAUSE HE SAID IT!" I am taken aback at how loud he gets, but he lowers his voice immediately. "Sorry, but Dee don't just say that to anybody. If he say it, he mean it, okay?" I shake my head in disbelief. He couldn't honestly think it was just that simple.

"You can tell someone you love them all day long, Damien. But when you continuously cheat on them, all that shit goes out the window. For real." I was trying not to get angry at his ignorance, but he wasn't about to make Dominique out to be an angel just because he was his brother.

"Well I don't know he cheated. He never tell me that," Damien says quietly. I chuckle.

"Yeah," I say with a sarcastic laugh, "I had my suspicions but when I walked in on him and another bitch having sex in our home…" I shook my head and began tearing up just thinking about it, "It was over for me at that point." Damien appeared to be in shock, as if he'd never expect his brother to do something like this. Neither did I. "And to think I actually went out of my way that day to look good for him and apologize for accusing him." The look on Damien's face has changed to one of confusion.

"You mean *that* day?" he asks, his eyes wide. The way he asks tells me that he knows something I don't. He referred to "that day" as if it was significant, and I didn't like it.

"Yes…that day. Why? What about that day, Damien?" I question him. He bursts into a fit of laughter and can't get his words straight so he can speak. This only annoys me even more. I spend almost five minutes trying to get him to stop laughing long enough to tell me what's going on.

"Dominique was not at home that day," he manages to get out. I'm so confused by that and I'm starting to think he's making a joke that isn't funny at all.

"He wasn't." It sounds like more of a statement than a question.
"No, no, no, no, no," he says, still shaking with laughter. "*I* was

there. With Casandra."

It takes a minute for his words to fully register in my brain. Even when they did, I didn't want to believe it. Over and over in my head, I repeated *'please don't let this be true, please don't let this be true, please don't let this be true'*.

"Damien," I say, grabbing his arm with my left hand and his chin with my right. I force him to look me in my eye and get serious. "What are you saying? Are you saying what I think you're saying?"

"I'm saying… I have sex with Casandra. Dee was not there." I wince.

Could that be possible? Could I have walked in on Casandra having sex with Damien and not Dominique cheating on me? I know I didn't get a good look at his face, but I would know my own man if I saw him right? I'd know my own best friend even if I saw her from a distance with her back facing me, right? I would never make a mistake like this, right?

"Damien…I need you to think really, really hard about this. Are you sure?" He has stopped laughing when he realizes the seriousness in my voice, and he nods his head quickly. "Casandra wasn't even staying in my house at that time, how would she be there? Why would she be there?"

"I don't know." He throws his hands up as if to say he is totally innocent in the matter. "I just know she use a spare key…under the uhhh…the mat? In front of the door? And she can't bring me to her dorm no more cause her roommate don't wanna leave the room." My spare key under the welcome mat at the front door of our house. Nobody knew about it except Casandra and Dominique.

"And you are 100% sure about what day this was?"

"Yes, she tell me it was okay cause you were out getting your hair and nails done so we don't have to worry about you walking in on us."

"Oh my God..."

Tears begin to stream down my face immediately because the only thing I can think about is how I tore into Dominique about his infidelity and I drove him away. I think about the fact that the past five months of depression and pain could have been completely avoided, and me and Dominique could still be together like we're supposed to be.

I think about everything he's been doing to prove to me that he's not the cheating man I thought he was. Then I think about how Casandra knew the entire time and didn't tell me anything. I didn't want to believe that she sabotaged me, but what else could you call it? It definitely explains all the strange behavior she's been having. I scream.

"Téa, calm down. People start to look at you," Damien says, glancing out his window. "You want me to take you home?" I wipe my tears with my jacket and practically blow steam.

"Yes. Take me home, please."

Casandra was about to feel my wrath. I used the short ride home to organize all my jumbled thoughts and everything I wanted to say to her. I convinced myself that violence is not the answer, but I couldn't be held responsible for what I might do to her when we're finally face-to-face.

"Wait outside," I tell Damien. I run up the front steps with a quickness and unlock the door. She's laying on the couch, resting in front of the television. I can't tell if she's asleep or not, but I don't really care.

"Casandra! Casandra!" I yell her name at the top of my lungs as I make my way over to the couch. She opens her eyes slowly and turns her head, searching for where my voice is coming from.

"CASANDRA!" I yell again. "Get up, bitch!" She sits up straight on the couch when she hears my harsh words. I'm still walking towards her and am only a few feet away now.

"Are you okay?" she asks, her eyebrows furrowed.

"I don't wanna sucker punch you, so I'ma let you know right now that I'm about to hit yo ass," I spit. She drops the blanket that was wrapped around her body and starts to stand.

"Téa, c'mon---." CRACK.

The unmistakable sound of her nose being fractured brings me temporary joy and I watch her hit the ground with pride. The feeling doesn't last for long as the pain from my blow hits all four of the fingers on my right hand. The adrenaline flowing through my blood makes me forget about it instantly though.

"What the fuck!" Casandra spits a stream of blood onto the carpet.

"I'm not done with you either, and you gone clean that shit up too," I say. There is fire in my eyes and fear in hers. "Now that I got that shit off my chest, let's talk."

Casandra is still a bit disoriented and leans on the table to try to help herself up. I don't offer my help. I just watch her struggle to her feet and look at me like I'm the one who's insane.

"You better tell me what the fuck is going on right now because you not gonna swing on me again with no retaliation. I'm telling you that right now," she says, grimacing from the blood that has begun leaking from her nose.

"Oh, don't you know, Casandra? Why would I just barge in on you and sock you in your face? Huh? What could you have possibly done to me that...I don't know...I may just now be finding out about? What could that be?"

I can see the blood rush from her cheeks instantly. She knows she's been caught and there is no escaping this. There is no lie she can think of.

"Téa...listen," she starts.

"SHUT UP," I interrupt her. I'm not here for her shit. I can't think of another time in my life where I've been so angry. "What excuse can you give me? Let me know!"

"There's no excuse...you're right. But it's not what you think." I cock my head at her, mockingly.

"How is it not what I think?"

"I didn't wake up one day and just decide to fuck with your life, okay! I feel terrible about this! I've been walking around with this guilt for months now! Why do you think I can't sleep at night?"

"Save all this suffering you went through, what about *me*?" My feelings of anger begin to turn to pain as I re-live all the hurt I had been through. "All you had to do was speak up when I told you what happened with me and Dee! That's all you had to do!"

"I wanted to, but it wasn't easy for me! I...I thought you would look down on me for giving it up to Damien after he made it clear he didn't want me." She looked down, undoubtedly expecting pity. "I didn't expect all this to happen, it just snowballed into something way bigger. I'm sorry, I never meant for you two to break up."

"You gonna have to think of something a whole lot fucking better than that, Casandra. You just let my relationship end over something petty as that? Are you out of your mind?"

I wait to hear her answer, but I get nothing. She just stands there looking helpless. Yeah, well I know that feeling. I was a lot more helpless than she is, and she deserves it a lot more than I did. When I speak again, my voice is weak.

"You saw how depressed I became after Dee left...you saw how Percy terrorized me...you saw what he did to me! You watched him tear me down and make me feel so little. And even after all of that. *After all of that!* You still couldn't find it in your heart to let me know what was really going on?" A large tear falls from my eye and splatters against the floor.

"I thought about it..." she says. "But honestly, I felt that I was doing the right thing. Because you know what... somebody needed to show you that you were making a mistake." I massage my temple with my fingertips and sigh.

"What does that even mean?" I ask.

"You were so blinded by love that you couldn't see Dominique is just like every other man. Him and Damien are just alike. He was gonna hurt you eventually, Téa, I just made it happen sooner." I look at her with squinted eyes.

"That's your brilliant explanation for letting me suffer? Because you *think* he would've eventually fucked up anyway?"

"It was only a matter of time." She looked so confident in her answer, it was almost laughable. Maybe under less extreme circumstances, I would've laughed.

"This is ridiculous. This doesn't explain anything and none of this makes any sense! My health and my livelihood was on the line." I start crying again. "None of that meant anything to you. It was more important to you to bring Dominique's "true colors" to the light. What is wrong with you? You were my *FRIEND*. You were my friend long before Damien or Dominique or any of this existed."

"That's right!" she yells suddenly. "I was your friend! And you forgot that! Right? You and Dee wouldn't even know each other if it wasn't for me! Dominique wouldn't have hung out with you and fell in love with you and started your perfect little life together if it wasn't for me being there for you when you were a pitiful mess that day! Do you remember *that*? I deserve to be loved too, Téa! I'm a good woman. I deserve a man who's gonna give me the world! And Damien thinks he's gonna just call me up and have casual sex with me whenever he wants? He thinks I'm his little plaything? What made *you* so deserving and not *me*? Huh! Since you have so many questions, that's my question for you! Is that fair?"

Through my teary, glossed-over eyes, I finally see Casandra for who she really is. I finally see that she was never my friend. Friends are never envious of you. Friends congratulate you. Friends don't destroy your life and other's lives because they can't have what you have. I could do nothing but pity her. My eyes slanted with concern for her well-being, if only for a second.

"You really are a crazy bitch," I whisper through the utter silence.

"Ha," she laughs although she is not humored, "Maybe that's why I'm alone."

"Get out," I say calmly. "Get out."

"That's fine, Téa. I don't need to stay here. It's bad for both of us. Look, I'm sorry for everything. I really am. I hope that you and Dee can be happy together and have lots of children and grow old together, because you know. You deserve it. You deserve the world. I'll come back tomorrow for my things."

I don't say a word as she grabs her shoes and leaves the house in her bare feet. I wash the tears from my face and get myself together because I know that now I have to make things right. I walk out to

Damien's car where he has been listening to the radio to keep himself entertained.

"Do you know where Dee is? Can you take me to him? Please take me to him," I say frantically.

"I don't know, Téa... I don't know where he would be but I will help you look around."

"Thank you. Thank you so much."

"I see Casandra... what did you do, girl?" he asks, comically.

"Don't worry, everything is fine. She's gone forever," I say with no emotion.

The rest of the car ride is silent. Damien drives by different clubs that he and Dominique frequented and even one bar. Nobody had seen Dominique and we couldn't get in contact with him because his phone was turned off. Evening was approaching when we finally gave up and decided to go home.

I knew Damien was tired from running around with me all day and I told him he could stay at the house with me if he wanted. When we stepped in the house, we saw none other than Dominique in the kitchen, fixing himself some food. My heart stopped at the sight of him. He had never looked more perfect to me.

"Hi, baby," he says with a mouthful of pizza. When Damien sees the pizza, he rushes into the kitchen without a question. I was somehow still stuck, frozen at the doorway.

"Dee..." is all I can say. Sound familiar?

"My phone die before I can call you back. But Casandra leave me a voicemail and I hear it when I charge my phone."

"So you know…"

He leans against the counter and crosses his arms over his chest with a sexy smirk on his face. His whole stature read *You fucked up big time but I forgive you, now come here.* He nods his head at me.

"But how did you get in?" He dangles my spare key in front of his face.

"I never dropped it off," he explains.

With teary eyes, I walk over to him and he picks me up and wraps me in the tightest, warmest hug I've ever received from him. It felt like the most familiar thing I've ever known in my life. More familiar than the home I grew up in as a child. More familiar than the bus route I took all throughout high school as a teenager. More familiar than the feeling of my art pencils in my hand when I was working on a new piece. *Home is where the heart is…*

"The entire time you were away from me, I continued to feel all your emotions. All your pain. Your joy. Your regret. Everything. I knew deep down that we would come back to each other."

I am soaking his shoulder with my tears and he is kissing my forehead and my ear and my nose, over and over again, trying to comfort me.

"I know. I felt it too," he whispers. I smile through my tears.

"It makes sense now. *You're my twin flame…* that's why we fell for each other so quickly. That's why you ran from me. That's why we were attracted to each other like magnets, even miles away…" I bury my nose in his neck and breathe in his musky scent.

"I love you," he says releasing me so he can look down into my face.

"I love you," I repeat. He uses his thumb to wipe away the last tears

I will cry for a while and kisses my lips fully. I was wrong about what I was feeling before. Nothing is more familiar than *this*.

We leave Damien where he is at the table, engrossed in his food, and head back to the bedroom that we used to share. The bedroom that we still share. I reclaimed what was mine that night and Dominique left his mark on me permanently. Our mind-blowing lovemaking session was the greatest of all time, and that hadn't changed. After an explosive climax, Dominique remained inside of me and stared deeply into my eyes.

"C'est la maison."

TEN
"1+1"

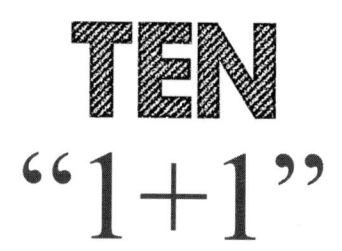

I fully expected to wake up from my dream in tears, my arms wrapped tightly around my own body. I'd cry for a few minutes, partly because of how beautiful it was and partly because I had to say goodbye to it. Then I'd pull myself together and try to return to reality. I awoke, instead, with my arms loosely circling Dominique's head, which lay firmly on my chest. We had fallen asleep that way, him on top of me with my legs tangled in his. His palms were still cupping my behind. I knew they had to be tingling...

As if it were on cue, the sun began to seep through the curtains and light up our entire bedroom. My surroundings matched my mood to a tee. I tried to wriggle from underneath Dominique's body, but this was impossible. One of his eyes flew open and he pulled me in tighter. I narrowed my eyes at him.

"Where are you going?" he asked, almost sounding like a pouting child.

"Nowhere," I say. *I don't plan on being away from you ever again.* Dominique kisses me between my breasts.

"Good, cause we gotta talk," he responds. Dominique slowly buries his head in my chest and I feel his warm tongue trailing across my nipple. I try to pull his head up but he resists.

"I thought we had to talk," I giggle, and he comes up for air.

"We do. It just been so long. I miss loving you…" he says. The corners of my mouth curve up into a knowing smile. "You know… I should never buy this house and don't let you see it first."

"It's fine… I was happy with it. I was happy just to have a house…"

"No. A woman make a house a home. I should let you decide where you wanna make your home. I should help you decorate our home. I didn't do enough."

"You can help me now…" I murmur. "We have a fresh start. This is the best time to change things around. I would know."

"Let's do it. But first, I wanna move everything out the family room so you can start your mural." I laugh while absentmindedly rubbing Dominique's shoulder in circular motions with my thumb.

"Why is that so important to you?" I ask.

"Because it was important to you. I see your eyes light up when you first tell me about it. Now you got the space, why you don't wanna do it?" he questions.

"I *do* wanna do it…I just don't know if I can…" Dominique's mouth twists up and his left eyebrow rises.

"Umm, I know you. You can do anything," he says.

"It's so hard to work with no inspiration, and lately I've had none." I can see him deep in thought, thinking hard about what we can do about this. Wanting to help me…and possibly upset that he himself can't be my inspiration.

"We just gonna have to find something to inspire you then." He shrugs. "Easy." My phone rings on the nightstand beside our bed and

Dominique grabs it for me. "It's your maman," he says.

"Hello?"

"Téa. What's going on? You might as well tell me, cause I already know something is wrong. Okay."

The tone in her voice is accusatory and it's definitely being directed at me. But I had no idea what she was talking about.

"You haven't talked to Casandra? Did something happen between ya'll, because she came back to Chicago in the middle of the night and says she's not going back to school this upcoming semester. She's dropping out and you don't know about it?"

"Well, I didn't know all of that. But Casandra is no longer my concern, Mami. I'll tell you about it later, not now." She sighs loudly through the phone and I can feel a lecture coming.

"So you choosing a man over your best friend," she says.

"Look…Mami," I laugh before I can even get my words out, "You don't even know the half, okay? If you knew, you would not blame me."

"I don't need to know about it, but it looks bad. I'm just saying, all these years ya'll have been friends and you gonna let it end because of him? I know you in love, but if this man has you ending life-long friendships, maybe he's not the one for you."

"I can't even do it right now, Mami. I'll talk to you later," I say, with my hand over my head. I'm praying I don't get a headache from this shit. Dominique takes the phones and hangs it up for me.

"She mad at you?" he asks.

"Yeah, but she doesn't get it. She thinks she knows everything, I can't tell her nothing."

"Sound familiar," Dominique says jokingly. I playfully slap him upside the head. Reaching up, I release my hair from the tight puff it has been in all night and begin to massage my scalp. I close my eyes and exhale because it feels so damn good to let it breathe. Dominique watches my soft, fluffy hair reach out towards the sun, and I feel him growing hard inside of me.

"Deeeee," I say in shock, but I'm not really surprised. He never could get enough of me.

Six weeks later

The kitchen was filled with the warm, chocolaty smell of cake baking in the oven. The aroma wafting into my bedroom made my mouth absolutely water, and I went downstairs to sit at the kitchen table and witness Vicky work her magic. Dominique and I had hired her two weeks ago after searching around for a chef that could prepare us healthy meals while we were both much busier with work. I set my laptop on the table so I could continue to work while I admired her baking skills.

Vicky was only two years younger than me and in her third year of college, studying culinary arts. Only looking for volunteer hours and no pay, she ended up being just what the doctor ordered. And since we were so close in age, I found myself having personal conversations with her. We had taken up chilling out on the couch and talking for an hour or so after she finished her work. I found it very comforting these days with no other woman in my life I could really talk to and relate to.

I didn't usually disclose such personal information to people I had just met, but she knew all about the Casandra disaster. I didn't give her all the dirty details, but she knew enough to give me feedback.

She felt that it was a shame a friendship that lasted so long should end the way it did. Well, she wasn't the only one. But Casandra hadn't reached out to me to try to fix it and I honestly wasn't sure I wanted her to. I was still very angry about it. I didn't need a person like that back in my life.

"Who told you chocolate cake was my favorite?" I asked Vicky with a silly smile on my face.

She covered her mouth with her hand as if someone was listening to us and said, "I'm not supposed to tell."

This could only mean that Dominique specifically told her to bake a chocolate cake for me. But the rich smell of the chocolate suddenly became overpowered by a scent that made me feel sick to my stomach. My tummy felt funny like when my grandma would have sweet potatoes in the oven. I couldn't stand the smell.

"What else are you cooking?" I say, covering my nose and scrunching my face up. But the only other thing she pulls out the oven is the cornbread she made to go with dinner. She frowned as she tilted the pan so I could see.

"You don't like this?" I moaned my response.

Dominique walked through the front door with Damien at that moment and I tried to forget the churning feeling in the pit of my stomach. I smiled from ear to ear so he wouldn't think I was about to get really sick like last time. I was crying internally, hoping that familiar pain wasn't about to come. Not only was I unprepared to deal with it, but this would also mean that I was still having problems and something could seriously be wrong.

"What you doing, baby?" Dominique kneeled in front of me to kiss my forehead, which made me perk up a little bit. I continued to hide how ill I was feeling.

"Just gridding this picture so I can start this new, really big portrait. It's taking forever. I think I'm gonna go upstairs in a few and take a nap."

"Oki. Before you do that, I need you to do something for me," he says. My eyes rest on the tip of his nose, and it's doing that cute puffy thing I love. I kiss it and beam at him.

"Of course, my love. What do you need me to do?" I ask.

"I need you to wear this for me," he says and holds up his hand.

There is a ring in it. It isn't sitting in a pretty little velvet box. It is only resting between his index finger and his thumb. I look up into his eyes and notice that they are filled, threatening to spill over. The reflection of the ring is glimmering in his pupil. I realize that Vicky and Damien are standing beside us, smiling down at me. I know instantly that they were in on it all along. They both knew that this was about to happen. Dominique had kneeled down in front of me several times, but who knew this time would be different?

"I know you say you don't want marriage," he starts, "So this not an engagement ring. But it's a promise ring. Right now, I promise to be with you and only you forever. And hopefully, I can buy you another ring one day when you change your mind. But to me, you are already my wife."

Vicky is practically squirming and jumping up and down with excitement. I know they are waiting for my response, but my mind is completely blank. I know what I want to say but my brain won't tell my mouth to say it.

"Will you wear it for me? Will you be my wife?"

Dominique presses me. I hold my ring finger out and allow him to slide the ring onto it. I just stare at it with huge eyes. I feel Dominique kissing my cheek. He whispers, *Je t'appartiens*, in my ear. Out of the corner of my eye, I see Damien congratulating Dominique with a shoulder squeeze and a half smile. I inhale sharply and my breathing starts coming in short bursts.

"Are you about to cry?" Vicky asks. "Oh my God! If you cry, I'm gonna cry!" she exclaims. Dominique laughs and reaches out to comfort me before my tears come.

But my body lurches forward and I heave all over his Jordans.

▪▪

I turn the volume down on the television when I see that Dominique is calling me. He and Damien had gone back out of town to do more workshops and make some club appearances, and the last three days without him were tough. I was having flashbacks of how lonely I was when he was on tour with Beyoncé. Thankfully, I had Vicky to keep me company and it was a little better than before. There was definitely an abundance of food for me to eat.

"Hey, baby," I answer, "Hold on for a second."

I pause when I see a familiar face on my television screen, and turn the volume back up so I can hear. I watch as Percy is escorted out of a house in handcuffs and lead to a squad car. Vicky starts to ask me what I want for dessert tonight, but I put a finger to my lips and shush her.

"Pop singer, Percy Brown, was arrested today outside of his San Francisco home following the brutal beating of his girlfriend, Cherry Moore. The 911 call, made by a neighbor, came shortly after 7pm when screams were heard coming from the third floor and a window was broken, shattering glass all over the sidewalk outside. A relative of the victim, who was called before the altercation got physical, stated that it allegedly began when Brown got upset at Moore for coming home later than the time they had agreed upon."

"I knew one day he would snap," a witness says into the microphone, "You can just tell when you see him walking down the street that he had some demons."

"Moore sustained severe head injuries," the reporter continues, "including a large gash that required 38 stitches. She was taken to the hospital immediately and charges have been filed."

I exhale deeply, my eyes wide in amazement. It had been only a little over two months since I stopped dealing with Percy. Thank God I did... that girl could've easily been me. At least now he was going to jail where someone could treat him the way he's been treating women.

"I'm back, baby," I say into the phone, and make my way towards the bathroom.

"What take you so long?" he says in a pouty voice. I smile to myself...

"Nothing. How are you and Damien doing?"

I listen to him go on and on for the next ten minutes while I take care of my business. It makes me feel good not hoping, but knowing, that he is far away staying completely faithful to me. He called to check in with me throughout the day because he wanted to, not because I asked him to. I had to admit sometimes he talked so much on the phone that I would start to zone out. I was doing this now. But when I hear the tone of his voice change to an excited one, I listen up.

"So anyway, they want this tour to be all about Les Gémeaux bringing dancers together from all over the world. And they gonna show it on ABC channel," he finishes.

"Oh my God!" I can't hide my excitement. "Oh my God! That's so good!"

"I know, baby, it's gonna be *big*," he replies, coolly. I can hear him smirking through the phone.

"Wow... this is a game changer, Dee. You and Damien are doing so well for yourselves." I beam with pride. Everyone told them their careers would be over after spending so much time with Beyoncé and they were proving them all wrong. "When does everything happen?"

"Well next year, 2015," he says. "But I just had to tell you now about the surprise." I stand and walk over to our bathroom sink and check all three pregnancy tests lying on the counter. I had a bit of a surprise to disclose myself.

■■■

On my birthday, Dominique and I spent the evening together back in Chicago. Leaves had already begun falling from the trees but the weather was warm and the sun was out. Just the way I liked it. Dominique pulled my hand up to his and kissed it tenderly without making eye contact. I smiled in return. We walked quietly up the pathway to my mami's house and waited for my little sister to come running to the door, nearly knocking us over with her excitement.

We were met with warm hugs and kisses, steamy green tea, freshly baked cookies, and millions of questions. What was it like living in California? Had I met any superstars? When would Dominique be touring again? Why did we decide to come back when the weather was about to get colder? Dominique and I exchanged smiles, hinting that we knew something everyone else didn't. We answered their questions respectively, then I left to use the bathroom.

I turned the water on so that nobody would hear me in case I got sick. I sat on the toilet and cried. I didn't know why I was crying. I was not sad. No... I was the happiest I had ever been in my life. In six months, I'd know a feeling even happier than this one. I would have a gift; the gift of unconditional love for an eternity. I laughed out loud through my tears and dried my cheeks before moisturizing them with cocoa butter. I looked in the mirror and tried to make a face that would make me appear less pregnant. Nothing worked.

I walked back to the family room slowly and Dominique was standing, waiting for me. He grabbed me by the hand and reached down to rub my pudge of a baby bump. My sister ran to me and unbuttoned my jacket. Screams. My mami is crying. She knows what I've been through the past year, afraid that I could never give birth to my own child. Despite her judgments about us not being married, my aunt cannot help but be happy for us. I laugh as my sister sits me on her lap so she can rub my belly properly.

Is it a boy or a girl? We don't know. We only hope the baby is healthy. Dominique takes me outside to get some fresh air for a while. He strokes my face as he plants a kiss on the tip of my nose. He tells me I have never been more perfect. We are making plans to visit Paris and tell his family the news. Our baby was conceived on June 18th. That means he or she will be born in Spring. What will we do about the dance tour? Dominique wants me and the baby to come with him. There is no way we cannot be by his side every step of the way. And I agree.

I want to cheer him on from the sidelines when he performs. I want to bring him back down to earth when he starts to forget where he started from. I want to relieve him when things get stressful and rub his back when he is tired. I want to do everything right this time. It was time for me to comfort my man as he comforted me when I needed it most. With the love our new baby would bring, nothing would be strong enough to tear us apart ever again.

NOTE TO DOMINIQUE

Dear Dominique,

I am writing this letter as I watch you hold our son in your right arm and deliver a speech to countless young dancers from all over the world. You are as animated and loveable as ever and three month old Dominique, who you have affectionately nicknamed Nico, adores you.

I love to see his chubby fingers pull on your twists in an attempt to balance himself as he teethes on your cheekbone. You love it too, and you chuckle in the middle of your sentence. The love in your eyes when you turn to him and smile makes your warning not to "slob on Daddy while he's working" hard to take seriously.

I know you will hand him off to me in a few minutes and you and Damien will begin your session. You have come so far, baby. The both of you have. I couldn't be more proud to call you my King and call Damien my brother. Over the past year, I've watched you grow from an impulsive, naïve young man into the thoughtful, motivated, loyal man I knew you could be.

It has been a long, educational few months and there were times when we both wanted to give up, I know. But we made it through baby. We kept working at it and working at it, and we have our *family now because of it.*

As you know, I wasn't the easiest person to be around when you came into my life. When I met you, I was able to have fun again. I was able to enjoy things that had become tasks to me, but were exciting activities for everyday people. You accepted me as I was.

My depression didn't scare you away, it made you want to love me more. And I'm grateful for that. You took on a difficult job that nobody else in my life had tried to. You helped me grow into a better woman. Baby, making love to you is as magical as it was the first time. Your touch still sends a tingly feeling through my entire body.

When I look at our son, I see you and it warms my heart. I cry tears of joy sometimes knowing that I get to wake up next to you. During the worst part of my life, I kept myself motivated by saying that it can only get better. One day, I will know what it feels like to be truly happy. I know that time has come.

You are my protector, my best friend, my soul mate, my inspiration, my happiness. You are so beautiful. You continue to hold everything together, refusing to be shaken by negativity. I admire that. I strive to be more like you and you motivate me to work harder at being a good person. What more could a woman ask for in a companion?

Shakespeare once said, "Uneasy lies the head that wears a crown." I'm here to tell you that you are wearing that crown, baby. You are wearing it like no other can. I love you.

Sincerely,

The undying melody playing on your heart strings
Your Queen, Téa

THE END

MUSIC THAT HELPED INSPIRE THE STORY

1. "Closer" by Corinne Bailey Rae
2. "The Truth" by India.Arie
3. "(Lay Your Head On My) Pillow" by Tony! Toni! Toné!
4. "For Real" by Amel Larrieux
5. "You Got It On" by Justin Timberlake
6. "Where I Wanna Be" by Donnell Jones
7. "Out My Mind, Just In Time" by Erykah Badu
8. "Sometimes I Cry" by Eric Benét
9. "Ex-Factor" by Lauryn Hill
10. "The Air That I Breathe" by Maroon 5
11. "Free" by Destiny's Child
12. "1+1" by Beyoncé
13. "Lost Queen" by Pharrell Williams
14. "Carousel" by Michael Jackson

MEET THE AUTHOR

Tanaé B. is a 22 year old writer, born and raised on the south side of Chicago. "Carousel" is her first published work, but she has been writing short stories, poems, and songs from the age of 6. She is currently working as a freelance portrait artist while writing her second novel. Please visit http://iamtanae.tictail.com to view Tanaé's visual works and get in touch with the author!

Printed in Great Britain
by Amazon.co.uk, Ltd.,
Marston Gate.